THE NEW PAGANISM

Also by Harold Lindsell

The Peoples' Study Bible (KJV)
The Peoples' Study Bible (TLB)
The Harper Study Bible (RSV)
The Harper Study Bible (NAS)
The Battle for the Bible
Free Enterprise: A Judeo-Christian Defense
A Handbook for Christian Truth

THE NEW PAGANISM

Harold Lindsell, Ph.D., D.D., Ll.D.

1817

Harper & Row, Publishers, San Francisco

Cambridge, Hagerstown, New York, Philadelphia, Washington
London, Mexico City, São Paulo, Singapore, Sydney

Acknowledgments can be found on p. vi.

THE NEW PAGANISM. Copyright © 1987 by Harold Lindsell. All rights
reserved. Printed in the United States of America. No part of this book
may be used or reproduced in any manner whatsoever without written
permission except in the case of brief quotations embodied in critical
articles and reviews. For information address Harper & Row, Publishers,
Inc., 10 East 53rd Street, New York, N.Y. 10022. Published
simultaneously in Canada by Fitzhenry & Whiteside, Limited, Toronto.

FIRST EDITION

Library of Congress Cataloging-in-Publication Data

Lindsell, Harold, 1913-
    The new paganism.

    Bibliography: p.
    Includes index.
    1. Apologetics—20th century.   2. Civilization, Christian.   3. Christianity
and culture.   4. Paganism—Controversial literature.   5. Evangelism.
6. Enlightenment.   7. Civilization, Modern—20th century.   I. Title.
BT1211.L56   1987   261   87-45187
ISBN 0-06-065272-1

87 88 89 90 91   HC   10 9 8 7 6 5 4 3 2 1

To some of my former associates who served *Christianity Today* while I was its editor from 1968 to 1978. From them I learned much and to them I am greatly indebted for their labors that helped to make the magazine one of the world's finest publications:

L. Nelson Bell (deceased)
Russell Chandler
Eugene Kucharsky
Arthur Matthews
Richard Ostling
Edward Plowman

ACKNOWLEDGMENTS

The following publishers have generously given permission to use quotations from copyrighted sources: From *The Invisible War*, by Donald Grey Barnhouse. Copyright © 1965 by Zondervan Publishing House. Reprinted by permission. From *The Word of God and the Mind of Many*, by Ronald Nash. Copyright © 1982 by Zondervan Publishing House. Reprinted by permission. From *The Enlightenment: An Interpretation—The Rise of Modern Paganism*, vol. 1, by Peter Gay. Copyright © 1966 by Peter Gay. Reprinted by permission of Alfred A. Knopf, Inc. From "John Locke," "Thomas Paine," and "History of Medicine and Surgery" in *Encyclopaedia Britannica*, 14th edition. Copyright © 1967. Reprinted by permission. From "Edward Gibbon," "Herman Samuel Reimarus," and "Humanism" in *Encyclopaedia Britannica*, 15th edition. Copyright © 1983. Reprinted by permission. From *Thomas Jefferson: An Intimate Biography*, by Fawn M. Brodie. Copyright © 1974 by W. W. Norton & Co., Inc. Reprinted by permission. From *The Autobiographical Writings of Benjamin Franklin*, edited by Carl Van Doren. Copyright © 1945 by Carl Van Doren. Copyright renewed © 1972 by Margaret Bevans, Barbara Klaw, and Anne Ross. Reprinted by permission of Viking Penguin, Inc. From *The End of the Historical–Critical Method*, by Gerhard Maier. Copyright © 1977 by Concordia Publishing House. Reprinted by permission. From *The Divine Relativity*, by Charles Hartshorne. Copyright © 1982 by Yale University Press. Reprinted by permission. From *A Common Faith*, by John Dewey. Copyright © 1934 by Yale University Press. Reprinted by permission. From *Pornography: Marxism, Feminism, and the Future of Sexuality*, by Alan Soble. Copyright © 1986 by Yale University Press. Reprinted by permission. From *Confessions of a Theologian*, by Carl F. H. Henry. Copyright © 1983 by Word Books, Publishers, Waco, Texas 76796. Reprinted by permission. From *God, Revelation and Authority*, by Carl F. H. Henry. Copyright © 1983 by Word Books, Publishers, Waco, Texas 76796. Reprinted by permission. From *A Christian View of Men and Things*, by Gordon H. Clark. Copyright © 1981. Reprinted by permission of Wm. B. Eerdmans Publishing Co. From *Matthew: A Commentary on His Literary and Theological Art*, by Robert Gundry. Copyright © 1982. Reprinted by permission of Wm. B. Eerdmans Publishing Co. From *Old Testament Survey*, by William LaSor, David Hubbard, and Frederic Bush. Copyright © 1982. Reprinted by permission of Wm. B. Eerdmans Publishing Co. From *Christian Reflections*, by C. S. Lewis. Copyright © 1967. Reprinted by permission of Wm. B. Eerdmans Publishing Co. From *Christians and Marxists, The Mutual Challenge to Revolution*, by José Miguez-Bonino. Copyright © 1976. Reprinted by permission of Wm. B. Eerdmans Publishing Co. From "The Scenario of Cosmic Evolution," by Eric Chaisson in *Harvard Magazine*. Copyright © 1967 by *Harvard Magazine*. Reprinted by permission. From "The Death of God," by Allen Spraggett in *The Toronto Daily Star*. Copyright © 1966. Reprinted by permission of *The Toronto Star* Syndicate. From "The Politics of AIDS," by Joseph Sobran in *National Review*. Copyright © 1986 by National Review, Inc. 150 East 35th Street, New York, NY 10016. Reprinted by permission. From "God Save This Vulnerable Court," by Richard John Neuhaus in *National Review*. Copyright © 1986 by *National Review*, Inc. 150 East 35th Street, New York, NY 10016. Reprinted by permission. From *Insights and Oversights of Great Thinkers*, by Charles Hartshorne. Copyright © 1983. Reprinted by permission of University of New York Press. From *Essays Moral, Political and Literary*, by David Hume. Copyright © 1963. Reprinted by permission of Oxford University Press. From *Baker's Dictionary of Theology*, ed. Everett F. Harrison. Copyright © 1960. Reprinted by permission of Baker Book House. From Kant, "What Is Enlightenment?," trans. Peter Gay, in *Introduction to Contemporary Civilization in the West*, 2 vols., 2nd ed. (1954, I, 1071-76). Used by permission of Columbia University Press.

Contents

Foreword

Popular thought—what the French call *vulgarisation*—quite consistently maintains that modern secularity is rooted in the Renaissance era. For contemporary pagans, this attribution is comforting, for it ties their current beliefs to the dynamism of the age of exploration and to what Burchhardt called "the discovery of the world and of man." For today's pietists, it offers the delicious possibility (as one of that ilk has asserted) of finding the source of twentieth-century pornography in Michelangelo's nude "David"!

Remarkably, the fine historical scholarship of Harvard's Myron Gilmore (*The World of Humanism, 1453–1517*) and of Michigan's Albert Hyma (*The Christian Renaissance*) has not killed this persistent stereotype. Perhaps Harold Lindsell's excellent volume will succeed where they have failed—by the different but equally compelling route of showing that today's "secular humanism" is the product not of the Renaissance of the sixteenth century but of the so-called enlightenment of the eighteenth, that misdescribed Age of Reason or *siècle de lumières*.

Harold Lindsell is probably best known as a journalist (editor of *Christianity Today* in its halcyon days) and theological controversialist (*The Battle for the Bible*). But he is first and foremost a scholar-historian (he received a Ph.D. in history from New York University). Since joining the M.A. faculty at America's unique Christian law school, the Simon Greenleaf School of Law, and later assuming the chairmanship of that program, Dr. Lindsell has had the opportunity to return to pure academics. Students have reveled in his courses on Marxism, secular humanism, and the history of ideas. Now the reading public who cannot benefit from such superb instruction face to face have in their hands the next best thing: a book offering, from the vantage point of classic evangelical theology, the first balanced treatment of how our society became secularized—and (hardly less important) what we can do about it.

JOHN WARWICK MONTGOMERY
M.Phil. in Law (Essex), Ph.D. (Chicago), Th.D. (Strasbourg)
Dean, The Simon Greenleaf School of Law,
Anaheim, California, and Strasbourg, France

6 January 1987
The Feast of the Epiphany

Introduction

The Post-Christian Age is here. There can be no doubt about that. What this means remains to be explored. But more than that, we need, as Christians, to understand how this came to pass. I am not speaking here of the Christian church in relation to the whole planet. I have in mind the Western world in particular, for there has never been a Christian Age in places like China, India, Japan, Southeast Asia, and others parts of this globe. These areas are still pagan vis-à-vis the Christian perspective, that is, their peoples by and large make little or no use of the Judeo-Christian tradition.

The purpose of this book is to document the fact that Western culture today is dominated by paganism. The word "paganism" is far better than the term popularly bruited abroad, secular humanism. The reason is plain enough. The term "humanism" has many meanings and not all of them are bad. There is a Christian humanism that is biblical and should not be sacrificed on pagan altars by misuse. The choice of the word "paganism" can best be discussed in terms of two weighty words: Zeitgeist and Weltanschauung.

Webster defines Zeitgeist as "the general intellectual, moral, and cultural climate of an era." The West at one time could be described as being committed to the Judeo-Christian tradition. Today that no longer is true. It is now committed to a New Paganism that has effectually displaced the Judeo-Christian tradition and brought into being what I have called the Post-Christian Era. I cannot speak of the Post-Christian Era for places like Japan, China, and India, for they have never had their paganism supplanted by the Judeo-Christian tradition as the ruling and reigning constituent in their culture.

The second word, Weltanschauung, is defined by Webster as "a comprehensive conception or apprehension of the world, especially from a specific standpoint." Different groups or cultures have different Weltanschauungs, different world and life views, and there probably always will be any number of them wholly different from the Judeo-Christian option. This opens up for discussion the question whether Christianity is the only true option or whether some other option is to be preferred above Christianity or whether all options, including Christianity, are unacceptable. It is the thesis of this book that Christianity is the only true faith and that all other religions are false despite apparent similarities, even those cults that use the Bible but add to it and by this process devitalize it and make it quite different from traditional orthodoxy.

I will demonstrate that the society and culture of the Western world, for a millennium and a half, was distinctively indebted to the Judeo-Christian tradition and that this tradition represented a Zeitgeist and Weltanschauung unknown in history before to any other nation or group of people. In short, Western civilization was the by-product of the Christian gospel, and no one can understand the history of the West without understanding the role of the Christian church in that history.

What the Christian church contributed to Western civilization has now been lost and the role of the Christian church has been displaced with another and alien Zeitgeist and Weltanschauung that now function in direct opposition to what Christianity has stood for from the beginning. Thus we live in a Post-Christian Age in the West and the displacement of the church from its leadership role in Western history was brought about by the Enlightenment, known in German as *die Aufklärung*. This eighteenth-century movement was responsible for the severest defeat the Christian church has suffered in its history. It represented a return to the paganism the Christian church found itself faced with at Pentecost. The shift from a culture functioning within the Christian tradition to a civilization opposed to the Christian faith and in principle opposed to all religion has now taken place and it has reached an ascendancy or full flowering that bodes ill for the future.

Since I live in the United States, the emphasis will be given to the Enlightenment's impact on American society and culture, but Europe or the total West will not be excluded from consideration. Indeed it may be said that whatever has transpired in

America is even more true about Europe, where the Enlightenment dug in so deeply and imprinted so indelibly its paganism on its peoples. In a sense, Europe has become an even greater mission field than America, we shall see in due time.

Certainly one group of Christians in America has signally failed to understand and appreciate what the Enlightenment has accomplished in its midst. I have in mind those who call themselves evangelicals. These people are important in American religious life and have captured the attention of the media—a few years ago it was the Year of the Evangelical, according to *Time* magazine. Evangelicals have generally remained faithful to historic orthodoxy and they have given special credence to the "born-again" phenomenon that has saturated the American scene, although the term has been appallingly applied to disparate activities having no relevance to Christianity. As a result the term has lost its meaning for far too many people, but this is not the worst aspect of the current situation.

Evangelicals on the whole do not really see that the church is back where it was at the first Pentecost. Consequently they do not know the pressing needs for the defense of the Christian faith and for any assault by the Christian church on the strongholds of paganism. They do not see that the situation is virtually identical to that of the church today in China, Japan, and India. Christianity in America is a minority force and at best can be said to be countercultural—it runs "counter" to the prevailing "culture."

The controlling elements of American culture today are pagan, and the influence of the pagans is not declining; that influence is increasing daily, so that the media and educational institutions of the land may be said to be pagan too. And these forces control the future of the nation. An alarm needs to be sounded so that at least evangelicals will see more clearly what they face. It is only then that they can devise programs and procedures to do what is required in the present situation. A revolution is called for. And it will be an all-out struggle against deeply entrenched forces that have awesome power. To reverse what has taken two hundred years to bring to power will be costly and the process will produce convulsions we have not experienced for generations.

It is my purpose, then, to survey the Christian scene to show how the church has gotten where it is today, how it all came about. To do this we must first take a look at how God brought the church into existence. We will survey the Old and New Testaments to determine what the basic and unalterable doctrines are, based on the fact that the Bible itself proclaims that there are truths that are the same yesterday, today, and forever. This is the first step.

The second step is to look at the divine mandate of what the church is supposed to do. Thus the second step begins at Pentecost and carries us through to the Protestant Reformation. When we do this we will, of necessity, have to pinpoint those conditions in the church that occasioned the rise of the Reformation.

The third step is to look at the Reformation itself and chart what it accomplished and how it functioned in a world that differed from that of medieval Christendom. The rise of the Protestant churches and the spiritual vigor of the movement contributed greatly to the advance of the Christian faith around the globe. The missionary outreach of the Protestant churches was spectacular; its pervasive influence was to alter the history of the world. But it also raised questions in people's minds that would bring us to the fourth turning point in the history of Christendom, the Enlightenment, which came about in the eighteenth century.

The Enlightenment will constitute the major consideration of this book. Attention will be given to the major components of the movement that produced a defeat for the church and the virtual end of Western civilization under the rubric of the Judeo-Christian tradition. In place of it we have witnessed the rise of the New Paganism. And the presuppositions of this paganism constitute a new Zeitgeist and Weltanschauung that function as a crucial opponent of historic orthodoxy. Wherever anyone accepts the basic views of the Enlightenment, it means the end of the Christian faith as we have known it through the centuries. All this simply means that the tenets of historic orthodoxy are antithetical to the tenets of the Enlightenment. To accept one standpoint means to deny the other.

When I have developed the evidence to support the theses of

this book, there still remains the need to show that the presuppositions undergirding the Enlightenment viewpoint can be shown to be falsely founded. And a program of action will be devised to show the best, and indeed the only, alternative to the Enlightenment is a biblical orthodoxy delivered from theological liberalism and neo-orthodoxy, which themselves are partakers of the Enlightenment mentality that has led us to the current impasse. It is to this end that we undertake our task.

1. The Christian Faith

Webster's Ninth New Collegiate Dictionary defines a pagan as "a follower of a polytheistic religion (as in ancient Rome)," or "one who has little or no religion and delights in sensual pleasures and material goods: an irreligious or hedonistic person." Clearly paganism stands in opposition to the Judeo-Christian tradition and the Christian faith; without this qualification the definition loses any real meaning. And when we talk about the relationship of the Christian faith to paganism we must first ask what the Christian faith is, where it came from, what it regards as its essential purpose, and what its final or ultimate goal is.

GOD AND THE CHRISTIAN FAITH

Christianity begins with God. It claims that God is the great Communicator and that He has chosen to reveal Himself to humankind whom, as we shall see, He has created for His own glory. There is no way humankind could have known who God is or that He exists unless God had revealed Himself by His own choice. This information comes to us through a book called the Bible. It professes to be the source of religious knowledge for Christians.

Once we say that God has made Himself known through the Bible, we must know what the Bible is and decide whether the Bible is a trustworthy source of religious knowledge. Historically, and especially since the Reformation, the Bible is a book that has in it sixty-six books from Genesis through Revelation. It is divided into the Old and the New Testaments. It is a trustworthy communication, for it has God as well as humans for its authorship. Whatever the state and condition of the human authors of the Bible, Christians have always recognized that the third person of the Trinity, the Holy Spirit, is the divine author of the Bible, or the Scriptures. Because this is so, the

Bible writers were preserved from error, so that what they said is the Word of God and thus is trustworthy in all of its parts. This means that it not only is theological truth, but it is true on whatever matter it speaks, whether that be science, cosmology, history, or anything else.

We learn from the Bible that God is one in essence and subsists in three persons, the Father, the Son, and the Holy Spirit. This is a difficult doctrine to understand. It transcends human reason, but that does not make it untrue. One divine said that "he who would try to understand the Trinity will lose his mind but he who would deny the Trinity will lose his soul." Whatever may be the difficulties of the Trinity, it cannot be denied that the Christian church has been trinitarian through the ages and the Bible itself supports the doctrine.

The God of the Bible is said to be holy, righteous, just, omnipotent, omniscient, and omnipresent. He is also Truth. This God who has revealed Himself in the Bible, which is the Word of God written, has also revealed Himself in the person of Jesus Christ, who is the Word of God incarnate. That is, God has become flesh and dwelt among us. Christians have always affirmed that whoever has seen Jesus Christ has seen the Father, according to the testimony of Jesus Himself. Thus there are two Words of God: the Scriptures and Jesus Christ. And no one can know the historical Jesus except through the Word of God written that reveals Him.

All of this does not tell us where the church came from and to this question we learn from Scripture that God is the creator who made all things for Himself.

GOD THE CREATOR

The Bible proclaims that God made all things by the word of His power. God called the cosmos into being. Since He is infinite and omnipotent, this could be done by the simple statement "Let there be," and whatever He wanted to be was immediately. In any event God is a spirit, not a material being, and matter did not exist before God created it. The first act of God was to create the cosmos. How old, then, is the cosmos?

Scientists tell us that the cosmos is billions of years old. We need not dispute that theory, but we do need to ask how it stands up in terms of biblical revelation. This question is of great import when we come to the question of the origin of humankind. Apart from the theory of evolution, whether it be theistic or nontheistic (and which remains unproved and is unprovable, as we shall see later), the history of humans on the planet Earth is one of recent origin. How can this be explained if the original creation of the cosmos was billions of years ago?

Donald Grey Barnhouse in his book *The Invisible War* offers a quite reasonable explanation of what some think to be an enigma of gigantic proportions. He starts with Genesis 1:1, which says, "In the beginning God created the heavens and the earth." Then he argues that verse 2 is separated from verse 1 by a lengthy period of time, whatever may be the true age of the cosmos. Using the analogy of Scripture, that is, interpreting Scripture with Scripture, Dr. Barnhouse offers very persuasive evidence to show that his claim is sustainable. This is his proposal:

On the one side of the abyss stands the phrase, "In the beginning God created the heavens and the earth." We come to the other side and read the second verse as it is found in the King James Version: "And the earth was without form and void and darkness covered the face of the deep." The revisers in both the English and American revisions, not satisfied with the terms, "without form and void," have given us the better translation "waste and void," though the *RSV* has gone back to the King James rendering. Still another translator interprets the Hebrew as "a wreck and a ruin." . . .

Just here the importance of the comparative method of Bible study is seen. In Isaiah 45:18, we read that God did not create the world as it is found in the second verse of Genesis: "For thus saith the Lord that created the heavens; God himself that formed the earth and made it; he hath established it, he created it not *tohu* . . . " Here is the same Hebrew word as in the second verse of the Bible. It is a formal statement: God did not create the earth as it is portrayed in the description that has commonly been called chaos. The great French translator, Abbe Crampon, boldly renders it thus: "He hath established it Himself and did not make it as a chaos (*Qui l'a fondee Luimeme et qui n'en a pas fait un chaos*)." It is noteworthy that the Revised Standard Version has adopted this reading. "He did not create it a chaos."

This categorical statement is sufficient to prove beyond a shadow of doubt that the first and second verses are separated by an interval. We might read the first and second verses from Genesis and the one from Isaiah as follows: "In the beginning God created the heavens and the earth. And the earth—though God most certainly did not create it that way—became a wreck and a ruin, and darkness covered the face of the deep."

That we have a right to translate the verb by the continuing form "became" is amply demonstrated by the fact that this precise form is thus translated in other parts of the Old Testament, as for example, "Lot's wife looked back and she became a pillar of salt" (Gen. 19:26). . . .

It should be pointed out, perhaps, that the knowledge of this explanation of the Scripture is nothing new. Dr. Thomas Chalmers of Scotland observed that there must be a considerable interval of time between the first two verses of Genesis. And we read in the notes of Crampon, who is perhaps the greatest scholar produced by the Roman Catholic Church in modern times and who works in the shadow of all the church fathers, the following: "Verse two refers to the indefinite interval of time which separates the primordial creation from the organization of the terrestrial globe as the author is about to describe it. This interval gives every latitude for explaining the transformations which matter has undergone according to the diverse scientific hypotheses." If the Church had followed these great students, Protestant and Catholic, there would not have been so great a furor concerning the modern theories of science, and it would have been much easier to winnow the wheat of truth from the theories and to throw out the chaff of speculative hypothesis.[1]

Nowhere are we told what happened to cause the original creation to become a void. Anyone may theorize in the endeavor to satisfy a curiosity common to all of us. But it is safe to say that no proof for any theory can be produced since no one who was there, if there were any intelligences present in that original creation, has left us a record of the happenings. Even God's re-creation is beyond the grasp of inquiry, since neither animals nor humans were created during the first five days recorded for us in Genesis 1. The only way we know what happened comes to us by revelation from God through Moses, who authored the Pentateuch.

GOD CREATES HUMANS

On the fifth day of the re-creation God made the first human in his own image, fashioning Adam from the dust of the earth and giving him a soul that was immortal. Whatever may be the judgments of current scholarship about the historicity of Adam, it is virtually impossible to claim that the Bible itself allows for Adam's nonhistoricity. Using the analogy of Scripture, we learn that the Chronicler claimed that Adam was the first man (see Chron. 1:1). If he were not, then a mythical man could not produce nonmythical children. The unbroken succession of the Chronicler establishing the link between Adam and such people as Abraham, David, and the rest is clear evidence that the Chronicler believed that Adam was the first man.

Luke does the same. He traces the genealogy of Jesus back to Adam, who is called the son of God (Luke 3:23ff.). No hermeneutic can deny that this was what Luke was asserting, unless one decides that Luke was perpetuating a myth either consciously or unconsciously. But it is difficult to suppose that modern scholars can deny the testimony of the Bible at this point without placing themselves above the Bible as its judge. Unless they can prove beyond a shadow of doubt that they are the conveyors of information that is demonstrably true and the witness of those in the Bible is demonstrably false, readers are faced with the choice of choosing between two schools of thought that oppose each other. Certainly, then, those who choose to accept the witness of the Bible are at least no worse off than those who choose the view of the scholars. In fact those readers are very well off if they have started with the proposition that the Bible is trustworthy in all of its parts. And they are also consistent.

Theology traditionally has agreed that God also created Eve to be the wife of Adam and that God placed the first pair in the Garden of Eden, which was the paradise of God for humans. The creation of humankind was followed by what we call a covenant.

GOD'S COVENANT WITH ADAM

God made a covenant of works with Adam in the Garden. It was an agreement between the Creator and a man, a free moral agent. Adam was given the privilege of eating of the fruit of the Garden except for the tree of knowledge. This prohibition was given to make it clear that Adam's responsibility was to offer God perfect obedience. Moreover he was warned of the consequences of disobedience if he should eat of the forbidden fruit. But Adam disobeyed and thus reaped death for himself and for the human race of which he was the federal head (Rom. 5:12, 18). Every covenant has a seal. The seal of God's covenant with Adam was the tree of life. It was the outward sign. From that tree Adam was separated because of sin. But there was more to it than that.

Adam of necessity was created conditionally immortal, that is, he would live and continue to live indefinitely so long as he was obedient to the command of God. As a result of this transgression, he died spiritually immediately and would die physically in due season. Had God foreclosed the issue by rendering a final judgment against Adam and Eve then and there, there would have been no children and no human race. God, however, would not be defeated by Satan, who was the agent of Adam's sin. Had God done nothing to make the redemption of Adam and of the human race possible in the future, Satan would have been victorious. This God would not allow. Therefore a doctrine of redemption was called for.

THE DOCTRINE OF DIVINE REDEMPTION

In Genesis 3:15 there is the first promise of a Redeemer. The conflict of the ages is predicted, a conflict between the seed of the woman and the seed of the serpent. The Redeemer will finally bring ruin to Satan and his seed, although in the process Satan will bruise the Redeemed (which took place at Calvary). Isaiah 53:10 further reveals that Satan's maltreatment of Christ the Redeemer was in accord with the permissive will and all-wise plan of God the Father.

One part of God's immediate judgment of Adam was his exclusion from the Garden of Eden. Another was the curse of God placed on the ground, so that by the sweat of his brow Adam and all humans after him would labor for their food. And God promised Eve that childbearing would be difficult. Following this the human race was enlarged by the birth of children to Adam and Eve. In those early years sisters married brothers until the earth was more fully peopled, at which time

God was to prohibit such marriages. But the institution of marriage itself was set up by divine mandate and was to be terminated only by the death of either spouse.

THE FLOOD AND THE TOWER OF BABEL

In the course of time a conflict raged between the wicked human sons and God their Creator. God proceeded to exterminate the wicked human race except for the family of Noah, but it was not done capriciously. For more than a hundred years, while Noah was building the ark, people were given the chance to repent and turn from their sins against their God. At last the patience of God was exhausted and judgment fell. The Flood killed off all human life on the planet Earth except for the family of Noah. And God began to replenish the earth through Noah. When the Flood was ended, God affirmed to Noah and thus to all humankind that the earth would never again have a flood that would destroy all human life. This covenant had for its sign the rainbow.

Shortly after the Flood was over the Noahic family produced sons and daughters whose ways displeased God. The outward sign of their disobedience was the effort to build the Tower of Babel. God stepped in again and confused their language, so that from that point onward people were divided by language barriers. Language was a divine gift in the first place and there is no other explanation for the existence of various languages among humans. Theories of language have been adduced, but they are of little help in determining the source from which languages came once the notion that they came from God has been discarded. Subsequent to this confusion of tongues God furthered His plan of redemption by calling to Himself a man by the name of Abram, later called Abraham.

GOD'S COVENANT WITH ABRAHAM

Many liberals think the first eleven chapters of Genesis are myth or legend and that real history had its beginning with Abram. There was a time when some liberal scholars did not think Abram was a historical person, but that viewpoint has been effectively demolished. Few scholars today would deny the historicity of Abram, whatever their views about Genesis 1–11. Understanding the significance of the covenant that God made with Abram is vital for understanding the balance of the Old Testament and indeed the New Testament as well.

God was at work in the hearts of humankind before the time of Abram. From the beginning of time and after the Fall, men and women who had faith in God were redeemed and became members of the body of Christ. God's plan of salvation was already in operation, but the fuller details of that plan were as yet unknown to people. The next step in the unveiling of what God was going to do came during the days of Abram, whose name was changed to Abraham once the covenant of God with him was made.

God's covenant with Abraham had in it several significant elements. Abram was a believer who had been justified by God through faith and made righteous. God ordained that through his loins there should come the Messiah who would be the Redeemer of humankind. Furthermore God promised that in Abraham all the nations of the world would be blessed. Moreover, the covenant required the blood sacrifice of animals for atonement, by which the demands of the law would be satisfied and the holiness of God vindicated. The notion of substitutionary sacrifice by the blood of bulls and goats, awaiting the sacrifice of Jesus Christ as the Lamb of God, was clearly in view even from the days of Adam. And now we see this more specifically demonstrated in the covenant God made with Abraham.

Abraham's grandson, Jacob, was the father of twelve sons; from these came the twelve tribes of Israel. Among those twelve sons, Levi and Judah were chosen for special purposes in the unveiling of God's plan. From the loins of Judah should come the Messiah, the Lord Jesus Christ. And from Levi would come the priesthood.

In the plan of God Jacob's family came to Egypt when Joseph, the eleventh son, was second only to the Egyptian pharaoh. As history unfolded, Jacob's descendants became slaves in Egypt. They prospered and grew so great in numbers that they presented a danger to Egypt, whose blood lines or racial distinctness was being challenged. However, the preservation of the

Hebrews in Egypt enabled a tiny minority to become a large horde, which God would fashion into a nation and through whom would come the church of Jesus Christ in later ages.

At His appointed time God raised up Moses, who led the people of Israel out of Egypt to the Promised Land or Caanan. It was during this period that further developments of great significance took place. God was setting up a theocratic state over which He would be king. Such a state had to have three elements essential to any state: territory, which was Caanan, people, who were the Israelites, and sovereignty, so that the nation could sustain itself against enemies from without and within. It was also necessary to set up a human government, a system of laws by which the people would be governed, and a priesthood, to care for the spiritual needs of the people and to fulfill the demands of a holy God who was to be worshiped and obeyed by His subjects.

In this connection it is vital to note the source from which the legal system and the governmental forms were derived, because later on the church, which would be established at Pentecost, was to face a Greco-Roman world quite different from the world of the Israelites. In Moses' day there was no Rome or Greece. These civilizations had not developed yet; therefore they could contribute nothing to the development of the state of Israel. From the human perspective, Moses had knowledge only of Egypt. He was raised and steeped in the Egyptian tradition. But that tradition was to contribute nothing to the new state God was bringing into being. Whence, then, did Moses gain the knowledge and insight to lay the foundations for the new state he was to establish?

The only possible answer is that God, who is both transcendent and imminent, was using Moses as the agent of divine revelation. It was God Himself who laid the foundations for the state of Israel, and its beginnings came when God gave Moses the Ten Commandments on Mount Sinai. They were not devised by Moses. They were written by the finger of God on the stone tablets and were expressions of what is basic to the nature of the Giver. All of Israel's future was tied up to these commandments, which were and are and shall forever be basic to any society.

The commandments served a twofold purpose. They revealed the unchanging fact that God is at work in this world and demands that all worship and obey Him. Second, the commandments laid down the laws governing human relationships without which no state can survive ultimately. Any society that permits lying, stealing, cheating, coveting, and sexual license will become anarchic in the long run. This is the surest guarantee of the demise of nations that permit these conditions to prevail. Moreover, God went beyond the Ten Commandments and laid down a more detailed system of law governing the behavior of the citizenry.

In the Israelite theocracy right on to and through the kingship period, law and religion were interconnected. Disobedience, whether it was of a spiritual nature or had to do with human natural relations, required the giving of animal sacrifices to propitiate God and to render justice to those who had been injured by the acts of another. The law went so far as to require sacrifices for sins of ignorance. From this we learn that choices have consequences, even when the choices are made in ignorance and lead to results the chooser never consciously intended. The relationship between law and religion in Israel can best be seen by an understanding of the Levitical priesthood.

THE LEVITICAL PRIESTHOOD

God set aside Aaron, the brother of Moses, and Aaron's seed to be the priests of Israel. The sacrificial system by which animals were offered and their blood sprinkled had its precursor in the Passover celebrated by Israel just prior to leaving Egypt. In the wilderness journeys of the Israelites the sacrificial system was fully instituted and regularized by Moses under God.

At the heart of Israel's religious observances lay the Tabernacle, which would later on give way to the Temple built by Solomon. In the Tabernacle was the Holy of Holies, and included in that area of the tent was the mercy seat, to which only the high priest had access once a year when atonement was made by the sprinkling of blood on the horns of the altar. But of greatest significance was the fact that the Shekinah glory of God filled the holy place. God was really present among His people in the Tabernacle. God was far off, but He was also near, and the tent was the divine dwelling place.

Israel's theocracy was fully set up in Moses' day. The revelation of God in the five books of Moses, the Pentateuch, laid the groundwork for a clearer understanding of the divine plan of salvation. While that plan was not yet enlarged as it would be in the New Testament after the incarnation, death, and resurrection of Jesus Christ, it did contain in principle all of the basic elements of a theology of salvation.

THE POST-MOSAIC ERA

Subsequent to the death of Moses, the taking over of Caanan by the Israelites, and the era of the Judges, the history of Israel was intertwined with the monarchy. Israel was desirous of aping the surrounding nations and asked for the monarchy to be established. God allowed for them to do so with the proviso that His prophet Samuel identify the one who would be king. Saul was selected and installed to rule over the people of Israel. Later he was demoted from the kingship for disobedience. In his place the prophet Samuel, under God, anointed David to be Israel's king. This choice was indelibly connected with the coming of Jesus Christ.

King David came from the lineage of Judah and it was from the tribe of Judah that God was to choose the one who would be the Messiah. The tragic story of the history of Israel after King David is recited in the history books of the Old Testament, which are followed up by the writing prophets, major and minor, until we come to the close of the canon with Malachi. The writing prophets provided additional information about the incarnation of the Messiah to come—His birthplace, His virgin birth, and more than forty other details connected with His life, death, and resurrection.

This period was also marked by the judgment of God on the unbelief of His people. That judgment included the virtual disappearance of the Northern Kingdom or the ten tribes of that region. Judah remained intact, but the seventy years' captivity in Babylon fell to its lot, followed by the return of the remnant and the building of the second Temple. The fortunes of the kingdom were at a low ebb. This accorded with the prophetic word that the Messiah should come as a root out of a dry ground.

Daniel was one of the prophets to whom the word apocalyptic can be applied. His divine vision looked down the ages and foretold not only the prophetic circumstances in the immediate future of Israel, but also what would happen during the closing days of the age and the Second Advent of Jesus Christ.

Malachi marks the end of the Old Testament writing prophets. From the end of his age to the beginning of the new age that started with the incarnation there was a lapse of four centuries. During this period there were prophets, but they were not writing prophets, and the canon of the Old Testament was complete.

THE NEW TESTAMENT ERA

The era of the New Testament spanned a century. During this period of time Jesus was born, lived, taught, died, and was raised from the dead. The details of Jesus' life have been recorded for us in the four Gospels. These Gospels and the other works that follow comprise the canon of the New Testament. Together they complete the canon of the New Testament and mark the closing of it, by which we mean there was no more revelation and there will be no more revelation to humans by God. The Bible has a back cover, if we may speak colloquially.

From the New Testament we learn quite plainly that Jesus was born of the virgin Mary, that He lived a sinless life, that He died a substitutionary death on the cross for humanity's salvation, and that He rose again in the same body and ascended into heaven where He is seated at the right hand of the Father in glory. He is also coming again in glory and great power to consummate the age and end history as we know it. There will be a final judgment that will see some sent to the Lake of Fire and others to dwell forever in the presence of God in the New Jerusalem, which comes down from God out of heaven. In short, the Bible gives us a full-orbed theology beginning with the Old Testament and concluding with the New Testament.

Jesus spoke of a new age and in doing so referred to the

establishment of the church as we know it in the New Testament. It was to have its inception at Pentecost, at which time the people of God would be baptized by the Holy Spirit into the one body. The Spirit would seal every believer, indwell every believer, and fill every believer, and also make His power available for service to those who met the requirements for the release of that power. The ordinances or sacraments of the church were given, the Great Commission to take the gospel to every creature was mandated, the officers of the church were established, and the Christian church was on its way.

This marks the end of our first segment, what the Bible says, and leads to the second segment of our approach to the Enlightenment, the church's mandate. God's full-orbed revelation of Himself and of His intentions and plans became inscripturated in the Bible. This inscripturation ended when God formed and fashioned His church and sent it forth into the world. That church, which had nothing in its establishment that came from the Greco-Roman world into which it was thrust, came face to face with paganism at its worst. It was called upon to witness to a pagan world and to demolish that paganism and establish a new culture based on the Judeo-Christian tradition. And it was to do this against the greatest odds and with the intention of making disciples of the people to whom it came, bringing spiritual healing by the forgiveness of sins and a return to a right relationship to God the Creator. Would it win or lose in this gigantic task and what would the end result be? This is the question.

2. Christianity Versus Paganism

In what the Bible calls the fullness of time God sent His Son, Jesus Christ, into the world. His life, death, and resurrection were pivotal events in the history of redemption, which had its beginnings in the Garden of Eden. This redemption of God found its fulfillment in Jesus Christ. The Kingdom of God came into history, Jesus Christ was installed as present and future King, and the consummation that was to occur at the end of the age was known by God. But before that consummation could take place, the church came into being and was the vehicle God was to use to evangelize the world. All history before the incarnation was designed to prepare the world for the coming of the gospel and to set the stage for the flourishing of the work of God.

The backdrop or preparation of the world for the coming of the gospel included God's arrangements that embraced Israel, Greece, and Rome. Each contributed something to the divine plan that was to have its new beginnings at Pentecost. Israel was the custodian of God's revelation in the Old Testament. This revelation included the fact that Christianity is the one true religion and that all other religions are false. The Old and the New Testaments together were the irreducible components making up the true faith. Christianity was not a new religion but the fulfillment of what had preceded it—Judaism.

Greece provided a universal language known throughout the Roman Empire. This was Koine Greek, not classical Greek, and it was the lingua franca of the Empire. It also provided the pagan conceptual frameworks of Greek philosophy, which reached its height in the centuries subsequent to the closing of the Old Testament canon.

The Romans provided stable government, a system of roads superior to any before it, and the Pax Romana. The latter meant that travel around the Roman Empire was safe, so that the progress of the gospel would not be impeded by a state of war and the dislocations that go with it. All of this did not mean that the gospel would encounter no difficulties or that its progress would be swift and unimpeded, for the Christian Era was launched into the sea of paganism.

GREEK AND ROMAN PAGANISM

By way of generalization regarding Greek religion, Albert Henry Newman in *A Manual of Church History* says:

[It] was a polytheistic personification of the powers of nature resting on a semi-pantheistic conception of the world. Their gods and goddesses were the embodiments no less of the baser passions of the human soul than of the nobler qualities, and the moral ideals of the people were low. The idea of sin as an offense against a holy God and as involving guilt was almost wholly absent. Sin was conceived of rather as ignorance, as a failure to understand one's true relations. There is no adequate recognition of the personality of God or the personality and responsibility of man.[1]

Among the best-known Greek philosophers were Pythagoras, Socrates, Plato, and Aristotle. In Jesus' day Stoicism, Epicureanism, and Skepticism were the leading philosophies.

Pythagoras used mathematics as the basis for his speculative system. Apparently he thought that the cosmos is in an eternal state of flux and that its movements are cyclical. People and events are repeated. A variation of Pythagoreanism was encountered by the Christian church in Alexandria and elsewhere during the early centuries of Christianity.

Socrates believed that virtue could be taught, since its absence was a matter of ignorance and not of human nature, as Christianity holds. He accepted the existence of the gods and of a divine principle over and above these manifestations of deity. However, deity for him had no distinct personality and he apparently thought the universe was either monistic or semipantheistic. Plato indicated that Socrates had developed a substantial argument for the immortality of the soul.

Plato came as close to Christianity in his philosophy as any of the others. He had an influence on Jewish thought before the

Christian Era and on some in the early Christian church. He developed the notion that ideas are archetypes of the divine thought or plan and that all material objects are an imperfect reflection of those ideas. He was committed to the Good, the Beautiful, and the True. Some think he represented these high ideas to a point where he called them gods. He identified his Demiurge, or world-builder, with the notion of the Good. Even though Plato at times implied a belief in the personality of God, his system was fundamentally pantheistic.

Eusebius said of him: "He alone of all the Greeks reached the vestibule of truth and stood upon its threshold."[2] Bishop Westcott said: "Plato, more than any other ancient philospher, acknowledged alike the necessary limits of reason and the imperious instincts of faith, and when he could not absolutely reconcile both, at least gave to both a full and free expression. And so Platonism alone, and Platonism in virtue of this character, was able to stand for a time face to face with Christianity."[3]

Aristotle, who was a disciple of Plato and the teacher of Alexander the Great, was perhaps the greatest intellect of the Greek world. In the realms of logic and dialectics he reigned supreme. A practical-minded philosopher, he rejected Plato's theory of ideas, arguing that the abstract principle derived from contemplating the individual person or thing rather than that the individual person or thing was subsequent to the idea itself. He held that moral action has happiness for its aim and this is attained by living a life controlled by reason.

The Stoicism founded by Zeno was centered around materialistic pantheism. Matter is real but motionless and unformed. Force comes into play and shapes matter, and the working force in the universe is God. The human soul is part of this ultimate essence. It survives the body and is reabsorbed into the deity at last. This viewpoint was ably represented in the writings of Seneca, Epictetus, and Marcus Aurelius, whose writings may have been influenced by early Christian viewpoints.

Epicureanism and forms of Skepticism were strongly represented in Roman life at the beginning of the church. Epicureanism was skeptical and rejected all mythical forms and conceptions. This included a denial of the supernatural and any belief in the immortality of the soul. Pleasure in the present life was the supreme goal. It was the leader of the Skeptics, Pyrrho, who said that each of two contradictory statements can be maintained with equal plausibility, thus obliterating any distinction between right and wrong, virtue and vice. It eliminated any sort of moral or religious restraint and this was to work perversely and sap the foundations of Greek and Roman society.

The religion of the Romans was related to that of the Greeks, but it differed in that the Romans looked at life through a different pair of spectacles, so to speak. The Romans were utilitarian, unimaginative, and practical. Their basic approach to religion was encompassed by a pantheistic worship of nature. Form rather than feeling was important and the exactness with which devotion to the gods was performed was what counted in securing help from them.

Once the Roman world came into contact with that of the Greeks, the latter had an immense influence on the former. In the century before the incarnation, Greek rationalism, skepticism, agnosticism, and atheism found a ready acceptance in the mind-set of Rome. The Romans took over the religion, the culture, the luxury, and the license of the Hellenists. They went even further by attributing deity to their emperors and enforced worship to them, no matter how evil those emperors were or how degrading was their influence on the people in general.

This was the kind of world into which the Christian church was thrust—pagan to the core. If the Christian faith was to be effective, it would have to meet the challenge of paganism at every level. Would it be able to do so? Before we can trace the effectiveness of the church in evangelizing, a word needs to be said about what happened in the Judaism out of which Christianity came.

THE FATE OF JUDAISM

Jesus' first disciples were Jews. The gospel came first to the Jews and multitudes of them were won over to the Christian faith, with Jesus as the fulfillment of Judaism. Men like Paul, Peter, John, and the writers of the four Gospels provided leadership for the church both with respect to evangelism and also to the writing of the New Testament, which was to complete the canon of Scripture and end God's inscripturated revelation for all time.

Paul became the great apostle to the Gentiles. In the Old Testament it was evident that Judaism was regarded as a missionary faith. God promised Abraham that in him all the nations of the earth should be blessed. Isaiah says that the "God of the whole earth shall he be called" (Isa. 54:5). But Judaism was never caught up in that divine intention and never did become a missionary people, as did the church after Pentecost. Rather, the Jews did not acknowledge Jesus Christ as their Messiah on the whole, and they became enemies of the gospel. From their perspective this was quite understandable, for if Jesus was not the Messiah then those who followed him were preaching and teaching what was false. The time would come when the church, which was nurtured in the womb of Judaism and which was dynamically connected with the synagogues around the Roman Empire, would separate itself from Judaism. In that sense there was competition between Jew and Christian. Since Judaism after Pentecost was reclusive and did not have missionary zeal, it was quickly outnumbered by the church. But more than that, something else transpired that virtually removed Judaism from the center of the religious stage.

Jerusalem was destroyed in A.D. 70 under the leadership of Titus and Vespasian. Israel shortly thereafter ceased to be a nation. This event marked the beginning of the Diaspora, or Dispersion, in which the Jews were relocated to the four corners of the earth. Israel disappeared as a nation and its people would remain nationless until recently. The Jews had no territory, no government, no sovereignty, and no concentrated mass of people. In short, they lost their nationhood. Christians have always regarded this as a fulfillment of the prophetic word in Deuteronomy 28:63ff. This was the divine judgment that followed the refusal to accept Jesus as the Messiah. The term "the Wandering Jew" properly designated the condition of that race of people, and the persecution the Jews have endured across the centuries has been looked upon as a part of the divine judgment. But always the Scriptures, Old and New, have forecast a time in the future when the Jews en masse will turn to Jesus Christ as their Messiah. It does appear that God's judgment on Judaism removed it from center stage. That was beneficial to the church in that it no longer had Judaism as its chief competitor. This was important, for the Christian faith was in its beginnings small, unimportant, and as yet not fully developed from a doctrinal perspective. Let's look at some of the doctrinal aspects of the Christian faith immediately after Pentecost.

DOCTRINAL CONTROVERSIES IN THE EARLY CHURCH

The early disciples went about preaching the gospel and urging people everywhere to turn to Jesus Christ for salvation. Two questions arose immediately about the person of Jesus Christ. The first had to do with Jesus' relationship to God, the second with Jesus' human nature.

From the outset Jesus Himself proclaimed His own deity. This was accepted by the early church, but it opened up the question about the nature of God in terms of the Trinity. Since Judaism and Christianity held firmly to the belief in one God, if Jesus was also God in what sense did this violate the concept of one God? The church wrestled with this problem and from the biblical data came up with the doctrine of Trinitarianism: that God is one in essence but subsists in three persons, the Father, the Son, and the Holy Spirit.

The subsistence in three persons ruled out the views of those who were modalists. They believed that God is one in essence and in subsistence. Therefore they taught that God revealed Himself first as Father, and then as Son, and then as Holy Spirit. In this way they tried to destroy the concept of three persons and what they thought was tritheism or three Gods. But orthodoxy then and now insists on one God in three persons, even though in recent thought this viewpoint is still contested. Once the doctrine of the Trinity had been established, there still remained questions about the incarnate person of Jesus. Who was He?

The early church grappled with Christology and defined the person of Jesus Christ as consisting of one person in two natures, a perfectly human nature and a perfectly divine nature. Various church councils clearly rejected the notion of two persons, a theory that may have been inherent in Nestorianism, and opted for two natures in one person. Obviously the two natures in one person was in a sense mysterious and difficult to understand, but no less so than the doctrine of the Trinity. If the nature of the Godhead required attention, so did the nature of the human person.

THE ANTHROPOLOGICAL PROBLEM

The question about human nature centered around the differences between the ideas of Augustine and Pelagius. Augustine held that the person is spiritually dead and is born with a sinful nature. Thus the sin of Adam was imputed to the entire human race and all are conceived in sin and born into this world as sinners who are lost and undone. Pelagius denied the imputation of guilt from Adam and held that all people are born into this world without guilt. They become sinners by choice, for they have perfect freedom to choose between good and evil. Every newborn person is created pure and has the same perfect freedom to choose for or against God as did Adam in the Garden of Eden. It is voluntary and thus a choice against God can be avoided.

Augustine's view required divine grace as essential for human salvation. This is unmerited and irresistible. All of this involved questions about predestination, foreknowledge, and divine election. It also raised questions about whether the atonement was universal or limited only to the elect. Semi-Pelagianism was to be more commonly accepted, a viewpoint that stood somewhat midway between Augustinianism and Pelagianism. The problem of free will versus predestination was to rise again in the Reformation and is to this day one about which Arminians and Calvinists continue to differ. But it is safe to say that whether one adheres to the notion of free will or foreordination, all are agreed that Christianity is the only way to salvation, and that it is secured by faith in Jesus Christ.

Thus it was that the church came into history, formed and fashioned by God with officers who were elders (or bishops or presbyters) and deacons and given the sacraments or ordinances of baptism and the Lord's Supper (or Eucharist). This infant church was commissioned to go to the ends of the earth with the gospel, beseeching people everywhere to repent, turn from their sins, and receive Jesus Christ as their Savior and Lord.

The world of that day was governed by a Weltanschauung that was wholly antithetical to Christianity. And its Zeitgeist, its general intellectual, moral, and cultural climate, was consistent with its Weltanschauung—pagan to the core. The church was sent into this kind of world to sound the death knell to paganism and put in its place a civilization that would be consistent with the Weltanschauung of the Christian faith. Would the church succeed in doing this?

THE SUCCESS OF THE CHURCH IN EVANGELISM

Pentecost marked a milepost in human history. It was a turning point in history that was to alter the course of human events from that day to this. By it the church effectively superseded the pagan culture into which it had been thrust and put in its place a Western civilization based on the Judeo-Christian viewpoint. This did not happen immediately. Why and how it took place is a story unprecedented in the history of humankind.

Two of the mainsprings for the surprising advance of the Christian faith included the followers of Jesus Christ and the advent of the Holy Spirit. Jesus had given the church the Great Commission to evangelize the entire earth. But this commandment would be of no use whatever unless those to whom it was given gave themselves to the task. From its earliest days the church was a missionary church intent on spreading the good news of Jesus Christ throughout the Roman Empire, which was geographically the largest empire ever assembled up to that time. In a short space of time churches were planted in various parts of the Roman Empire. The apostle Paul, of course, was a key leader in this advance. Subsequent to his death, a passion similar to his was displayed by the Christians who continued the work of evangelization. But the activities of the Christians hardly account for the dramatic success of the enterprise. The Holy Spirit, the third person of the Trinity, was the divine agent or viceregent of Jesus Christ who supervised and empowered the disciples of Jesus.

One of the most important aspects of the Spirit's work was the divine attestations that accompanied the preaching of the gospel. Signs and wonders were performed by the Christians under the guidance and with the power of the Holy Spirit. Sick people were healed, blind and lame people were restored to health, and even the dead were raised. These acts lent credence to the preaching of the Word. It was no coincidence that through the ages before the church came into being, God gave external, confirming evidences of the divine power so that people were without excuse. Moses and the burning bush, Elijah and the fire from heaven, the miracles performed by Moses before Pharaoh, the healing of Naaman the leper, and many other signs and wonders by Jesus in the flesh attested to the genuineness of the true faith. This was the Spirit's work. But there was more than even that, important as it was.

Jesus prophesied that the Spirit sent by the Father and the Son would bring conviction of sin and of righteousness and of judgment. This would lead people to repentance and faith in Jesus Christ as their Savior. Moreover regeneration, or the new birth, was the work of the same Spirit. By faith those who were dead in trespasses and sins were made alive and became new creatures in Christ Jesus. The Word of God and the Spirit of God were instrumental for the spiritual success of the mission of the church. In tandem the work of the Spirit and the human efforts of the Christians were an unbeatable combination. So the faith spread rapidly.

Three hundred years after the beginning of Christ's public ministry the church had brought the Roman Empire to its knees in worship of the Redeemer. Under Constantine in the fourth century there was the commencement of a state church and what was to become a church state. Nowhere in Scripture was there any data to support the establishment of the church as an earthly kingdom. Jesus had said plainly that His kingdom was not of this world. In terms of eschatology Christ's kingdom would someday be established and the kingdoms of this world would become the kingdom of Christ and he would reign forever and ever (Rev. 11:15). But this was the "not yet," while the prince of the power of the air was still free to work in the sons of disobedience (Eph. 2:2). Only after Satan was defeated at last would that glorious age of Christ's eternal kingdom come. The union of church and state was to bear fruit at a later date that was to produce grave difficulties both for the church and for the state. The history of the Holy Roman Empire (which was neither holy, Roman, nor an empire) illustrates the constant struggle between popes and emperors for supremacy. Henry VIII of England, for example, clashed bitterly with the Catholic church of his era. The vexing problem of church and state in recent United States' history bears continuing witness to this controversy.

Through missionary activity the gospel spread and churches were formed in the Middle East, North Africa, all of western Europe, Scandinavia, England, Scotland, Ireland, and Russia. Ecclesiological developments led to the establishment of the five patriarchates, an office dating from the sixth century for the bishops of Alexandria, Antioch, Constantinople, Jerusalem, and Rome. In early times these bishops were looked upon as equals, but Alexandria, Antioch, and Jerusalem declined so that Constantinople in the Eastern world and Rome in the Western world became the leading patriarchates. This eventuated in a division that marked the rise of Rome to a dominant position in the Christian church. Rome and Constantinople engaged in a struggle for primacy that ended with Rome as the eventual victor.

For our purposes we need not spend time on the struggle between the two major patriarchates except to say that the Eastern Church was geographically limited and became a more or less self-contained entity. It could not easily move into Europe, which had been preempted by Rome, and it did not become involved in any widespread missionary outreach to the east of its perimeters, where the Roman Empire itself had never spread.

DOCTRINAL DEVELOPMENTS IN THE ROMAN CHURCH

The Roman Catholic church of the West did the work of evangelization in Europe and became the progenitor of Western culture and civilization. With the development of the papacy the Roman church became a powerful force in the political realm. It claimed for itself a role in political life by asserting that the state was the moon and the church the sun. The state was therefore subject to the church and was, in effect, to be ruled by the church. Through the use of excommunication it was able to curb recalcitrant monarchs. It also claimed to have the power to crown monarchs and to take their crowns from them. This was resorted to in several instances. The height of this usurpation of power came in the reign of Boniface VIII (1294–1303).

In 1302 Boniface issued the bull called the *Unam Sanctam* from its opening words. It was the result of a quarrel between Boniface and Philip IV of France. The document illustrates the most extreme claims of the papacy in the most extravagant form. It declared that there was "one holy Catholic and Apostolic Church" outside of which there was "neither salvation nor remission of sins." The pope was stated to be the head of the church. Therefore to reject the authority of the pope was to cease to belong to the church. The bull distinguished between the "spiritual sword" and the "temporal sword," claiming that both were committed to the church. Since the spiritual was over and above the temporal, it was evident that the temporal power was to be subject to the spiritual power. The conclusion stated that it was necessary for salvation that every creature be subject to the Roman pontiff.

None of this could be traced back to the Scriptures and thus the bull represented an addition to Scripture. This was a far distant cry from the humble fisherman Peter, whom the Roman church claimed to have been the first pope and through whom by way of the episcopacy all popes thereafter had the supreme power that had been given to him according to the papal understanding of the keys of the kingdom in Matthew 16. But this was only part of the great and grave changes made in and by the Roman Catholic church under such earlier popes as Leo the Great (440–465), Gregory the Great (590–604), Hildebrand (Gregory VII, 1073–1085), and Innocent III (1198–1216).

The seizure of political and spiritual power by the papacy brought people under the sovereignty of the church and destroyed their freedom. The Roman church made many other changes for which there were no scriptural precedents. In the spiritual realm these changes were to lead to the rise of reforming sects and then to the Reformation itself. What were some of the changes that ultimately precipitated a crisis for the Roman church?

One major change lay in the area of hermeneutics, that is, in the area of the interpretation of the meaning of Scripture. The

Roman church was led by popes who spoke officially from the seat of Peter. Whatever was spoken from that seat was infallible and forever binding on the Roman church. And whoever dissented from the rulings of the pope lost his or her salvation and was anathema. Excommunication was the lot of many who did this, and the establishment of the Inquisition, which had both spiritual and political power, led to the use of torture and death to deal with dissidents. Religious freedom to be something other than a Roman Catholic was lost. Atheists, agnostics, and dissenters felt the heavy hand of the church on them and on their families and their worldly possessions. Force, rather than persuasion, was used to make converts. And since there was no salvation outside of the church, all those who were outside were heathen.

Moreover, the doctrine of salvation itself was modified and this was to lie at the heart of the Reformation later on. According to the new doctrine, people were said to be justified by faith plus works, despite the clearest teaching of the apostle Paul in Galatians and Romans to the contrary. The salvatory pattern was further modified by adding five additional sacraments to those of water baptism and the Lord's Supper. These provided the church with oversight of all its members from the womb to the tomb. Sins were divided into venial and mortal; mortal sins cut one off from the church unless and until there was perfect contrition on the part of the sinner. What was still more restrictive was the teaching that only the priests had the power to forgive sins.

The development of the Mass marked a further addition to Roman Catholic teaching that had no support in the Bible. The church taught that Christ was ubiquitous, which is quite correct. This means that wherever Christ is His body must also be there. From this fact the church moved on to declare that in the Mass Christ was really present in His body and blood. In the doctrine of transubstantiation the wine and the bread became the actual body and blood of the Redeemer, even though they retained their original outward form. This was a miracle performed when the priest elevated the host. Curiously this meant that wherever the Mass was celebrated Jesus Christ was really present and He could not be separated from His body. In that event, when different Masses were being celebrated in different places at the same time, Christ would then have to be omnipresent so far as his body is concerned and there would have to be two Christs or more at the same time, a curious anomaly.

Still another important addition to the teaching of the church was the doctrine of purgatory, a teaching that took away from the perfectness of the atonement of Jesus Christ on the cross of Calvary. Except for a certain few, all those who died in the faith went to purgatory where they had to work off the effects of their transgressions through suffering until full satisfaction had been rendered to God, at which time they would attain to perfection or sainthood and thus stand in the presence of a holy God. However, there were some saints who attained sainthood in this life and who had more merits than they needed, called works of supererogation. This constitutes a treasury of merit that belongs to the church and can be dispensed by the church to shorten the time one spends in purgatory. These helps are called indulgences and can decrease the length of stay in purgatory. Indulgences make possible the remission of the temporal penalty for sins and are available in consideration of prayer and other pious works by the faithful. Inasmuch as the church has an inexhaustible treasury of merits to dispense, one wonders why a plenary indulgence should not be given to all by papal fiat. It was the sale of indulgences, the profit from which went to build greater churches in Rome, that caused Martin Luther to tack his Ninety-five Theses to the church door at Wittenberg.

Still other additions made to the theology of the Roman Catholic church caused difficulties and helped ensure some sort of revolution, or at least schism, in the church. One can mention clerical celibacy, Mariolotry (which assigned to the mother of the historical Jesus the role of coredemptrix), auricular confession, simony, the scandalous lives of many of the popes, and a spiritual deadness among the laity among the many things that made the faith unattractive to those outside and inside its boundaries.

At Pentecost the church was thrust into a pagan world. It won a great victory over paganism and brought Western civilization as we know it into being. Europe was given the gospel and churches were established. While this was happening and while faithful souls were still being used by God to further the divine plan of the ages, the developing Roman Catholic church was seen by many to have become apostate. This required remedial action either by reformation from within or by establishing a new church or churches based on the original apostolic tradition that had been modified so greatly by the Roman Church. And the latter happened, as we shall now see.

3. The Reformation

If Pentecost represented a cataclysmic change in the world situation, it can be safely said that the Reformation brought about another turning point in the history of redemption. Instead of one church in the West, numerous other churches were to appear, and the changes in the role of the churches were to have worldwide implications. Whereas the world outside of the churches was fixed in bondage to paganism in a variety of forms, the Reformation was, in the long run, to send the church of Jesus Christ to the ends of the earth with the message of the gospel.

Before the Reformation came to western Europe in the sixteenth century, earlier dissenting movements had challenged the supremacy of the Roman Catholic church. They were not able to reform the Roman church and so had to exist outside the boundaries of that church despite persecution that resulted in the death of thousands of people over some centuries. Before we get to these sects, however, one other challenge to the Roman church deserves mention.

MUHAMMADANISM

Muhammadanism (Islam) was the only distinctively non-Christian religion that successfully obliterated a part of the Christian church during the period between Pentecost and the Reformation. Muhammad was an Arab and thus a descendant of Abraham who was born about 570 and who was acquainted with the Christian and the Jewish faiths. Following his own conversion from polytheism to monotheism, he had a vision from heaven and a book, the Koran, came down out of heaven according to his story. This book was to become the sacred scriptures of the new faith.

The theology and ethical precepts of this faith are not of interest here, but the expansion of Muhammadanism was to eradicate the Christian church in some areas of the world where the church had been strong. North Africa had a strong church. Indeed Augustine came from that region of the world. Alexandria had what was perhaps the greatest religious library of its day. The successors of Muhammad embarked on a program of world conquest and overran Palestine, Syria, and Egypt. Constantinople barely escaped from the onslaught of the conquerors in 668 and 717. The Muslims also overran Persia, Afghanistan, and part of India. In 707 North Africa fell to the invaders and the church was essentially wiped out there until today.

The operating principles of the Muhammadans can be seen from the story of the burning of the library at Alexandria. The conquerors said that if the books were in agreement with the Koran they were superfluous; if they disagreed with the Koran they were useless and harmful. In either event the books were to be burned; so they did and the valuable library was lost forever.

Around 711 the Muhammadans secured a foothold in Europe when they occupied the southern portion of Spain. They set up the califate of Cordoba after they had subjugated the Visigoths. Then in 732 they crossed the Pyrenees, threatened the Frankish kingdom, and expected to house their horses in St. Peter's in Rome. Fortunately for the West, the forward progress of Muhammadanism was stopped by their defeat at the hands of Charles Martel in the battle of Tours in 732. It would be a long time before Spain was fully returned to the Roman church under Ferdinand and Isabella. Had the boundless ambitions of the Muhammadans, who believed they were unstoppable, been achieved, the history of western Europe and the Roman church would have been quite different. However, there were other peoples in the sphere of the Roman church who were just as much a threat to that church as the people of Islam were. The story of these pre-Reformation sects helps to make the coming of the Reformation understandable.

PRE-REFORMATION SECTS

The story of the Albigenses, a heretical rather than an evangelical sect, presented a challenge to the Catholic church. They were Manichaean dualists who held to the two principles of good and evil. They retained the New Testament and the prophetic parts of the Old Testament but interpreted them allegorically. They taught that Jesus Christ was an angel who had a phantom body. He did not suffer, die, or rise again. His redemptive work lay in teaching people the true Albigensian doctrine. They rejected the sacraments, denied the existence of hell, purgatory, and the resurrection, and palpably hated the Catholic church. They also condemned marriage and forbade the use of meat, milk, and eggs.

The Catholic church acted vigorously against the Albigenses and were successful at last in extirpating them. Despite the church's condemnation of the Albigenses by the councils at Reims (1148) and Verona (1184) and the Fourth Lateran Council (1215), they spread rapidly. In fact, by the middle of the twelfth century virtually all of southern France was anti-Catholic. Innocent III started a crusade against the Albigenses, promising those who extirpated the heretics their territory, the spoils of the war, and a plenary indulgence. A large army was gathered and city after city was decimated, their inhabitants slaughtered. The work went on for years until the region was almost depopulated. Some fled to Spain and others went to the Netherlands, which was the home of many heretics until the Reformation.

Other movements during this period included the Bogomiles, the Cathari, the Joachimates, the Spirituales, the Amalricians, the Beghards and Beguines, the Petrobrusians and the Henricians, the Arnoldists, the Humiliati, the Poor Men of Lombardy, the followers of Marsilius of Padua, the followers of Peter Chelcicky, and the Brethren of the Common Life. These movements were symptomatic of the increasing difficulties in the Catholic church that were eventually to lead to the Reformation. Three movements are of special interest to those in the evangelical tradition: the Waldensians, the Lollards (Wycliffe), and the Hussites.

Peter Waldo was a wealthy merchant who, along with his followers, went about preaching and teaching the Word of God. The archbishop of Lyons forbade these laypeople to preach and teach. When they refused to stop their ministry, the Council of Verona (1184) excommunicated them. Meanwhile their numbers increased over the south of France, in Piedmont, Italy,

Spain, and the Rhine Valley. Innocent III instituted a crusade against them in 1209. In 1211 some eighty Waldensians were burned at Strassburg. Waldo died in Bohemia and left behind him a strong company of believers in the evangelical theological tradition. When the Reformation dawned, they made contact with the Reformers; they have remained outside the Roman Catholic fold and have been numbered among the Protestants ever since.

John Wycliffe was a fourteenth-century English reformer who earned the title of the "Morning Star of the Reformation." He believed that all Christians had the right to read and interpret the Word of God for themselves. To this end he began the translation of the Bible into English, a work that was carried on by his disciples Nicholas of Hereford and John Purvey. Wycliffe quickly earned the enmity of the Catholic church when he, among other things, asserted that the pope's claims to primacy could not be supported from Scripture and that his salvation was no more guaranteed than that of any other person. His language became more violent as he charged that the pope and the Catholic hierarchy were the Antichrist and he called the pope's adherents the "twelve daughters of the diabolical leech."

Wycliffe spent the latter years of his life in writing and preaching. He died in 1384. The Council of Constance declared him a heretic. His bones were dug up from the consecrated grounds in which they lay and burned and the ashes were thrown into the Severn River. He left behind him the Lollards, who were his followers. They spoke out against clerical celibacy, transubstantiation, pilgrimages, and indulgences. They too argued that the pope and the hierarchy were unscriptural, that auricular confession exalted the pride of the priests who used these conversations for vicious purposes, and that prayers for the dead are a false foundation for alms. One Roman Catholic writer observed that when you saw two men on the road, one of them was likely to be a Wycliffite. These "Poor Priests" were persecuted, harried, and sometimes burned at the stake. But they made their contribution as pre-Reformation reformers.

John Huss was also a fourteenth-century reformer in Bohemia. He studied the writings of Wycliffe and was numbered among the pre-Reformation Protestants. Educated at the University of Prague, Huss was to become rector of the University in 1401. He was regarded as a menace to the Roman Catholic church because of his biblical preaching and teaching. Pope Alexander V issued a bull forbidding preaching in private chapels and requiring the burning of Wycliffe's writings. Huss continued to preach and also to defend Wycliffe. He wrote a great work on the church and retired from Prague. He was summoned to appear at the Council of Constance, which convened in 1414. He was given a safe-conduct guarantee by Emperor Sigismund.

When the Council met it was learned that a priest of Prague, James of Misa, was giving the communion in both kinds. (The worshipper received both the bread and the wine, whereas the custom was for the priest alone to drink the wine and the worshipper to receive only the bread.) His actions were attributed to the teaching of Huss. On November 28, 1414, Huss was thrown into prison, charged with heresy. He was later refused a fair trial and was burned to death in July of 1415. The reasons behind this treatment were many.

Huss zealously defended Wycliffe, who was called a heretic. He was the leader of a group of people who were threatening the existence of a hierarchical church. His denunciations of the Roman Catholic clergy brought them into disrepute. Bohemia's (and Huss's) desire for political freedom was looked upon as a tendency toward freedom from ecclesiastical authority. Almost any one of these was sufficient for the Roman church to take steps to rid itself of Huss.

The Reformation was about to begin. It would be imprudent to suggest that only religious factors were responsible for that movement, which was to alter the face of the whole globe in due season. Economic, political, and social difficulties also played a role in the movement away from the Catholic church that led to the establishment of Protestant churches and furthered the spread of the gospel far beyond the borders of Europe. While the Reformation would never have taken place without the presence of these other factors, that is, if the issues at stake were simply religious, time does not allow for a detailed description of them. Our central thesis has to do with the Enlightenment, so only a short résumé of the Reformation is required. Martin Luther was first and foremost in the genesis of Protestantism, and to him we go for a clue concerning his dissent from the Catholic church.

MARTIN LUTHER

Most readers know of Luther's birth and background. The key moment for us is when he nailed his Ninety-five Theses to the church door at Wittenberg on October 31, 1517. While indulgences lay at the heart of Luther's protest, we can generalize as to what his objections were to the Catholic church. Indeed Luther's attack against the abuses involved in the sale of indulgences was hardly new. This practice had already been criticized widely and was in some measure responsible for the Reformation's popular appeal when it came about.

Apart from the corruption of Rome, Luther repudiated the Romish teaching that salvation is secured by faith plus works. He reiterated his belief that we are saved by faith alone under the Latin label *sola fide*. He also stated the case for the Bible alone under the label *sola scriptura*. The Roman church had added tradition to Scripture and believed each to be without error and binding on all believers. Luther opposed the papal claims to supremacy and stood against the theory that the apostle Peter had been the first pope. He attacked the dogma of transubstantiation and clerical celibacy and sought the end of papal power in Germany. He also sought a radical reform of the religious orders. Luther also attacked the Mass, pilgrimages, the doctrine of purgatory, relics, and the invocation of saints.

By no means was Luther a schismatic; he sought to work for changes within the church. A showdown came when he was forced by the papacy either to recant his "errors" or be excommunicated by the church. He refused to recant and was excommunicated, which meant, according to the teaching of the Roman Catholic church, that he had lost his salvation and could not get to heaven unless and until he repented and performed an act of perfect contrition. This he never did, so that from the Roman Catholic viewpoint (at that time at least) he was lost forever.

Lutheranism spread widely and encompassed the Scandinavian countries, Germany, and Germanic-speaking peoples elsewhere in Europe. In those regions where Lutheranism constituted a majority, state and church were intimately connected. The faith was to spread across the ocean and take root in the United States. It existed in other European countries, and, following the missionary advance later on, Lutheran churches came into being around the world. The Lutheran Reformation was only part of the story. John Calvin added another element to the reform movement.

JOHN CALVIN

John Calvin was born July 10, 1509. While Martin Luther was excommunicated by the church of Rome, Calvin withdrew from it, having pronounced it to be no true church of God. His magnum opus, *The Institutes of the Christian Religion,* appeared in first draft either in 1534 or 1535 when he was in his mid-twenties. The definitive edition appeared in 1559. It was this work that became the cardinal document of the Reformed churches that were to spring up around much of Europe and Scotland as well.

In the dedication of *The Institutes* to Francis, king of France, Calvin observed:

For where the glory of God is not made the end of the government, it is not a legitimate sovereignty, but a usurpation. And he is deceived who expects lasting prosperity in that kingdom which is not ruled by the sceptre of God, that is, his holy word; for the heavenly oracle cannot fail which declares that "Where there is no vision the people perish."[1]

In the same dedication Calvin asserted that "we forge no new Gospel, but retain the very same whose truth was confirmed by all the miracles ever wrought by Christ and the apostles."[2] As over against the teaching of Rome, "We assert, on the contrary, first, that the Church may exist without any visible form; secondly, that its form is not contained in that external splendour which they foolishly admire, but is distinguished by a very different criterion, viz. the pure preaching of God's word, and the legitimate administration of the sacraments."[3]

Later he argued that the Roman church was not a true church:

As this is the state of things under the Papacy, it is easy to judge just how much of the Church remains there. Instead of the ministry of the word, there reigns a government, compassed of falsehoods, by which the pure light is suppressed or extinguished. An execrable sacrilege has been substituted for the supper of the Lord. The worship of God is deformed by a multifarious and intolerable mass of superstitions. The doctrine, without which Christianity cannot exist, has been entirely forgotten or exploded. The public assemblies have become schools of idolatry and impiety. In withdrawing ourselves, therefore, from the pernicious participation of so many enormities, there is no danger of separating ourselves from the Church of Christ. The communion of the Church was not instituted as a bond to confine us in idolatry, impiety, ignorance of God, and other evils; but rather as a means to preserve us in the fear of God, and obedience of the truth.[4]

A few pages later Calvin added these words:

While we refuse, therefore, to allow the Papists the title of the Church, without any qualification or restriction, we do not deny that there are Churches among them. We only contend for the true and legitimate constitution of the Church, which requires not only a communion in the sacraments, which are the signs of a Christian profession, but above all, an agreement in doctrine. Daniel and Paul had predicted that Antichrist would sit in the temple of God (Dan. 9:27; 2 Thess. 2:3,4). The head of that cursed and abominable kingdom, in the Western Church, we affirm to be the Pope. . . . We by no means deny that Churches may exist, even under his tyranny; but he has profaned them by sacrilegious impiety, afflicted them with cruel despotism, corrupted and almost terminated their existence by false and pernicious doctrines, like poisonous potions; in such Churches, Christ lies half buried, the gospel is suppressed, piety exterminated, and the worship of God almost abolished. . . . To conclude I affirm that they are Churches. . . . But, on the other hand, because of those marks, which we ought chiefly to regard in this controversy, are obliterated, I affirm, that the form of the legitimate Church is not to be found either in any one of their congregations, or in the body at large.[5]

Given these statements of John Calvin, it is clear that the only remedy for him was to leave the Roman church and to set up another church. He agreed with virtually all of the points made by Martin Luther against Rome. Like Luther he stood for *sola gratia* ("by grace alone"), *sola scriptura,* and *sola fide.* He proclaimed the universal priesthood of all believers and rejected the notion of baptismal regeneration.

The great body of Reformed churches sprang out of the bosom of this reformer. His emphasis on the sovereignty of God, the doctrine of election as foremost in the order of the divine decrees, and the consequent acceptance of a limited atonement lay at the heart of his view on predestination. It was here that Luther and Calvin differed, the former emphasizing divine synergism and the latter divine monergism with regard to the salvatory process. These differences did not hinder either of them from preaching the gospel to all, nor did it prevent either of them from being responsible for two of the greatest church movements in the Reformation, movements that persist to this very day. Another strand that went into the Reformation was Zwinglianism.

ULRICH ZWINGLI

Zwingli was born in 1484 and thus was contemporary with Luther and Calvin. A member of the Roman Catholic church, he foretold the overthrow of indulgences and other papal abuses. He had a pension from the pope, which enabled him to study the Latin classics and philosophy. Like Luther he thoroughly approved individualism and freedom of thought.

The humanism of the Renaissance prospered in Switzerland and the University at Basel was a center for advanced thought. Erasmus spent much of his time at Basel and influenced Zwingli, Oecolampadius, Capito, Pellican, Hedio, and Denck, all of whom advanced the reform movement. Humanism was the order of the day, but it was founded on Scripture and could be said to have for its central frame of reference a devotion to the humanities and a keen interest in culture. Its chief danger lay in the possibility that scholarship uncontrolled by the Scripture might lead to a secular rather than a religious spirit and become an enemy rather than a friend of the Christian faith.

Zwingli had been ordained a priest of the Roman church in 1506 and, like so many of those who were celibate, he lived a sinful life as a secret fornicator. In 1518 when he was chief preacher in Zurich, it was reported that he had seduced the daughter of a respectable citizen of Einsiedeln. He acknowledged his guilt but asserted that the woman was a harlot; he averred that he was careful never to seduce a virgin or a nun.

When he finally wed publicly in 1524, he had been secretly married for two years to Anna Reinhart, who then became his wife in a public ceremony.

As early as 1519 Zwingli in his lectures took issue with the Roman church over purgatory, the invocation of saints, and monasticism. In a public disputation in 1523 he defended his views against the church quite successfully to an audience of some six hundred. He argued that the gospel is the sole basis of truth and rejected the sacrifice of the Mass, celibacy of the clergy, the invocation of saints, and times and seasons of fasting. Before his death Zwingli was defending the right of anyone to preach the gospel regardless of church authority, for example, by those who were not invested to do this by the Roman Catholic Church. He also preached and taught and wrote against the Mass as a sacrifice and insisted it was only a memorial meal. He held the church universal to be invisible and said Christ was the only head of the church. In 1525 in his book *Commentary on True and False Religion,* he laid down his own views most completely. He was opposed both to Roman Catholicism and Anabaptism.

In 1531 in a battle against the Catholic Forest Cantons the followers of Zwingli were decimated and Zwingli himself was slain. His body was cut into pieces and burned and his ashes were mingled with those of swine and then thrown to the wind. Yet so far as Switzerland is concerned, the Reformation movement was indebted to Zwingli. And the Anabaptists he opposed also played a role in the Reformation and stood for things opposed by the other major reformers.

THE ANABAPTISTS

The Anabaptists may be said to have followed to their logical conclusions the principles laid down by Lutheranism and Zwinglianism. Both had repudiated church tradition and all human authority and had insisted that the Bible is the only rule of faith and practice. Consequently they aimed at restoring evangelical Christianity in its pure and primitive form.

The Anabaptists yearned for churches filled only with regenerate people and to this end insisted that only those who made a credible profession of faith in Christ and who voluntarily submitted themselves to water baptism could be church members. Personal faith was a prerequisite to baptism.

It might be said that wherever there were two Anabaptists gathered together there were three opinions. Their varieties were numerous and their differences many. Depending on the leader of any given group, the Anabaptists were given to idiosyncrasies. Yet it may be said that certain principles were more or less common to all of them:

1. They leaned in the direction of communism; in terms of self-denial and brotherhood they desired to follow what they thought was the example of the apostolic churches—the absolute community of goods. Some were satisfied with regarding their goods subject at all times to the demands of Christian charity.

2. They were opposed to infant baptism, which they regarded as unbiblical, indeed antiscriptural, and quite incompatible with the desire to maintain churches of the regenerate only. They regarded infant baptism as "the pope's first and highest abomination."

3. They insisted that only regenerate people should be church members. For unregenerate people to celebrate the ordinances and to participate in what was limited to the true believer was looked upon as an abomination.

4. They passionately believed in absolute freedom of conscience and were strongly opposed to any connection between church and state. They also thought that no Christian should occupy the office of magistrate.

5. Oath taking was said to be expressly prohibited by the words of Jesus. The truth could be spoken without the need for an oath.

6. They were opposed to war in any form and were willing to suffer death rather than bear arms. This also included objections to capital punishment.

7. They generally insisted on free will, the necessity of good works, forms of asceticism, and separation from those who did not meet their standards, and they practiced connectional church government while holding that each local congregation was a true church and not subject to any external authority.

It is safe to say that Anabaptist views were to have a significant impact on the thinking of many in the future. Their individualism had implications in the fields of economics as well as politics and religion. They were opposed by Lutherans, Zwinglians, and Calvinists for a variety of reasons, but they could not be stamped out and remained a challenge to those who were less radical and more conventional.

THE CHURCH OF ENGLAND

In a sense the Church of England does not seem to fit into the Reformation pattern, yet it became a worldwide body and had a significance in history far beyond the numbers of those committed to it as members.

At the heart of this church lies the figure of Henry VIII, who reigned in England from 1509 to 1547. He was originally a Roman Catholic and the author of a book defending the seven sacraments of Rome. Yet when he wanted his first marriage annulled by the Roman church and was unable to gain the consent of the pope, he demitted the church, founded the Anglican church, and married for the second time. Thomas Cranmer assisted Henry in his endeavors and became the archbishop of Canterbury. He was responsible for setting up the forms for the Church of England, producing the first and second editions of *The Book of Common Prayer* in 1549 and 1552, the English Ordinal, and a statement of doctrine, the *Forty-two Articles*. Henry, a repressive and absolute despot, "never spared a woman in his lust, or a man in his anger." Nor did he spare the Roman Catholic church, which he bested in his struggle for supremacy in England.

In 1538 Pope Paul III published a bull in which Henry's kingdom was placed under the interdict. This forbade the allegiance of Henry's subjects, anathematized Henry and his favorites, and exhorted Catholic princes to seize Henry's realm. This did not bring Henry to his knees, however, and the struggle between Protestants and Catholics for England continued.

In the long run the Protestants emerged victorious and the Church of England became the established church; English kings and queens had to be members of that church and were crowned by the archbishops of it. Inasmuch as the English became the leading overseas colonizers, wherever they went the Church of England went with them. It became a worldwide church and in due season archbishops of that church were appointed in various geographical areas of the world.

In the United States, members of the Episcopal Church in the U.S.A., part of the Anglican Church (Church of England), though few in number, played an important role in the political, social, and economic spheres of our nation. The prestige of the church, its liturgy, and its oftentimes wealthy parishioners attracted people who were high in the social order of the nation.

CONCLUSIONS

The Reformation represented a crucial junction point in the history of the Christian church. There was a shift in every sphere of life resulting from the losses suffered by the Roman Catholic church and the gains made by the Protestants. It was a major factor in opening the door wide to the Enlightenment of the eighteenth century. A new age had dawned and new beginnings were moving forward dynamically to reshape the world in which we live.

The Reformation broke the religious monopoly of the Catholic church in the West. Now other expressions of the Christian faith were made available to people. The wide variety expressed by the differences between Lutheranism, Anglicanism, the Reformed faith, and the Baptists gave people options they had not had before. The so-called breaking of the seamless robe of Christ, by which it was alleged that the unity of the church had been rent asunder, was not quite accurate. Long before the Reformation that seamless robe had been rent by the division of the one church into the Eastern and Western churches and by the rise of many small but important movements inside and outside of the two major manifestations of the faith. At the same time it is true that the increasing number of denominations did alienate Christians from each other and did produce a spirit of competition as well as friction based on strongly held theological convictions. Differences about infant baptism, the

Lord's Supper, and ecclesiology as well as Calvinism versus Arminianism did lead to divisions that seemed to be irreparable.

The Reformation also made clear the imperfections in the Catholic church. The Reformation churches were in revolt against Catholic teachings that had no support in the Scriptures. That the revolt happened showed that the Catholic church was not likely to institute major reforms from within. Once the Reformation occurred, however, it led to the Counter-Reformation by the Catholics.

The Counter-Reformation produced the Council of Trent. The Catholic church in this council hardened its stand, solidified its doctrine against that of the reformers, and authorized repressive means everywhere to overturn the Reformation. It served to drive a still deeper wedge between the Catholic church and the new emerging churches and to create a spirit of hostility that exists in some quarters even to the present hour. The rivalry and the tensions of the consequent struggle afforded the enemies of the Christian faith in any form an opportunity to inveigh against God and Christ. It also aided the non-Christian religions, whose members looked upon the Christian divisions as an opportunity for them to spread their own beliefs.

From the political perspective, the Reformation broke once and for all the monopoly the Catholic church had over the rulers of the West. The religious strife that eventuated from the Reformation gave rise to the Thirty Years War from 1618 to 1648. It was surely one of the worst wars of all time and it was a result of the religious differences between Catholic and non-Catholic forces. The Peace of Westphalia in 1648 ended the strife and established the right of the prince to determine the religion of his subjects. Each prince could tolerate or exclude dissent according to his own pleasure. The map of Europe was remade as a result of the war. The Catholic church by no means approved the terms of Westphalia.

At Westphalia the papal nuncio, Fabiana Chigi, did all he could to prevent the bishops and Catholics who were present from signing the treaty. The pope himself protested in the form of a bull saying that what had taken place was "prejudicial to the Catholic religion, to the divine worship, to the Apostolic Roman See—in granting to heretics and their successors, among other things ecclesiastical goods, in permitting heretics the free exercise of religion, the right to ecclesiastical offices, dignities," and so on. He declared that the various treaties were "perpetually null, void, and of no effect, iniquitous, unjust, condemned, reproved, frivolous, without force and effect" and no one was bound to observe their provisions.[6] In short, the pope said the Roman church was free to use any and all means in the future to destroy all religious opposition.

The Reformation changed the educational patterns of Europe permanently. Education had been a church function and it was controlled by the Catholics everywhere. There was no education to speak of that was not involved with religion. The great universities served as an arm of the church for the education of the clergy. There was no such thing as secular education. All this was to change as the Reformation opened the door wide for the establishment of educational institutions by the different Protestant churches. And this in turn was to lead sooner or later to secular education divorced from any church. The influence of education and teachers on the future of any community cannot be overestimated. It may be said that as the schools go, so goes the nation.

The Reformation broke the Roman pattern against religious freedom and dissent. The very existence of Protestant churches, which had come into being over and against the opposition of Rome, produced a substantive change of dramatic proportions. Once the Protestant churches claimed their freedom to dissent and freedom to believe other than what was taught by Rome, they opened the doors to wider dissent and to irreligion as well. If the Protestant churches had the right to disagree with Rome, then the people of those communities also had the right to dissent from the Protestant teachings. Religious freedom carried with it the risk that people could become anything they chose to become—adherents to the ethnic religions or any of a variety of new sects that came into being, skeptics, or even atheists. Moreover the very notion of religious freedom of necessity included the right to disseminate and to propagate religious ideas of every sort, whether they were in accord with community standards or not. This dangerous precedent had its roots in the Reformation and was to bring forth its own fruit in the years ahead. Since religious freedom has implications in the fields of economics, politics, and social life and behavior, there was no church that could render compelling decisions to determine what the civilization of a people should or would be.

One factor introduced into Western civilization prior to the Reformation had profound consequences. I refer to the invention of printing from movable type by Johannes Gutenberg (1390–1468). It certainly helped the Reformation itself, for it made the Bible available in German and in English. The availability of the Bible was instrumental to its study and its study in turn led to a comparison of the teachings of the Roman church with the teachings of Scripture itself. The widespread dissemination of printed materials popularized the Reformation among the people generally. And with the advent of the humanism of the Renaissance the printing press was to make available to scholars and people alike Greek and Roman classics that were steeped in paganism, a fact that had definite implications for the Enlightenment.

Last, we may say that the Reformation broke the Roman monopoly of power and the quenching of dissent by the use of force whether applied by the church itself or by the state through the church. Once persecution for dissent ceased, the door was opened wide for inquiring minds to pass adverse judgment against the Christian faith, whether Roman or Protestant. Now people were freed from the threat of persecution and death for heretical opinions. The fear of the consequences of publicly expressing dissent now annulled, human minds could roam over the whole landscape of life and use either reason or revelation to approach life and answer questions.

Even as Pentecost was a turning point in the history of Christendom, so the Reformation was another turning point that brought vast changes. But the end was not in sight. The next strategic turning point in God's plan of the ages was to be the Enlightenment, to which we now turn our attention.

4. The Enlightenment

I have traced the rise of Western civilization as it had its origins in the Pentecost experience of the church. The church had entered history at a time when paganism was rampant and superbly represented in the Greco-Roman world. Yet the church was able to assault and finally overturn that paganism and in its place bring to fruition a civilization based on the Judeo-Christian tradition. At the center of Western culture lay the Roman Catholic church, which over the years had altered the apostolic traditions by addition and reinterpretation. This led to the Reformation, which brought about extensive changes.

The Reformation, as we have seen, broke the Roman Catholic monopoly in Europe and new churches came into being. We took note of the changes the Reformation wrought and made mention of the Renaissance or the New Learning, which opened new doors of inquiry and centered around a humanism that was in accord with Scripture. Gradually the changes brought about by the new freedom under the Protestant view of the universal priesthood of all believers and the religious freedom that resulted from the doctrine allowed for dissent without persecution. This meant that neither the Catholic church nor the Protestant churches were able to prevent the rise of viewpoints that were, in effect, heretical from the standpoint of both communities.

Great and important as the differences were between the Catholic and Protestant churches, many basic doctrines were held in common. Both believed the Bible to be the revelation of God and agreed that revelation was over reason. They were trinitarian and believed that Jesus was God, was born of the Virgin Mary, died on the cross of Calvary for people's sins, and rose from the dead in the same body. But voices were now being heard that attacked the Christian faith about matters Catholics and Protestants held in common, as well as about matters that were peculiar to Catholics and to the individual Protestant churches.

By the middle of the eighteenth century, there was a clearly defined and significant movement in process that has been called the Enlightenment, or the Aufklärung in German. This movement in two centuries was to do what it took the church at Pentecost three centuries to do. It would reverse what the early church had done and bring to Europe and to the West in general the New Paganism; this New Paganism has dislodged the church from its key religious and cultural position and brought about what we now call the Post-Christian Era. In doing this the Enlightenment steeped itself in the writings of the Greco-Roman world into which Christianity entered at Pentecost and added to those writings new and compelling ideas that took root and flourished in the Western world.

The Enlightenment battled with Christianity in a life and death struggle. While the victory of the Enlightenment did not erase the church from history and the West, it did unseat the church from its primary position in Western civilization and break its hold by installing a new Weltanschauung that stood in opposition to Christianity, and that in turn brought the West under the control of a new Zeitgeist that was secular and anti-Christian. Whoever fails to understand what the Enlightenment did cannot understand the role of the church in modern culture. Until the fact of the demise of the church as a primary factor in Western civilization is seen, the need for another reversal will not be perceived and no orderly plan will be put into operation to effect any change.

First, it is necessary to look at the Enlightenment to see what it consisted in and what it stood for and who the key actors were. It will also be necessary to take careful note of the charges leveled against the Christian faith, charges that have been accepted by multitudes and that must be assessed and answered if the Christian faith is to recoup the ground it has lost in the past two centuries. Right now, in the Western world, the Christian faith exists in a sea of paganism and the situation is not getting better. It is getting worse. Quantitatively, Christianity in the Western world may be better off than in places like Japan, China, and India. But qualitatively, churches all around the world are living in the midst of a dynamic and challenging paganism that is powerful, sophisticated, and on the march. In the so-called non-Christian nations the ethnic religions have rebounded and increasingly present a greater and greater challenge to the Christian faith.

Few textbooks of church history supply adequate information on the Enlightenment. Many of them do not index anything on such people as Diderot, Condorcet, d'Alembert, and even Voltaire. The Encyclopedists are hardly, if ever, mentioned. The one historian who has contributed more to my own understanding of the Enlightenment and its meaning for the church in the twentieth century is Peter Gay, who teaches at Yale University. His two-volume work *The Enlightenment* has more material than any other work of which I have any knowledge; the subtitle of the first volume is "The Rise of Modern Paganism." In my own reading of evangelical works I have never found any scholars in this tradition who have tackled his work seriously or who are even acquainted with it. I pleaded guilty to the same failure until recently when I was challenged to approach the study of the influence and effect of the Enlightenment on the modern church. Professor Gay himself is a serious advocate of the major theses of the Enlightenment and gives no hint of any acceptance of or genuine interest in historic orthodoxy.

It is fair to say that I have drawn on the writings of Peter Gay and owe him a greater debt than words can express. He has clarified my thinking and sent my attention in directions I regard to be less known and explored by evangelicals than I think necessary. I hope that my own discussion of this subject will quicken the interest of a host of younger historians who can start where I leave off and fill in the gap I think wider and deeper than most of us who are called evangelicals imagine. It is with some trepidation that I open the study of the Enlightenment with the *philosophes* (French, "philosophers").

THE PHILOSOPHES

In his overture to his work Peter Gay says:

There were many philosophes in the eighteenth century, but there was only one Enlightenment. A loose, informal, wholly unorganized coalition of cultural critics, religious skeptics, and political reformers from

Edinburgh to Naples, Paris to Berlin, Boston to Philadelphia, the philosophes made up a clamorous chorus, and there were some discordant voices among them, but what is striking is their general harmony, not their occasional discord. The men of the Enlightenment united on a vastly ambitious program of secularism, humanity, cosmopolitanism, and freedom, above all, freedom in its many forms—freedom from arbitrary power, freedom of speech, freedom of trade, freedom to realize one's talents, freedom of aesthetic response, freedom, in a word, of moral man to make his own way in the world. In 1784, when the Enlightenment had done most of its work, Kant defined it as man's emergence from his self-imposed tutelage, and offered as its motto *sapere aude*—"Dare to know": take the risk of discovery, exercise the right of unfettered criticism, accept the loneliness of autonomy. Like the other philosophes—for Kant only articulated what the others had long suggested in their polemics—Kant saw the Enlightenment as man's claim to be recognized as an adult, responsible being. It is the concord of the philosophes in staking this claim, as much as the claim itself that makes the Enlightenment such a momentous event in the history of the Western mind. . . . The Enlightenment was a volatile mixture of classicism, impiety, and science; the philosophes, in a phrase, were modern pagans.[1]

Before we discuss who the philosophes were and what they believed and propagated, it is important to see where they were coming from and which ancients they learned their first lessons from and took as their models.

GREEK AND ROMAN BACKGROUNDS OF THE PHILOSOPHES

The philosophes owed a great debt to the ancient pagans of Greece and Rome. They regarded the Greeks and the Romans as the finest specimens of those who brought about the first "Enlightenment," which was later supplanted by Christianity. In some ways, of course, the Greeks and the Romans had an influence on Christians, particularly those who were steeped in the Greek and Roman classics. But Greek and Roman paganism was unable to halt the incursion of the Christian faith, which ultimately triumphed and brought into being the Judeo-Christian civilization of the West.

The triumph of Christianity over Greek and Roman paganism lasted for more than a millennium and a half. During this period the writings of the ancients lay buried, oftentimes unread and unknown. The advent of the printing press changed all this. The presses in the eighteenth century spewed forth copies of these ancient works and did so at a time when educated men and women read Latin, at least, and Greek and other languages as well. Titus Lucretius Carus was a favorite of the philosophes. His book *De rerum natura,* which was Epicurean in its approach and emphasis, was to be found in virtually every library of the philosophes. Voltaire was known to have had at least six editions and translations of the work in his possession.

The old paganism of the Greeks and the Romans was now to become the source of inspiration for the new Enlightenment. Most of the presuppositions underlying the viewpoints of the old pagans were taken over by the new pagans, but to them were also added ideas resulting from the rapid advance of knowledge in the sciences and in philosophy. New avenues of thought were opened; new insights were brought forth; new data were advanced against the Christian faith; the new age made it appear likely that what the Christian faith had done to the old paganism would now be done to the Christian faith. That faith, for the first time, was faced by old and new tools of schooled minds greater than anything the church had experienced in its history.

The writings of the Greek and Roman pagans would have been of little help had there not been gathered at this time in history an elite group of trained scholars with excellent minds, facile pens, persuasive speech, passionate unbelief, and above all a sense of desire and intention to crush religious faith. An all-out war was fought between those who placed the Bible over humans and revelation over reason and those who put reason over revelation and humans over the Bible. And how the philosophes were influenced by Greek and Roman thought is important for us to see.

The Greeks

Denis Diderot, one of the foremost exponents of the Enlightenment, told Catherine the Great that the Romans had been taught by the Greeks and that both of them belonged to the philosophes. Despite the fact that probably most of the less well instructed philosophes were most moved and helped by the

Roman Stoics, Epicureans, and Eclectics, their indebtedness to the Greeks was substantial whether they acknowledged it or not. The Greeks, who themselves had been held in bondage to a large pantheon of gods for centuries, did perform a useful service by demythologizing the gods. The apostle Paul in Acts 17 gives notice of the then still current acceptance of many gods; he who pointed out that the existence of counterfeit gods pointed to the one true God incarnate in Jesus Christ. By this approach Paul was saying that the destruction of mythological gods did not carry with it a necessary conclusion that all gods are mythical. There might be the One True God and this One he proceeded to make known to the Greeks.

The Greeks, notably Thales, did contribute to the advance of knowledge by introducing the scientific method to philosophy. It has been said that Thales was the first one worthy of being called a philosopher. His was an inquisitive mind, representative of a spirit of inquiry that was a Greek contribution. But the Greeks differed from the Christians in that their morals were derived from human nature rather than from the being and mind of God.

David Hume said that the historians Thucydides and Xenophon were the first writers of real history. He found in their writings a clear-cut distinction between superstition and thought, that is, the difference between myth or fable and history or reality. And one might add that Hume was thereby suggesting that the Christian faith was mythical, not historical.

Petrarch, the Italian poet and humanist of the fourteenth century, a precursor of the Enlightenment, took the term "dark ages," which had been applied to pre-Christian times, and laid it squarely on the back of the Christian faith. This constituted a denial of the historicity of the Christian faith based on the notion that it was grossly superstitious.

To the philosophes Greek philosophy represented the conquest of myth by reason. Socrates' precept, "Know thyself," was accepted by the philosophes and interpreted by them to mean that mind and self-mastery belonged together, a view that had in it a virtual denial of metaphysics. Aristotle and Plato were not as popular with the philosophes as were the Romans. Nevertheless what they contributed was carried over into the thought process of the Romans and later followers of them in diluted forms, and thus it influenced the philosophes whether they were aware of it or not. But basically the philosophes chose the Romans over the Greeks.

The Romans

It may be that the influence of Roman writings can be accounted for in some measure by the fact that Latin was at the heart of the curriculum for the student world. Without Latin the Catholic church would have been lost. Its ritual, its edicts, and its own writings made use of Latin. Thus the Roman world was accessible to every schoolchild, every scholar, and every politician.

The Roman world was pagan to the core. Christianity confronted that world with the gospel and advanced the claim that Christianity alone is the true religion and the only way by which people can get to heaven. The average man or woman in the Roman Empire was not an atheist. Rome had a surfeit of gods and goddesses. While we may attribute this to mythology among both the Greeks and the Romans, there is still one possibility that should not be overlooked. Given the biblical teaching of Adam's sin and fall, humankind was prone to invent gods and goddesses to replace the God they had lost and now did not know. One can surely say that behind the mythological and counterfeit gods there was the real God. The apostles ran into this problem and endeavored to disclose the God of the Old and New Testaments to replace these pagan deities.

In Acts 14:11 Luke says that the pagans in Derbe and Lystra, cities of Lycaonia, cried out that "the gods are come down to us in the likeness of men." Acts 17 speaks of "certain philosophers of the Epicureans and of the Stoics" who said Paul was a babbler who set forth strange gods. They drew him to the Areopagus where he talked about Jesus to the crowd gathered there. These incidents provided Paul with an opportunity to evangelize. Had they been atheists, he would have had to argue first about the possibility that God might exist. As it was, he had a common ground on which to start his preaching. They believed in gods. And all Paul wanted to do was to tell them that their notion of the existence of gods needed to be corrected and to show them that there is one God and that Jesus Christ is the divine Son of God.

As we now come to consider the indebtedness of the philosophes to the Roman literary lights we must remember that the latter were pagans. But we also must remember that they were human beings who still bore the image of God however defaced and that they were beneficiaries of a primitive revelation that had been twisted and turned so that the knowledge of the true God was missing. Their errors and misconceptions still pointed back to something true that had been scarred and distorted. Behind their errors there was truth they did not understand.

It makes less of a difference than we suspect whether the truth is asserted by Christians or non-Christians. For a pagan to say that stealing is wrong does not render that notion useless because it was spoken by a pagan and not by a Christian. Truth is truth wherever it may be found. Thus we will see that the Roman pagans who were to influence the philosophes were not wrong in all they said. Some of their insights were and are true and will always be true. They coincide with Christian revelation at that point. But just because they said true things does not make them Christians when they were actually pagans.

Later we shall see that the philosophes misunderstood this and consequently claimed that Christian writers were inconsistent to use the thoughts of any pagans. This would lead to the conclusion that anyone outside the Christian faith could not possess any knowledge that would be consistent with Christian revelation. Neither Scripture nor thoughtful Christians have ever said this.

This brings us to a short discussion of the paganism of Rome, its leading writers, and the impact their writings had on the philosophes in the eighteenth century. For our purposes we will look at a few of the celebrated Romans who were generally read and followed by the philosophes—Ovid, Horace, Lucretius, Virgil, and Cicero.

OVID

Ovid (Publius Ovidius Naso, 43 B.C.–A.D. 18) was educated at Rome where he studied rhetoric but gave himself over at last to poetry. He may be regarded as either among the last of the

Augustan poets or among the first of the poets of the Silver Age of Latin literature. He went through three marriages and was involved in some fashion not known to us in the adultery of Augustus' granddaughter. She was banished and so was he. Augustus banned his works from the public libraries.

Some have called the twelfth and thirteenth centuries the "age of Ovid." His works were widely read in the schools. They were entertaining as well as instructive—he had a gift for epigrams, terse, sage, or witty and paradoxical sayings often removed from their original settings. During and following the Renaissance his writings were an integral part of the education of the day and an acquaintance with his writings was normally expected of any educated person.

Ovid was a hedonist who authored *Ars amatoria,* an immoral poem that was condemned by Augustus as destructive of the morality he was trying to advance among the people in the Roman Empire. He was a pagan who, says Peter Gay, "recommended religious belief on grounds of convenience." He quotes *Ars amatoria* as saying, "It is convenient that there should be gods; and since it is convenient, let us think they exist." Peter Gay then adds his own statement that "Polybius, Cicero, Sextus Empiricus, Varro, all agreed that false myths were socially useful."[2] Ovid was a gifted poet, a much studied exponent of the arts, an author read by multitudes, and a pagan.

HORACE

Horace (Quintus Horatius Flaccus) lived from 65 to 5 B.C. His father was a freed slave. Horace spent most of his life in Athens and was a contemporary and friend of Virgil. He was noted for his ability to create memorable phrases. His epigrams were striking and found their way into the writings of many other authors including the philosophes. He extolled the emperor and his family and composed short formal hymns to the gods and goddesses.

Peter Gay remarks that "Diderot, whose knowledge of Horace was unsurpassed, prized him as 'the most sensible and delicate author of antiquity' and bitterly resented those of his contemporaries who mouthed the famous phrase *ut pictura poesis* without knowing a single other line from Horace." Gay adds:

But after all it was hardly Horace's fault that his poetry had been despoiled to furnish copybook maxims for the trivial moralizing of the eighteenth century. And in fact, to the philosophes, Horace meant more than this: he was a master of the art of living; he was the urbane advocate of moderation, free alike from doctrine and fanaticism, a free spirit who took from the schools what he needed and tested his reading by experience. He had described himself as "a hog from Epicurus' herd," but he was enough of a Stoic to detach himself from slavish dependence even on Epicurus. Being everyone's disciple, he was no one's; living in the interstices of doctrine, he achieved an ideal individuality that moved the philosophes to imitate not merely his writings, but his style of life as well.[3]

Diderot thought enough of Horace to emulate him in his own production *Le Neveu de Rameau,* which was patterned after the *Satires* of Horace. Horace was indeed a true pagan whose influence on the philosophes was important.

LUCRETIUS

Lucretius (Titus Lucretius Carus) lived in the first century before Christ; he was an author whose contribution to the Enlightenment was considerable. His life is shrouded in mystery and of all his writings only *De rerum natura* survives. But that work alone makes him a marvel of his age and the darling of the philosophes. Virgil paid tribute to him in these words: "Happy is the man who can know the causes of all things, and has trampled underfoot all fears, inexorable fate, and the clamor of greedy hell."[4]

Perhaps no other writer of that age campaigned as vigorously against religion as did Lucretius. Fiercely polemical, he argued that science and science alone provided the answers to the riddle of the universe. Religion, to him, was based only on superstition derived from ignorance and maintained by force. An exponent and defender of Epicurus, he endorsed the notion of passionless gods who had no part or role in the present operation of the universe. Science and right reason are handmaidens whose working together makes religion unnecessary, indeed useless.

It was Lucretius who claimed that no one can create something out of nothing. The universe is infinite in size and changeless atoms control all things. Whatever happens is the result of matter and void. The human soul is made of matter. It is born, grows, and dies with the body. Sense perception tells us what we know. It perceives the existence of matter and reason leads one to suppose that it exists in the form of atoms.

He thought that priests and prophets exercised power by frightening believers with the threat of eternal punishment. He firmly believed in a natural order in which religion had no place and served no purpose. It was said that Voltaire had no less than six editions and translations of Lucretius' work and many other philosophes possessed copies of his masterpiece. As a materialist he foreshadowed Karl Marx. His views would be incarnated a thousand times over by the cult of scientism, which was based on naturalism and which was no friend of religion whether in the form of Christianity or the ethnic faiths of the East. His ideas would form an essential component of the Enlightenment, which would also place reason above revelation and science above metaphysics.

VIRGIL (VERGIL)

Virgil (Publius Vergilius Maro, 70–19 B.C.) was born of peasant stock, educated at Cremona, Milan, and Rome, and became the greatest Roman poet. He was the author of the *Eclogues*, the *Georgics*, and the *Aeneid*. One of his teachers was Siro, an Epicurean whose views appear in Virgil's earlier works but eventually give way to a world and life view consonant with Stoicism and neo-Pythagoreanism.

Perhaps no other Roman author was better known to students and scholars than Virgil. His works were studied by all who sought to master Latin. Unfortunately, Christian writings in Latin could not be compared to the writings, if not the ideas, of Virgil. No other literary reputation comes close to his. From the Christian perspective Virgil may well be the pagan who came as close to the Christian faith as any other ancient writer.

The content of Virgil's fourth *Eclogue* was taken by many of the early fathers of the church as a reference to the birth of the Messiah, Jesus Christ. Some of the church fathers theorized that, had he not been born before Christ's time, he would have become a Christian. By some he was called "a soul Christian by nature" if such was possible. It is, of course, true that even in the Old Testament there was room for those who were not of the stock of Israel to enter the kingdom of God by faith. In fact some have speculated that Plato may have been a true believer. But those opinions must await the judgment day. However the fathers found all sorts of ways to Christianize what Virgil said.

Suffice it to say that Virgil was known and used by Westerners in and outside the Christian camp. Milton's *Lycidas* is said to have had for its predecessor the fourth *Eclogue* of Virgil. The philosophes, in their use of Virgil, did not draw the same conclusions as did the early church fathers. They recognized in this poet a quest for a world and life view similar to theirs, one that was antithetical to that of the Christians. Many a student who was steeped in Horace and Virgil found greater delight in these classics than in the Bible or the theology of the Christian faith. Ironically, Gay says that in Winckelmann's Latin school at Stendal "the pupils studied everything, including Latin itself, to learn the true fear of God, but Winckelmann, for one, learned precisely the opposite; he was inattentive during theology classes and was punished for it, but to no avail. . . . Winckelmann, the greatest of eighteenth-century pagans, learned his paganism with much pain, deep secrecy, and inexhaustible delight, in a Christian school."[5]

Little did the fathers know that "baptizing" pagan material and taking the good from among the bad would lead younger people to take the bad and leave the good. And nowhere was this lesson to be found more true than in the Enlightenment which, in turn, was to overcome the Christian faith and bring Western civilization to its knees with the New Paganism.

CICERO

Cicero (Marcus Tullius Cicero, familiarly known as "Tully," 106–43 B.C.) was a statesman, lawyer, scholar, and writer. He, along with Demosthenes and Edmund Burke, are thought to be the world's greatest orators. He was born in Arpinum (Arpino) in a wealthy local family and was educated in Rome and Greece and served in the military under Pompeius Strabo, who was the father of Pompey. For us his greatest contribution lies in the area of philosophy.

Cicero was essentially a skeptic, although he agreed that myths, though false, are socially useful. The philosophe, Diderot, thought Cicero to be irreligious even though he maintained an outward appearance of a devout religionist. Gay remarks of people like Cicero: "Viewing with a smile of pity and indulgence the various errors of the vulgar, they diligently practiced the ceremonies of their fathers, devoutly frequented the temples of the gods; and sometimes condescending to act a part on the theatre of superstition, they concealed the sentiment of an atheist under the sacerdotal robes."[6] Even David Hume, whose style was somewhat similar, spoke of Cicero as a "penetrating genius."[7] Undoubtedly Hume found in Cicero his own mode of thinking.

It will be of interest to all Christians that up until the Renaissance the works of writers like Cicero lay buried in monasteries and libraries where they were untended and uncared for. During the Renaissance, leading humanists discovered these ancient treasures, which then were made available first to scholars and then to all who wished to buy books following the invention of movable type by Gutenberg. In 1345 Petrarch discovered Cicero's letters to Atticus, a discovery that saddened him because in them he found a Cicero he did not know. Toward the end of that century Coluccio Salutati, who was a Christian, a humanist, and a disciple of Petrarch came across Cicero's *Epistolae ad familares.* Later he wrote *De tyranno,* a work on political theory, the impetus for which sprang from his reading of Cicero. Thus, for better or for worse, Cicero proved to be one of the redoubtable figures who provided ammunition for the Enlightenment philosophes in their struggle against religion and Christianity in particular.

Many other Greek and Roman writers contributed to the education of the philosophes in the eighteenth century. Those mentioned here are simply illustrations of the richness of the pagan tradition from which the Enlightenment was to gather an impressive and formidable array of arguments and indictments against Christianity in particular and religion in general. The philosophes did not stop with the contributions of the pagan classicists. They added to them new insights and arguments unavailable to the classicists from the continual enlargement of knowledge garnered from the New Learning. The combination of the old paganism and new insights from the

New Learning was sufficient to undo the accomplishments of Christianity and bring forth from the Enlightenment a radical change—a Weltanschauung and a Zeitgeist divorced from the Christian perspective and standing in opposition to the Bible and to both Catholicism and Protestantism in Western culture and civilization.

Our journey has brought us from the beginning of time to the victory of the church over Greco-Roman paganism. We have witnessed the rise of Western civilization and culture and now we are about to witness its decline and fall starting with the Enlightenment and reaching what may well be its apogee in the latter part of this twentieth century.

WHO THE PHILOSOPHES WERE AND WHAT THEY THOUGHT

Some of the precursors of the Enlightenment philosophes were identified with the Renaissance, which had in it elements supportive of the ideas of the later philosophes. However, it would be a mistake to suppose that when the philosophes emerged as a force in the Western world, they were all of the same stripe. There were philosophes and there were philosophes.

In all probability some of the philosophes were Christians, that is, they had been regenerated. Yet they accepted notions that identified them with the Enlightenment. One excellent illustration of this trend was Archbishop John Tillotson of the Church of England. His sermon "His Commandments Are Not Grievous" indicated that he was a Latitudinarian who could embrace the Church of England while he attached little importance to matters of dogma, ecclesiastical organization, or liturgical practice. In effect his sermon was in accord with the philosophes' viewpoint, so that he was holding views that were antithetical to some of those espoused by the Church of England. His bland theology occasioned the observation by George Whitefield, the English evangelist who was orthodox in his theology, that people like Tillotson knew "no more about true Christianity than Mahomet."[8] Whether Tillotson was a regenerate is open to question, but he was a confessing

Christian whose breadth took him far beyond the boundaries of orthodoxy.

Many of the philosophes were atheists, or skeptics, or agnostics who had little if any use whatever for the Christian faith. Yet even some of these did not leave the sacred halls of the church in which they had been raised. They were infidels who functioned among believers and who oftentimes pretended to be what they were not. Of course, a number of the philosophes stayed clear of any church and made no pretensions of any commitment to anything that resembled Christianity.

There were still others who were what one might call transitionalists. They were on the forefront of the new age in the realm of science, human freedom, and reason above revelation, yet they did not see the inconsistency between what they thought and did outside of the church and what the church itself regarded as eternally true. Such a state could not continue indefinitely and those who followed after them would choose against the true faith in favor of empiricism, and other modes of thought that were fatal to the basic principles of Christianity. As so often happens, the apparently minor concessions of one age are taken as starting points by the successors of the tradition and are then modified further and further away from what the earlier forebears intended. Thus the orthodoxy of one age becomes the heterodoxy of the next and the bête noire of the third.

The true philosophes knew where they stood, where they had come from, and where they were going. They had for their goal the destruction of Christianity, which they regarded as superstition and nonsense. They elevated reason above revelation and humans over the Bible. Before we come to the philosophes themselves, we need to mention three important precursors.

PRECURSORS OF THE PHILOSOPHES

The philosophes of whom we shall speak shortly were preceded in their endeavors and propagandizing by Francis Bacon, Isaac Newton, and John Locke. These English pioneers were to become the patron saints of the French philosophes who readily acknowledged their indebtedness to these gifted savants. It is, of course, quite likely that the French philosophes would have come into their own one way or another, had they not been preceded by these men whose ideas they emulated and carried to their logical conclusion.

Bacon

The first of these Englishmen was Francis Bacon (1561–1626), who died a member of the Church of England and was thought to be an orthodox yet discriminating member of that church.

Bacon distinguished himself in law, literature, philosophy, and science. For our purposes he is best known as "the prophet of modern science." He was an empiricist, but it's hard to see how his attachment to the Church of England and his empiricism could exist under the same umbrella. Bacon himself had been preceded by Descartes, who, like Bacon, followed the empirical methodology. Bacon even carried his empiricism into the field of morals. He did not accept the notion of any absolute rules of conduct or of a *summum bonum,* or "highest good." This obviously meant that Bacon could not accept the Ten Commandments as absolutes for human conduct.

Many conclude that Bacon influenced John Locke as evidenced in Locke's work *An Essay Concerning Human Understanding.* Locke's conviction that ideas are the product of sensation and of reflection can be found in Bacon's *Novum organum* where he says:

Man, who is the servant and interpreter of nature, can act and understand no further than he has observed, either in operation or in contemplation, of the method and order of nature.[9]

A true empiricist would hardly be a metaphysician and no empiricist could accept the supernatural. Thus Bacon, whatever his attachment to the Church of England, was not of much help to guard that church from what the philosophes would have to say later against the Christian religion. He gave them more ammunition than he probably was aware of at the time he composed his various works. But Isaac Newton and John Locke advanced the cause of the philosophes, which made this English triumvirate important for the Enlightenment.

Newton

Isaac Newton (1642–1717) is known to us as a scientist, theologian, and Master of the Mint. He was converted to Christianity as a student at Cambridge. He became well known as the greatest physicist of his day. He formulated the law of gravitation, discovered differential calculus, and was the first scientist to correctly analyze white light.

His contribution was thought by some to bulwark and support the Christian faith. Others saw in his works, this new science, things that troubled them. John Donne observed that the "new philosophy" called "all in doubt" and that the cosmos, once stable and comprehensible, was now "all in pieces, all coherence gone."[10] Although Newton was a conforming churchman, he denied the doctrine of the Trinity (he believed the Bible taught Arianism) and thought that all who believed in the love of God should be entitled to Communion in the Church of England.

It is not beyond belief that Newton could be labeled a Christian pagan, since he entertained views antithetical to historic orthodoxy. However he was a circumspect in his behavior and took pains to avoid theological controversy. Whatever doctrines of the faith he did believe would be later sabotaged by the philosophes, who regarded his religious faith as idiosyncratic. They embraced his scientism and the empirical method but denigrated what faith he had. This brings us to the third of the great English triumvirate, John Locke.

Locke

Of the English men we have mentioned, Locke was probably the most important English philosopher. The *Britannica* says that Locke was "the initiator of the Age of the Enlightenment and Reason in England and France, an inspirer of the American constitution, and more than a quarter of a millennium after his death still a powerful influence on the life and thought of the west."[11] This is a fair representation of Locke's significance, for, as we shall see, he did have an impact on the philosophes probably greater than that of any other precursor. They started where he left off and moved more and more in the direction implied by his thoughts but not yet taken by him at the time of his death.

Locke was born in 1632 and died in 1704 before the Enlightenment had come into flower. He earned a B.A. in 1656 and an M.A. in 1658 at Christ Church, Oxford. He also received a B.M. in medicine in 1675, although he was averse to practicing medicine generally. He wrote in the fields of theology, morals, education, philosophy, and politics.

Locke was an empiricist who had been influenced by the writings of Descartes. He, in turn, was to influence many others who followed after him. John Toland, who was an unwelcome disciple of Locke, wrote a full scale work on deism. His book *Christianity Not Mysterious* was based on a simple rationalist proposition that the only good religion is one based on reason rather than on revelation. Anthony Collins also followed Locke and the master was glad to acknowledge him. He was a doughty opponent of the Christian faith not too far removed from Toland.

Locke did go out on a limb when he proclaimed that all a good Christian needed to believe was that Christ is the Jewish Messiah according to the Old Testament prophets who foretold this. It was Collins who went on to say that, unfortunately, it could be shown that what the prophets of the Old Testament foretold did not literally come true. He argued that whoever believed those prophecies was naive, for the arguments against the difficulties were invincible. It was not Locke who came to this conclusion, but one who followed the logic inherent in his thought, and carried it to its ultimate conclusion.

Some in the church felt intuitively that Locke was a deist even though he never said that of himself. David Hume, a pagan who came later, insisted that Locke was an Arian or Socinian. Edward Gibbon thought that Locke's reason had been affected by a belief in revelation, a belief he thought mistaken, evidence of weakness in a person's intellect, and a regrettable lapse in Locke's thinking.

Locke remained a mediator, the last in the long line of pagan Christians. His book on religion, characteristically entitled *The Reasonableness of Christianity*, was, not yet, not wholly, a naturalistic work. The book did not please the pious, who thought it scandalous that Christianity could be summed up by the Divinity of Christ, and revelation reduced to an exalted form of reason. But it did not satisfy the philosophes either: the title of Locke's book struck them as a contradiction in terms, and, largely on Lockean grounds, they repudiated any possibility of a reasonable revelation. It was a sign of their distance from Locke that while they quoted his other writings with delight, they generally passed over his *Reasonableness of Christianity* with respectful silence. Voltaire summed it up rather curtly with an entry into his English notebook: "Mr. Locke's reasonableness of Christian religion is really a new religion." And that was that.[12]

It is fair to say that Locke was involved in a logical inconsistency that he did not overcome either because he was unaware of his logical fallacy or because he did not want to jump the fence all the way as men like Toland did and his philosophe successors were going to do. Knowingly or unknowingly, John Locke was the seminal father of the paganism that exists today. The great defeat of the church rising out of the Enlightenment can be said to have occurred in a major way as a result of the activities and writings of Locke.

The triumvirate we have mentioned—Bacon, Newton, and Locke—were contributors to the viewpoints of the philosophes and to them we now come. And the first of the philosophes is Voltaire.

VOLTAIRE

Voltaire (pseudonym of François Marie Arouet) was a Frenchman educated by the Jesuits. He earned a reputation as an able, articulate, and prime opponent of the Christian faith. He enjoyed a literary career endowed with brilliance and wit, which he used to maximum advantage and by which he gained for himself both enemies as well as friends.

Voltaire was exiled following two stays in French prisons: the first for ridiculing the Regent and the second for a quarrel with the chevalier de Rohan. He then spent time in London, where the influence of deists and followers of the Enlightenment turned him away from the Christian faith. For some years he was careful in what he wrote and how he expressed himself, so that it was difficult for those who opposed him to say that what he wrote were his own opinions—his deftly expressed opinions came from the lips of his characters. When he turned against religion in general and the Christian faith in particular, he became a never ending critic of the Catholic church. In the closing years of his life, what up until then had been half hidden now became open and unadulterated venom against the Catholic church. Of Voltaire's later years Peter Gay says:

Nothing was safe: the Trinity, the chastity of the Virgin Mary, the body and blood of Christ in the Mass, all were cruelly lampooned to enforce a single point: "May this great God who is listening to me, this God who surely cannot have been born of a virgin, or have died on the gallows, or be eaten in a piece of dough, or have inspired these books filled with contradictions, madness, and horror—may this God, creator of all the worlds have pity on this sect of Christians who blaspheme him!"[13]

Voltaire regarded the Bible, the Old and the New Testaments, as accounts filled with childish absurdities and contradictions that could not be reconciled or believed. They were manifest deceptions to him or just primitive allegories, but certainly not history and not something to be believed or taken seriously. In his attacks against the Bible Voltaire offended both Catholics and Protestants. Yet the evidences do not show that he was an atheist, as many of those who held views similar to his had become. Whatever his belief in God was, it was not that found in Holy Writ. So far as the Christian faith is concerned, though, Voltaire might just as well have been an atheist. After all, the Scriptures do teach that Satan believes in God, but this does not save him. If anything, Voltaire might be thought of as a deist whose God was above this world, divorced from it, and having no influence on history or the course of events among humans. His personal life did not commend itself as consonant with the ethics of the Bible or the express commandments of God. No one can say that Voltaire's life did not bring changes in the Western world. It did and today we are seeing the effects of that life all around us.

Voltaire is probably better known in America than Denis Diderot, who was one of the key philosophes and one without whom the Enlightenment cannot be understood. Whether Voltaire is the greatest of the group is hard to say, but to Diderot we now turn our attention.

DIDEROT

Denis Diderot (1713–1784) came from a family that included a number of Catholic priests. His parents were pious Catholics and there was a time when Diderot considered entering the priesthood. Fortunately for the church and for him, he apparently never did begin training for the priesthood, although there is a tradition that he had entered a school for that purpose. He lost whatever faith he had and became a champion against anything and everything Christian. This must be understood within the context of the Roman Catholic church, which he knew so well and objected to so vigorously.

During his lifetime Diderot was at times a deist, a skeptic, and then an atheist. Yet he was not without doubts even with regard to atheism. He enjoyed the ceremonialism of the Catholic church and was moved by it despite his rejection of it as false. His own sister thought he was driven by a philosophic devil. In writings left from his love relationship with Sophie Volland there are evidences that he was unable to square his love for her purely on the basis of the blind encounter of atoms, a theory quite consistent with his atheism. His mind approved his atheism while his heart revolted against it. He also found difficult the notion that the person is innately good, a view that destroyed the idea of original sin. Because of his experiences among people, his faith in humanity was oftentimes shaken by how they lived and conducted themselves. Harassed by doubts, Diderot even in his last days did not repent of his denial of everything Christian.

A decade before his death he traveled to Russia and met with Catherine the Great, who purchased his library with the stipulation he could keep it until his death. This gave him money for the dowry of his only living daughter.

Diderot has been recognized as one of the most literate men of his age, a philosopher, man of letters, a brilliant and original thinker. His greatest contribution to the Enlightenment came from his editorship of the French *Encyclopédie*, of which d'Alembert was coeditor. This work was proscribed for its content, which ran counter to everything intrinsic to a culture and civilization based on the Hebrew-Christian tradition. It was filled with materials gleaned from the ancient Roman pagans.

Gay illustrates this strain in the mind and heart of Diderot by an excerpt from a letter Diderot wrote to Voltaire:

Other historians tell us facts to teach us facts. You do it in order to excite in the depth of our souls a strong indignation against mendacity, ignorance, hypocrisy, superstition, fanaticism, tyranny; and that indignation remains when the memory of the fact has gone.[14]

It is interesting that philosophes like Voltaire and Diderot who fought these negative qualities were convinced that the Christian faith was guilty of having breached all of them. On the other hand, few Christians opposed to what the philosophes stood for could really believe that these pagans practiced what they preached.

Diderot was consistent about one thing—his hatred for and opposition to the Christian faith, especially as it was expressed in the Roman Catholic church of his day. That he had the endorsement of this attitude by some Protestants who were equally opposed to Roman Catholicism admits of no doubt. But what Diderot said about the Catholic form of Christianity did not keep him from being wholly and unalterably opposed to Protestant Christianity as well. In fact his atheism could be said to include all ethnic non-Christian religions as well. All fell under his conviction that religion is false and comes from human imagination. It has no ultimate reality since it is a figment of a person's mind. Diderot's high calling was to disabuse all humankind of religion of any kind. And he was ever at work to accomplish that goal, which was also the goal of all of the philosophes however much some of them may have differed from him.

One fascinating aspect of Diderot's life was his estrangement from Jean Jacques Rousseau, whom he had introduced to the circle of the encyclopedists. Rousseau was more of a deist who struck down revealed religion and advocated a sentimental faith divorced from supernaturalism. His views opened the doors wide to humanistic liberalism of a later day. He died in 1778 without reconciliation with Diderot, who had been his mentor and who expressed no regret about his decease. In Diderot's atheism there seems to have been no ground for sorrow or for any emotion since there is no immortality and no judgment.

The estrangement says something about both men. Diderot objected to Rousseau's retirement from an activistic state, which reminded him of Christian monasticism. He thought Rousseau was deserting the true Enlightenment faith by doing this. Rousseau's responses to Diderot sounded critical of the life-style of the master—and this may well have represented a genuine clash of ideals rather than just a personality difference. In any event both of them were leading characters in the Enlightenment and their views were to fuel the fire that would lead to the rise of the New Paganism in the Western world.

One of the most curious aspects of Diderot's life came at the time of his death. This atheist was buried in consecrated soil at St. Roch through the intervention of his son-in-law. In death he lay among those who during their lifetime were as far apart from him as humans could be. Had they been alive, they would have chosen some other place to rest their bones rather than to be buried close to the great enemy of the faith they held to be true.

D'ALEMBERT

Jean le Rond d'Alembert was born in Paris in November 1717. He was the bastard son of the chevalier Destouches and Madame de Tencin. His education was provided for by his father. He studied in the Mazarin College of the Jansenists. Like so many of the philosophes, he ranged widely in his interests and attainments. He was a mathematician, a philosopher, and also a physician and a lawyer, although he neither practiced law nor medicine. He was also gifted in music as a science and as an art.

D'Alembert lived modestly and gave away half of his yearly income. He enjoyed pensions from the king of Prussia, the king of France, the French Academy, the Academy of Science, and from his own family. Whatever d'Alembert's contributions were in mathematics, for our purposes he was best known as the coeditor with Diderot of the *Encyclopédie*.

In 1756 d'Alembert visited with Voltaire, who entertained him along with leading Calvinist pastors, bankers, and physicians of Geneva. The Genevans candidly revealed much to the Frenchman, who listened more than he talked. They later came to regret their indiscretion. D'Alembert wrote a four-page article for the *Encyclopédie* on Geneva. It was far larger in scope than other articles devoted to more populous and larger countries.

It was explosive in its content and shook the Genevans to their bootstraps.

D'Alembert claimed that some of the Genevans no longer believed in the divinity of Jesus Christ. He said that some of the pastors of Geneva disagreed with Calvin over the burning of Servetus and interpreted the Bible in a purely rationalistic framework. To cap it all, he averred that some of the Genevans pastors had no more religion than a perfect Socinian. The response to the widely read article resulted at last in the resignation of d'Alembert from the *Encyclopédie*. Diderot accused him of desertion. Voltaire urged d'Alembert not to retract a single line from the article.

Peter Gay writes that Voltaire penned a note to a good friend that in Geneva "the reasonable Christianity of Locke is the religion of all the ministers." Voltaire later told his friend Tronchin that "you are cowardly enough to take it [i.e., the article by d'Alembert] in bad part."[15] Secularization was indeed making progress. The age was still religious in a limited sense, but religion was losing its hold on the people in a variety of ways.

One way in which Christianity was losing its hold was simply a lack of interest in anything Christian. Gay illustrates this with a quotation from Samuel Johnson, who spoke to young Boswell about a noted actor and wit, Samuel Foote: "I do not know, Sir, that the fellow is an infidel; but if he be an infidel, he is an infidel as a dog is an infidel; that is to say, he has never thought on the subject."[16]

Gay also pictures another character whose Christianity was described by Diderot in his correspondence with Sophie Volland. He was writing about M. de Montamy, who was a steward to the duke of Orleans and an able chemist. Diderot said of him:

No one is better informed than he is. No one behaves with better judgment or more moderation than he does. He is attached to his duties, to which he subordinates everything else in his mind. . . . He goes to Mass without believing it too much; respects religion and laughs up his sleeve at the jokes made against it; hopes for resurrection without being too sure about the nature of the soul. In general he is a large heap of contradictory ideas which make his conversation a pleasure.[17]

D'Alembert was a strong opponent of Christian orthodoxy and he properly deserves some of the credit for the demise of the activities of the Jesuits in France, which led to their expulsion from that country for a time. This occasioned his writing a book in 1766 titled *Sur la destruction des Jesuites en France,* in which he was critical of the Jesuits. While the Jesuits were urbane, sophisticated, talented, and well in tune with the Zeitgeist of the age, they were in large measure responsible for their own decline and expulsion from France. We might say they dug their own grave.

CONDORCET

Marie Jean Antoine Nicolas de Caritat, the Marquis de Condorcet (1743–1794), was born in Picardy and educated at the Jesuit college in Reims and the College de Navarre in Paris. He was a French mathematician, philosopher, and revolutionary.

Condorcet was influenced by d'Alembert to participate in the publication of the *Encyclopédie.* His reputation was secure by his election to the perpetual secretaryship of the Academy of Sciences and his membership in the French Academy and other European academies. He was noted for his biographies of Turgot and Voltaire.

He greeted the French Revolution with enthusiasm, but his independent spirit eventually resulted in his being outlawed and condemned. He died under strange circumstances—whether it was from exhaustion or poison is not known. His aim was not only to cause a revolution in politics but also in economics and social relations. He was a genuine polemicist and wholly a man of the Enlightenment.

Condorcet's philosophical fame derives from his *Equisse,* published posthumously in 1795. His basic thesis was the inevitable progress of the human mind toward ultimate perfection. Unfortunately, his theory cannot be sustained from any empirical evidence and was only the product of Condorcet's rich and suggestive imagination.

He said that humans started in a low state of barbarism with only a slight edge over other animals. According to him we can identify nine stages or epochs in the development to a higher form of life. Humans went from hunting and fishing to pastoral work and then on to agriculture. The fourth and fifth epochs corresponded to Greece and Rome. The Middle Ages were the sixth and seventh epochs. The eighth went from the invention of printing to the time of Descartes, who revolutionized the method of philosophical thinking. The ninth began with the great intellectual revolution—the Enlightenment—ended with the French Revolution of 1789, and had for its most important contribution the offerings of Isaac Newton, John Locke, the Abbe de Condillac, Turgot, Richard Price, and Jean Jacques Rousseau.

Eschatalogically, Condorcet saw a future epoch to be characterized by the absence of inequality between nations, the end of inequality between classes, and the indefinite perfectibility of human nature itself, intellectually, morally, and physically. This viewpoint had for its support the word of Condorcet, whose prophetic capacity, if accurate, would have given him a station not far removed from deity. He made no claim that he had any superhuman source for his opinion. Rather he demonstrated an intense aversion to all religion, which suggests that he was indeed an atheist. He thought Christianity had only contempt for the humanities. He said that Christianity "feared that spirit of investigation and doubt, that confidence in one's own reason, which is the scourge of all religious beliefs. It found the very light of the natural sciences hateful and suspect, for it is extremely dangerous to the success of miracles; and there is not a single religion that does not force its devotees to swallow a few scientific absurdities. Thus the triumph of Christianity was the signal for the complete decay of the sciences and philosophy."[18]

The best that can be said of Condorcet is that he was an amiable person, a good scholar, a splendid conversationalist, a genuine humanist, and an almost perfect pagan.

CONDILLAC

Étienne Bonnot de Condillac (1715–1780) was born in Grenoble, educated in Roman Catholic schools, and ordained to the priesthood at an early age. He came to know Jean Jacques Rousseau, who tutored his brother. He was deeply influenced by Diderot, whom he met in Paris. This brought him into direct contact with the Encyclopedists. Two of his books made him a center of attraction in the literary saloons and led to membership in Berlin Academy in 1752. He was elected to the Academie Francaise in 1768. Perhaps no other word can be said of him than that he turned out to be a Christian pagan.

It was Condillac who established firmly and systematically in French society the philosophy of Locke. He set forth with great skill the empirical sensationalism of Locke. Yet in his analysis of the human mind, despite his being a priest, he carefully omitted any reference to the active and spiritual sides of the human person. In his book *Traité des systemes* he attacked metaphysical systems vigorously. In *Traité des sensations* he departed from Locke, arguing that knowledge and faculty are transformed by sensation only, excluding thereby any other principle. He was a master of naturalistic philosophy which easily leads to atheism and determinism.

In all of this Condillac apparently insisted on the freedom of the will and the substantive reality of the soul as well as a heaven and an abyss. These were, of course, left over from his Catholic and clerical background. He stated that we never get outside ourselves—it is always our own thoughts that we perceive. It was from this sort of statement that Berkeley got one of his starting points. If Condillac's statement is correct, then there can be no revelation from God that stands outside of us. But if there is no revelation, then something outside of us has no way to get inside us and thus provide us with some things that are above and beyond us and do not proceed from within us.

Condillac's contributions in the *Encyclopédie* were significant and tightly knit him to the philosophes and the Enlightenment. It is interesting and suggestive that modern church historians do not see the importance of thinkers like Condillac and some of the other philosophes for the church in the present-day world. Williston Walker's *A History of the Christian Church*, recently revised by Norris, Lotz, and Handy,[19] has no mention in the index of Diderot, d'Alembert, Condorcet, or Condillac. A. H. Newman, a Baptist church historian, in his *A Manual of Church History*[20] barely mentions Diderot and d'Alembert but does not include either Condorcet or Condillac in his index. Moreover, they did not see or understand that the Enlightenment represented a return to the Greco-Roman pagan writers by the philosophes who were responsible for the victory of the New Paganism over the Christian faith, which had previously thwarted and overcome the paganism current in the apostolic age.

Ordinarily we think of philosophes as French, but we must remember that there are also thinkers from Britain who were members of the fraternity of the philosophes.

HUME

David Hume (1711–1716) was Scottish. He was born in Edinburgh and received his education there. He gained notoriety as a historian and philosopher. Whatever may have been his religious upbringing as one born in Calvinist Scotland, he ended up as a skeptic if not an atheist. He never married and in later life developed an enormous physical stature as a result of an affinity for food.

In his philosophy Hume was indebted to John Locke and George Berkeley. To him reason was the product of experience, which meant that he destroyed its claim to sole validity. He argued that the facts of reality are only made certain by probability. If this is true then there can be no metaphysics and neither the existence of God nor the existence of the physical world can be demonstrated by reason. To him theism was neither the first nor the highest form of religion.

Hume thought that immortality was at best doubtful and he had no objection to suicide. He was fully aware of the fact that he had destroyed any basis for real knowledge and thus he taught pure skepticism. When it came to miracles or the supernatural, Hume was a diligent and doughty opponent. He began with a presupposition that at no time in any age or any place had a dead person risen from the grave. He cast aside any and all historical evidence for miracles by asserting that even if a miracle were possible, this notion was offset by the possibility that the so-called evidence for such a thing includes the possibility of that evidence being a deception. He said that it was contrary to experience that a miracle could be true, but not contrary to experience that testimony could be false.

The views of Hume were applauded, derided, revised, or accepted and used by a variety of those who were philosophically minded. Among those indebted to Hume were his friend Adam Ferguson, himself a lapsed Christian and a former chaplain, who leaned toward the theory of the evolution of humans from lower forms of life. Ferguson was also a strong opponent of the Christian faith, Immanuel Kant, and Auguste Comte. Certainly Jeremy Bentham was following along lines laid down by Hume in his utilitarianism, which had for its central thesis the notion that the largest balance of pleasure over pain and the greatest happiness of the greatest number were the best and most desirable goals for human life.

Hume's belief that there is no demonstrable immortality did not seem to bother him at the time of his death. He was quite complaisant as death approached and saw no reason to alter any of his earlier views. In summary, from the Christian perspective, the words of Ronald Nash are helpful:

To argue as many Christians do, that reason can infer many of the divine attributes from features of the world, and that the Christian religion (or any religion, for that matter) is supported by miraculous events, is to exceed the bounds of human knowledge. These claims, according to Hume, must be rejected, as must the many assertions that Christians make about God in their creeds, items allegedly derived from special revelation. Without doubt, some Christians have overestimated the ability of human reason with respect to proofs about God's existence. . . . More serious, however, is Hume's denial of the possibility of any knowledge about God in general and the possibility of revealed knowledge in particular.[21]

GIBBON

Another British scholar and properly a member of the tribe of philosophes was Edward Gibbon (1737–1794), who is most noted for his work *The Decline and Fall of the Roman Empire*. When Gibbon was fifteen his father sent him to Magdalen College, Oxford. His stay there was disappointing. The authorities at the college hardly knew he existed. They did nothing for him intellectually or spiritually. Even his absences from the college went unnoticed. Left to his own devices, he began reading in theology and became a Roman Catholic when he was received into that church by a priest in London on June 8, 1753.

Gibbon's father learned of his turning Roman Catholic and shipped him off to Lausanne, where he came under the tutelage of the Rev. Daniel Pavillard, who was in the Reformed tradition. As a result of that experience Gibbon abjured his Roman Catholic faith and was readmitted to the Protestant communion on

Christmas of 1754. He himself stated that after this he did not concern himself with theology; he simply believed the tenets and mysteries acceptable both to Catholics and Protestants. It is quite doubtful that Gibbon was a Christian in the true sense of the term.

Gibbon's great work on the fall of the Roman Empire was and may still be thought of as unsurpassed in the field of history. He surveyed Roman history from the second to the fifteenth centuries from the standpoint of the prevailing humanism of the eighteenth century, that is, from the perspective of the philosophes with whom he associated and with whom he was in rather full agreement. The *Britannica* says of Gibbon:

The first quarto volume of his history, published on February 17, 1776, immediately scored a success that was resounding, if somewhat scandalous because of the last two chapters in which he dealt with great irony with the rise of Christianity. Reactions to Gibbon's treatment of Christianity have displayed various phases. Both in his lifetime and after, he was attacked and personally ridiculed by those who feared that his skepticism would shake the existing establishment. In the 19th century he was hailed as a champion by militant agnostics. Gibbon was not militant. He did not cry with Voltaire, "Écrasez l'Infâme!" ("Crush the infamy!") because in his England and Switzerland he saw no danger in the ecclesiastical systems. His concern was past history. One may say, however, with confidence, that he had no belief in a divine revelation and little sympathy with those who had such a belief. While he treated the supernatural with irony, his main purpose was to establish the principle that religions must be treated as phenomena of human experience.[22]

Gibbon had no affection for religion of any kind, let alone Christianity. Peter Gay states:

[Gibbon] noted that Roman statesmen had manufactured religious notions, forged religious documents, piously celebrated religious rites they secretly despised, all to keep the power orders in check: Augustus, said Gibbon, was "sensible that mankind is governed by names," and so, to preserve social peace, he gave the Romans names, both glorious and frightening. "The policy of the emperors and the senate, as far as it concerned religion," Gibbon noted with relish, "was happily seconded by the reflections of the enlightened, and by the habits of the superstitious, part of their subjects. The various modes of worship which prevailed in the Roman world were all considered by the people as equally true, by the philosopher as equally false, and by the magistrates as equally useful."[23]

This statement of Gibbon's reflects his own sentiments vis-à-vis Christianity. And one can assume that for him any religion that would keep the citizenry in check is to be regarded as useful or utilitarian even though obviously false. It is safe to say that Gibbon possessed the mind-set of the philosophes and was himself a strong and vocal advocate of the anti-Christian spirit that animated the leadership of the Enlightenment. In that sense he played a significant and important role in the defeat of the Christian faith in the West. Hume and Gibbon together represented the finest non-Christian minds and gifts, which they used so largely to reproduce the paganism of the Greco-Roman world in place of the Christian faith.

Now we must look at some of the German scholars whose impact on the Enlightenment was great and whose followers in the nineteenth century were to be identified under the label of German Higher Critics. Immanuel Kant was surely one of the most important members of the German Aufklärung and to him we now turn.

KANT

Immanuel Kant (1724–1804) was born in Königsberg, East Prussia, where he lived all of his life in relative seclusion, never leaving the province. He came from a Pietist family of Lutheran extraction. He was a professor of logic and metaphysics at the University of Königsberg from 1770. The writings of David Hume wakened him from his dogmatic slumber and turned him into a critical exponent of viewpoints quite at variance from traditional Lutheranism. This occasioned difficulties for him with the Prussian government.

In the tradition of Hume, Kant gave a new twist to the disjuncture between faith and knowledge. He maintained a personal belief in God, yet his own system made him a religious agnostic. He tried to meld the empiricism of David Hume with the rationalism of the Enlightenment. He argued that all knowledge is perceived by the senses (empiricism) but is then structured by the mind (rationalism). He ended by asserting that it is impossible for us to know ultimate reality. Thus he invalidated metaphysics. He also taught that the classical rational proofs for the existence of God (ontology, cosmology, and teleology) were invalid.

Curiously, Kant thought that the denial of the knowledge of God opens one door for faith. This idea provided a starting point for some who came after him such as Friedrich Schleiermacher, Albrecht Ritschl, and more recently Karl Barth and his "wholly other." He saw no need for a personal redeemer and found no place, as in traditional Christianity, for the historical as such. As humankind advanced in moral perception, Kant said that the practice of prayer was at best unprofitable. Miracles for him had no significance even if they happened.

Peter Gay was aware of the fact that for Kant theology became anthropology. When Kant asserted a natural human propensity toward wickedness, he disappointed Goethe, who thought Kant might be relapsing into the old Lutheran faith. He said that Kant had "slobbered" on his "philosopher's robe" and left on it "the shameful stain of radical evil," thus inviting Christians to "kiss its hem." Gay adds: "It was an interpretation as intemperate as it is doubtful, but it shows, with its very vehemence, how precious the Enlightenment's denial of original sin was to a perceptive contemporary."[24] Gay concludes that "Christian anthropology was that man is a son dependent on God. Whatever the philosophes thought of man—innately decent or innately power-hungry, easy or hard to educate to virtue—the point of the Enlightenment's anthropology was that man is an adult, dependent on himself."[25]

Along with Kant's denial of the propriety of metaphysics out went the notion of revelation. And without metaphysics and revelation there is and there can be no knowledge of God worthy of its name. Each person could construct his or her own god by whatever means he or she chose to.

Immanuel Kant was not alone in his endeavors. There were other Germans who walked by his side and fell into the same anti-Christian syndrome that was to challenge historical Christianity at the deepest levels and lead to the current impasse in the twentieth century. Two of those connected with the German

Aufklärung along with Kant were Hermann Reimarus and Gotthold Lessing.

REIMARUS

Hermann Samuel Reimarus (1694–1768) is remembered for his commitment to deism. He stated that "human reason can arrive at a religion more certain than religions based on revelation."[26] He labored as a professor of Hebrew and oriental languages in the Gymnasius Johanneum in Hamburg. His great work was still unpublished at the time of his death. Subsequently parts of its four thousands pages were published piecemeal and anonymously. Lessing edited and published parts of Reimarus' work too.

In the manuscript of Reimarus' great work was the title *Apologie oder Schutzschrift für die vernünftigen Verehrer Gottes* (Apologia or defense for the rational reverence of God). In that work Reimarus summarily dismissed miracles and revelation. He accused the biblical writers of fraud, contradictions, and fanaticism. Jesus, to him, was a mere human who suffered from messianic illusions. His dead body after Calvary was seized by his disciples and hidden away.

Reimarus worked his way through the Bible and came to the conclusion that from a rational perspective it was obviously false. In his *Third Fragment: Passage of the Israelites Through the Red Sea* he analyzed the scenario presented in the Exodus of the crossing of the sea. He said, "If we look at . . . the miracle of the passage through the Red Sea, its inner contradiction, its impossibility, is quite palpable." He went on from there to construct a situation based on his own assumptions and then argued that what is described in Scripture is utterly and completely false. Nothing in the biblical account, however, indicates that Moses used the plan Reimarus described. Moreover, as a deist Reimarus did not accept miracles in the here and now. Given his presuppositions and his scenario, one would have to agree with his viewpoint. But that is precisely what the difference consisted in between the philosophes and those in the historic Christian tradition; each held to presuppositions the other denied.[27]

Reimarus was a seminal contributor to the German critical school of the nineteenth century and influenced Albert Schweitzer in the views he expressed in *The Quest for the Historical Jesus*.[28] Reimarus had a marked influence on Gotthold Ephraim Lessing about whom a word should be said now.

LESSING

Gotthold Ephraim Lessing (1729–1781) was the son of a Lutheran pastor and came to fame by the publication of extracts from the unpublished work of Reimarus. A number of scholars entered the fray, supporting or opposing the views of Reimarus as well as those of Lessing. Lessing himself was a noted playwright who was often impoverished. At his death he was buried in a pauper's grave at public expense. In his literary works he profited much from his knowledge of the plays of Plautus and Terence, who were his ideal Romans.

According to Peter Gay, Lessing was not an untroubled pagan. His father, a distinguished Lutheran pastor, was tolerant, yet he rejected the theological innovations of his time. The son deserted the Lutheranism of his youth but he did so gradually and oftentimes with a sense of regret. He swung back and forth in his faith, favoring it when he read the treatises of its most offensive opponents and rejecting it when he read the works of those who supported it the most.

When Lessing worked his way through the *Apologie* of Reimarus, it served to convince him away from historic orthodoxy into the deism of this erudite scholar. Reimarus himself had passed through a painful time of recurring doubts about the Trinity, about the love of God who could permit eternal damnation for the unbeliever, and of Jesus Christ as the bringer of salvation.

Lessing's play *Nathan the Wise* portrays three men, one a Christian, one a Jew, and one a Muslim. Holding a sort of naive belief in the perfectability of the human person, it was the Jew who fared best in his work. He alone lived up to the ideal of what full humanity should be like. Lessing was to break with his earlier deism and move in the direction of the pantheistic philosophy of Spinoza. Thus he broke with the deism of the Enlightenment.

In his *Rettungen* (Vindications) Lessing argued that right reasoning, rather than faith or revelation, would lead humankind to truth and happiness. He rejected the notion that historical evidence is a sufficient basis for religious belief. For him the truth and value of religion are to be apprehended in experience. Thus those who live right will thereby show they have true religion. In effect he denied the idea of revealed religion and objective truth, becoming as it were the inventor of his own religion. Moreover he was convinced that Jesus was a purely human Messiah; he denied His deity and did away with the Trinity in the process. Whatever the differences between Lessing and other philosophes and no matter how much their viewpoints varied, he was still very much a member of that fraternity and an opponent of historic orthodoxy.

The plays of Lessing, while not centered in theology, were of such a nature that they conveyed to the audience ideas common to the Enlightenment. Probably more people were influenced by his plays than by the works more specifically related to religion as such. Since his plays had little or nothing in them supportive of the true Christian faith, it can be said that they contributed to the diminution of Christianity and were part of the general attack against the faith that was to lead to its paganization. Thus his labors mark him off as a pagan and a propagandist for unbelief.

AMERICAN FOLLOWERS OF THE PHILOSOPHES

This short survey of the European philosophes is normative for the Enlightenment, which captured the attention of numerous scholars, religious liberals, and many of those interested in science, the theater, philosophy, and the Greek and Roman classics. We now turn to an exploration of the influence and effect the European Enlightenment had on the American colonies at a time when they were preoccupied with seeking freedom from England and, once that was secured, with the task of establishing the United States of America and writing a constitution.

Since the American colonies had a close relationship with Europe and England, it is not surprising that the Enlightenment numbered among its followers some of the colonies' leading thinkers. If we are to understand the paganization of the West, which has included the United States, Canada, and Latin America, we must look to the influence of the European Enlightenment. We will see that the Enlightenment penetrated colonial America in a larger measure than some suspect and called forth a response from some of the brightest lights of Christian orthodoxy.

Deism, a child of the Enlightenment, did spread to America. How widescale that penetration was can be seen from a statement made by Jonathan Edwards, whose significance and contribution to American religious life cannot be overestimated. His statement itself makes it clear that deism was a major force among the intelligentsia of New England, for example. In Volume I of Edward's *A History of the Work of Redemption,* in *The Works of President Edwards* he said that the deists "wholly cast off the Christian religion and are professed infidels." They "deny the whole Christian religion." They "deny that Christ was the son of God, and say he was a mere cheat; and so they say all the prophets and apostles were: and they deny the whole Scripture. They deny that any of it is the word of God at all; and say that God had given to mankind no other light to walk by but their own reason."[29] This leads us to those American colonists who can be identified as sympathetic to or labeled as philosophes.

Jefferson

Thomas Jefferson in spirit if not in fact was the quintessential philosophe. He spent some years in France and was fully acquainted with the writings of the some of the philosophes as well as those of the Greek and Roman pagans. He had friends among the philosophes and sympathized with what they believed, but it is difficult to call Jefferson a Christian pagan. Rather he breathed out a spirit that was not at all congenial with the traditional faith of the Reformation or of the Roman Catholic church for that matter.

One of Jefferson's biographers, Fawn M. Brodie, says:

By 1773 John Locke's natural rights theories had become as commonplace for discussion as the Epistles of St. Paul, and for a surprising number of colonists the science of Newton and the political and legal teachings of Locke, Voltaire, Burlamaqui, Rousseau, Beccaria, Grotius, Pufendorf, and Vattel had edged out John Calvin altogether. For Jefferson the old Trinity was replaced by a new trinity, Newton, Locke, and Bacon.[30]

When the question of inoculation for smallpox was an item for public discussion, some of the clergy objected to its use, for the concept that sickness was part of God's will for those infected was quite common. "But Jefferson, who had ardently embraced the new science, could not attend and would not hide his head in the sand in this fashion. If death from smallpox could be avoided by the simple application of a bit of 'pus' in a scratch, what did the will of God have to do with death, whether from smallpox or in childbirth or any other cause? This was a question Jefferson certainly faced later on, as his new deism robbed him of one of man's oldest consolations in the perennial trauma of mourning."[31] In fairness it must be said that Jonathan Edwards, who was ever the noble defender of orthodoxy, approved of inoculation and himself died after he had been inoculated for smallpox. Inoculation could be approved both by deists and orthodox Trinitarians who objected strongly to deism. Anti-inoculation was not and never has had any support from the Bible.

Jefferson was strongly in agreement with Thomas Paine's *The Rights of Man* and saw to its printing. His note, which was attached to the material printed with Paine's book, gave Jefferson no end of difficulty. But that he and Paine shared similar sentiments could not be denied. When the news media expressed distaste that Paine, who was regarded as "the greatest infidel on earth," had been a guest of Jefferson's at the president's house, Jefferson stuck to his guns. "It showed how stubborn Jefferson could be about his friends."[32]

Jefferson later decided to make his own private edition of the New Testament. "He would strip away its 'corruptions,'" leaving out all references to the supernatural—the Virgin Birth, the miracles, the Resurrection, and the complexities of the crucifixion, including only, as he put it later, 'the matter which is evidently his, and which is as easily distinguishable as diamonds in a dunghill.' This project he began to carry out in the winter of 1804–05."[33] While Jefferson could have had no awareness of it, he was a progenitor of the modern school of redaction criticism, which has for its purpose the discovery of the historical Jesus, into whose mouth the authors of the Gospels have put words he never said and to whom they attributed acts he never performed. Jefferson did not have the benefit of the modern historical-critical methodology, which was to flower later, but he was engaged in the same sort of enterprise. When he was eighty-one years of age he wrote, saying that the apocalypse of John in the book of the Revelation was "the ravings of a maniac, no more worthy nor capable of explanation than the incoherences of his own nightly dreams."[34]

Jefferson was indeed a full-fledged philosophe in his thought world, whatever else he might have been in his life as president and as the founder of a great university. In his approach to education he exhibited great disdain for religion. "Still deeply suspicious of any religious sect save those of the Quakers and the Unitarians, he omitted religious instruction except as a branch of ethics, in effect outlawing the establishment of a divinity school."[35] Jefferson did contribute greatly to the establishment of the government of the United States and served the nation well as a president. But the absence of any religious convictions in the Judeo-Christian tradition was a serious flaw that made possible the decline and fall of the church in our generation.

Adams

John Adams was quite different from Thomas Jefferson, yet they were acquaintances and friends and worked together for the establishment of the United States following the American Revolution. Adams had been raised and lived in Massachusetts all of his life except for the times he spent as president and as a representative of the emerging republic in Europe.

Adams went to Harvard, as did a number of his progeny later on. The college had been started for the training of men for the Christian ministry, but by the eighteenth century it had been infiltrated by some of the same ideas as were held by the philosophes. When his son, John Quincy Adams, was ready for Harvard, he was interviewed by the president, three professors, and four tutors. He answered questions on Horace, the Iliad, logic, Locke, and geography. When admitted to the college, he studied Euclid and Terence among other subjects.[36]

Clearly Harvard was enmeshed in the writings of the pagan Greek and Roman world during the time John Adams and John Quincy Adams attended the college. Whether John Adams, the father, had been touched by the same influences of the

philosophes is uncertain. But the cultural influence of the philosophes was no less in evidence in Cambridge than it was in
Paris and London. The senior Adamses were concerned, as his
father put it, that he was "breathing now in the atmosphere of
science and literature, the floating particles of which will mix
with your whole mass of blood and juices." They feared life's
temptations and his mother wrote saying: "I hope you will guard
your brother against that pernicious vice of gaming too much
practiced at the university."[37]

That John Adams had more than just a speaking acquaintance with the writings of the philosophes is clear from a statement made by Jefferson's biographer. He records that "John
Adams had begun in 1759 reading the works of the great
men of the Enlightenment, admonishing himself in his diary
in January of that year: 'Aim at an exact Knowledge of the
Nature, End, and Means of Government. Compare the different forms of it with each other and each of them with their
Effects on the public and private Happiness. Study Seneca,
Cicero and all other good moral Writers. Study Montesquieu,
Bolingbroke.' "[38]

When it came to the Christian faith, John Adams was a
paradoxical figure. He firmly approved of the moral and ethical
traditions common to the Judeo-Christian faith. The idea of
humanity's perfectibility was, in his judgment, "mischievous
nonsense." The imperfectibility of man, Adams wrote Van der
Kamp, should not keep them from "our utmost exertions to
amend and improve others and in every way ameliorate the lot
of humanity: invent new medicines, construct new machines,
write new books, build better houses and ships, institute better
governments, discountenance false religions, propagate the only
true one, diminish the vices, and increase the virtues of all men
and women wherever we can."[39]

John Adams was far removed from most of the philosophes
when he advocated the propagation of the true religion, which
obviously meant Christianity as he understood it, and the dis-
countenancing of all other religions, which he regarded to be
false. But the paradox lay in the fact that Adams was fully in
agreement with most of the philosophes when it came to the
person of Jesus Christ. He moved far away from the traditional

faith of the Reformation and the New Testament in that regard. In a letter to Benjamin Rush, Adams wrote:

"The Christian religion, as I understand it, is the brightness of the glory and the express portrait of the eternal, self-existent, independent, benevolent, all-powerful and all-merciful Creator, Preserver and Father of the Universe. . . . It will last as long as the world. Neither savage nor civilized man without a revelation could ever have discovered or invented it. Ask me not then whether I am a Catholic or Protestant, Calvinist or Arminian. As far as they are Christians, I wish to be a fellow disciple with them all."[40]

Indeed, his biographer said he rejected the doctrine of the Trinity.

Adams and the philosophes were in full agreement when it came to the person of Jesus—none of them believed that Jesus is God. The philosophes, however, were consistent in that once they denied that Jesus is divine, they also scrapped the Bible in its entirety. They believed there was no revelation from God and generally that all religion was in vain. Adams's ancestors were sturdy Calvinists and from them he inherited a world and life view that would have been fully Christian if he had believed in the divinity of Jesus. He was inconsistent in that he held on to a great deal of the theology of the Reformation, but parted with that tradition at one of its pivotal points, the doctrine of the Trinity.

What Adams did not and could not know was that his views would later be formalized in the establishment of the Unitarian denomination in New England. This, in turn, would lead in the twentieth century to a conclusion which he could not have accepted, had he been alive. The Unitarians dropped from their vocabulary any acceptance of biblical revelation that was true and binding on humankind. Indeed many of them ceased to be theists and became cultural relativists. So grave was the situation for the Unitarians that they found themselves unwelcome even in the company of organizations that were by no means thoroughly orthodox but still unwilling to open their doors to non-Trinitarians. This was and is true for the World Council of Churches today; it does not admit Unitarians.

Whether John Adams understood it or not, traditional

Christianity has always held that whoever denies the divinity of Jesus Christ is not and cannot be considered a Christian. And whoever is not a Christian is a pagan. Adams's views on the Trinity, for good or for ill, logically tied him to the Enlightenment. In that sense he could only be called a Christian pagan. One is entitled to ask whether Adams might have changed his views, had he known where those views inevitably take those who embrace them. Unitarianism is one of the gifts of the Enlightenment and represents one aspect of the defeat suffered by the church as a consequence.

Paine

Thomas Paine (1737–1809) lived during the heyday of the Enlightenment and can be numbered among that illustrious group of philosophes as one who finally understood and approved of their basic principles. As an Englishman who emigrated to the American colonies on the advice and with the support of Benjamin Franklin, he was able to play an important role in the American Revolution.

Paine's father was a Quaker, but Paine was confirmed in the Church of England. He was a deist, although he was accused by many in the colonies of being an atheist, a viewpoint by no means popular at that time. Tom, as he was called, had a checkered career. He did not follow his father's trade of corsetmaking. He was a sailor, a teacher, and an exciseman. His first wife died and his second marriage was unhappy. He was a roving, adventurous spirit who thoroughly approved of and worked for colonial freedom from the English yoke.

When Paine came to America he first resided in Philadelphia, where he edited the *Pennsylvania Magazine* for a year and a half. During that time he became friendly with John Witherspoon, who was the president of the College of New Jersey (later known as Princeton), David Rittenhouse, the scientist, and Benjamin Bush, the physician-patriot who encouraged Paine to publish *Common Sense,* a book that set the pace for the colonial revolt against England. The book itself was an instant and perennial best seller with half a million copies in print, a phenomenal attainment considering the small population of the colonies at that time.

Paine published a number of other works that gave him an established position in the movement toward independence and the writing of the American constitution after it was seen that the Articles of Confederation were ineffectual. He returned to England and from 1787 to 1802 was either there or in France. His book *The Rights of Man* led to his being indicted for treason in England and occasioned his hasty escape from England to France, where he was elected to the revolutionary French Convention. But his book *Age of Reason* led to imprisonment for a season because of Robespierre's suspicion that Paine was traitorous. The cause was easy to find. The *Age of Reason* was partly written "lest in the general wreck of superstition we lose sight of morality, of humanity, and of the theology that is true."[41] Interestingly enough it was this book that caused many critics to argue that Paine was an atheist.

In 1802 Paine returned to America where he died in 1809, having alienated most of the friends he had made in his earlier years. As to his convictions vis-à-vis the Christian faith, it can be said that at best he was a deist. The *Britannica* article summarizes his convictions this way:

Paine expressed most completely the ideals of the Enlightenment, involving faith in the immutable law and order of nature as a divine revelation; the omnipotence of reason when there is freedom to debate all questions; tolerance; the equal rights and dignity of the individual; a religion of good deeds and humanitarianism; and peaceful cosmopolitanism.[42]

Since it was Benjamin Franklin who had urged Thomas Paine to come to America and who also sent with him letters of introduction, it is appropriate that we ask what role, if any, Franklin played with regard to Christianity. Was there any specific relationship between Franklin and the leaders of the Enlightenment in France or did he represent the English side of the movement?

Franklin

Benjamin Franklin was one of America's leading citizens during the eighteenth century. He was a publisher, businessman, author, philanthropist, inventor, moralist, scientist, civil servant, and above all a statesman. He influenced American religious life and especially popular morality through his work *Poor Richard's Almanac* (1732–1757). It contained sage advice and included forceful maxims fully in agreement for the most part with the Bible. Much of what he wrote stemmed from his own convictions expressed in his private *Articles of Belief and Acts of Religion* dated November 20, 1728.

In 1790 just prior to his death, Franklin wrote a response to a letter he had received from Ezra Stiles, the president of Yale College. In that letter President Stiles asked particularly what Franklin thought about Jesus Christ. Franklin began his response:

I confide that you will not expose me to criticisms and censures by publishing any part of this communication to you. I have ever let others enjoy their religious sentiments, without reflecting on them for those that appeared to me unsupportable or even absurd. All sects here, and we have a great variety, have experienced my good will in assisting them with subscriptions for building their new places of worship; and, as I have never opposed any of their doctrines, I hope I go out of the world in peace with them all.[43]

Earlier in his *Autobiography* he had written:

My parents had earlier given me religious impressions, and brought me through my childhood piously in the Dissenting way. But I was scarce fifteen, when, after doubting by turns of several points, as I found them disputed in the different books I read, I began to doubt of Revelation itself. Some books against Deism fell into my hands; they were said to be the substance of sermon's preached on Boyle's Lectures. It happened that they wrought an effect on me quite contrary to what was intended by them; for the arguments of the Deists, which were quoted to be refuted, appeared to me much stronger than the refutations; in short, I soon became a thorough Deist.[44]

In response to the query by President Stiles, Franklin continued:

You desire to know something of my religion. It is the first time I have been questioned upon it. But I cannot take your curiosity amiss, and shall endeavor in a few words to gratify it. Here is my creed. I believe in one God, creator of the universe. That He governs it by His Providence. That He ought to be worshiped. That the most acceptable service we render to Him is doing good to His other children. That the soul of man is immortal, and will be treated with justice in another life respecting its conduct in this. These I take to be the fundamental points in all sound religion, and I regard them as you do in whatever sect I meet with them.

As to Jesus of Nazareth, my opinion of whom you particularly desire, I think his system of morals and his religion, as he left them to us, the best the world ever saw or is likely to see; but I apprehended it has received various corrupting changes, and I have, with most of the dissenters in England, some doubts as to his divinity; though it is a question I do not dogmatize upon, having never studied it, and think it needless to busy myself with it now, when I expect soon an opportunity of knowing the truth with less trouble. I see no harm, however, in its being believed, if that belief has the good consequence, as probably it has, of making his doctrines more respected and more observed; especially as I do not perceive that the Supreme takes it amiss, by distinguishing the unbelievers in the government of the world with any peculiar marks of his displeasure.[45]

Since deism was a cardinal doctrine for many of those who can be numbered among the Enlightenment elite, Franklin must also be included in their number. Whether he got his deism from the Enlightenment or whether it was arrived at without the benefit of others is immaterial. Franklin adhered to what is an optimistic and undogmatic natural religion. For him nature rather than Scripture is the place at which human beings come to recognize God. Franklin was no supporter of historic orthodoxy and was, like so many others, at best a Christian pagan, which meant that he was no Christian at all.

SUMMARY: KANT ON THE ENLIGHTENMENT

So we come to the end of this short synopsis of the Enlightenment as expressed and understood by some of its chief figures. Summing up the information, we can turn to a statement made by Immanuel Kant. Peter Gay's view is correct: "No one figure embodies the Enlightenment, but if any one could be singled out, it would be Immanuel Kant."[46] Kant, in his *What Is Enlightenment?* says:

Enlightenment is man's emergence from his self-imposed nonage [which word means "period of youth, lack of maturity"]. Nonage is the inability to use one's own understanding without another's guidance. This nonage is self-imposed if its cause lies not in lack of understanding but indecision and lack of courage to use one's own mind without another's guidance. *Dare to know! (Sapere aude.)* "Have the courage to use your own understanding," is therefore the motto of the Enlightenment. . . .

If I have a book that thinks for me, a pastor who acts as my conscience, a physician who prescribes my diet, and so on, then I have no need to exert myself. I have no need to think, if only I can pay; others will take care of that disagreeable business for me. Those guardians who have kindly taken supervision upon themselves see to it that the overwhelming majority of mankind—among them the entire fair sex—should consider the step to maturity not only as hard, but as extremely dangerous. . . .

Thus it is very difficult for the individual to work himself out of the nonage which has become almost second nature to him. He has even grown to like it and is at first really incapable of using his own understanding, because he has never been permitted to try it. Dogmas and formulas, these mechanical tools designed for reasonable use—or rather abuse—of his natural gifts, are the fetters of an everlasting nonage. The man who casts them off would make an uncertain leap over the narrowest ditch, because he is not used to such free movement. That is why there are only a few men who walk firmly, and who have emerged from nonage by cultivating their own minds.

It is more nearly possible, however, for the public to enlighten itself; indeed, if it is only given freedom, enlightenment is almost inevitable. . . .

This enlightenment requires nothing but *freedom*—and the most innocent of all that may be called "freedom": freedom to make public use of one's reason in all matters. . . .

When we ask, Are we now living in an enlightened age? the answer is, No, but we live in an age of enlightenment. As matters now stand it is still far from true that men are already capable of using their own reason in religious matters confidently and correctly without external guidance. Still, we have some obvious indications that the field of working toward the goal [of religious truth] is now being opened. What is more, the hindrance against general enlightenment or the emergence from self-imposed nonage are gradually diminishing. In this respect this is the age of enlightenment and the century of Frederick [the Great].

A prince ought not to deem it beneath his dignity to state that he considers it his duty not to dictate anything to his subjects in religious matters, but to leave them complete freedom. If he repudiates the arrogant word *tolerant,* he is himself enlightened. . . . Under his reign, honorable pastors, acting as scholars and regardless of the duties of their office, can freely and openly publish their ideas to the world for inspection, although they deviate here and there from accepted doctrine. This is even more true of every other person not restrained by any oath of office. . . .

I have emphasized the main point of the enlightenment—man's emergence from his self-imposed nonage—primarily in religious matters, because our rulers have no interest in playing guardian to their subjects in the arts and sciences.[47]

Thus spake Immanuel Kant: the human being is autonomous and reason is supreme!

5. The Fall of the Church After the Enlightenment

The Enlightenment did not arise, peak, and decline like some other movements. Rather it became more widespread, moving forward and gaining momentum subsequent to the end of the eighteenth century. It was not to reach its full flowering until after the middle of the twentieth century, at which time its impact could be seen in the defeat of the church in the West. It took two centuries for its goals to be realized.

The Enlightenment's opposition to metaphysics, its denial of the supernatural, and its exaltation of reason over revelation found its classical expression in a world and life view (Weltanschauung) wholly inconsonant with historic orthodoxy; this was accompanied by an intellectual, moral, and cultural climate (Zeitgeist) in accord with this pagan world and life view. This meant that the West had lost its Judeo-Christian foundations and was now thoroughly pagan, although it did not mean that the Christian faith was obliterated. Rather it was a minority viewpoint in a society that was governed by paganism. The West had become pluralistic and was marked by two major viewpoints in opposition to each other, but the controlling viewpoint was pagan and anti-Christian.

FRANCE

In Europe the influence of the philosophes was felt most immediately in France. There the Enlightenment was a substantial force contributing to the French Revolution of 1789. The revolution itself was at least partly a revolt against the Roman Catholic church, which the philosophes opposed. Most of the French were inclined toward skepticism and were well aware of the corruptions and oppressions of the Roman hierarchy. The property and the privileges of the church were among the first to go under the revolutionary slogan of "liberty, equality, and fraternity." The French monarchy and the Roman church had been allied together, so both fell as victims of the times.

Albert Henry Newman summarizes the situation accurately when he writes:

> Excommunication and interdict had lost their force, for the people no longer believed that their temporal or spiritual well-being was in the hands of pope or priest, and they could smile at papal or prelatical anathemas. The confiscation of the estates of the church, the complete abrogation of ecclesiastical privileges, the proscription and persecution of the clergy because of their opposition to the revolution, and finally the legislative annihilation of the Christian religion with the attempt to obliterate all Christian institutions by changing the calendar, etc., grew out of the widespread popular conviction that the dominant form of Christianity, with which Christianity itself was identified, was the arch-enemy of human rights and the enslaver of men's bodies, minds, and consciences.[1]

Even though Napoleon became emperor and later there was a temporary restoration of the monarchy, France never recovered from the revolution so far as the Christian faith was concerned. It became and still is a pagan nation. The Catholic churches are virtually empty and Protestant Christianity is by no means an important force in French life. Nor are there any signs that suggest a renaissance of religion in that nation.

GERMANY

There was no unified German monarchy during the eighteenth century. There were only small German principalities and kingdoms, of which Prussia was the most powerful and the most significant. It was not until 1871 that Bismarck proclaimed King Wilhelm I of Prussia German emperor. During the Enlightenment Frederick II (known as Frederick the Great) was king of Prussia. He was a religious freethinker who was in thorough accord with the philosophes. He was a disciple of Voltaire and in some ways was more French than German. He wrote that "all religions are equal and good." He was an atheist and an epicurean, a cynic and an enemy of the Christian faith. He set the tone for the German future.

The Germans became the most substantial and learned opponents of historic Christianity. It was in their territory that school after school of skeptics and critics turned out one generation after another of advanced thinkers whose time was spent destroying the faith. Of course some German Christians were orthodox and did their best to reclaim Germany for the true faith, but they were unsuccessful and their efforts came to nought.

German universities ruled as the most popular seats of learning and students flocked to them for their doctorates. This was a time when no American universities offered graduate studies leading to the doctorate, so Americans went to German ones. German scholars were long on biblical criticism and short on faith. Reason was exalted above revelation and the Bible was regarded only as a purely human book. Scholars from other countries made contributions to the attacks leveled against the Scriptures, but generally speaking one can trace back to German scholarship virtually all of the errors that crept into the church and played a signal role in the decline of the church in the Western world.

Technically, the rise of higher criticism was central to the assault made on the Bible by its critics. The term *higher criticism* seems to have surfaced in the writings of Johann Gottfried Eichhorn, who pioneered in this field and who said many of the Old Testament books were spurious. In the years 1780–1783 he published a three-volume Old Testament introduction that was very influential in the years that followed its publication.

In a sense, higher criticism can support the Bible as well as oppose it. *Lower criticism* has to do with the text of the Bible itself; *higher criticism* has to do with how the Bible came into being, who wrote it, what the sources were from which it came, and what its meaning is. When this methodology starts by assuming that the Bible is true only after it has been studied by the scholars and that their study may show that parts or all of the Bible are not to be trusted, it becomes a critic standing over and above the Bible. It is human beings over the Bible rather than the Bible over human beings. And when the scholars can decide what is Scripture and what is not Scripture, then there is something above Scripture that is greater than Scripture itself. This is the point at which higher criticism becomes an enemy of the Bible. And the Germans are noted for this sort of approach to the Bible.

SCHOLARS IN THE LIBERAL THEOLOGICAL TRADITION

Ferdinand Christian Baur (1792–1860) was the founder of what is known as the Tübingen School. Many scholars studied under him and the influence of this school was widespread. Baur himself was a disciple of Schleiermacher and Hegel. He roused a storm of protest when he argued that except for Galatians, 1 and 2 Corinthians, and Romans, all of the other epistles attributed to Paul were not written by him. He also denied the apostolic origin of the Acts of the Apostles. He pioneered an antitheistic, nonsupernatural approach to the beginnings of the Christian faith. He was a radical Bible critic.

David Friedrich Strauss (1808–1874) was a pupil of Baur who was also influenced by Schleiermacher and Hegel. He applied the "myth theory" (that the Gospels have in them some legends, fables, and/or fiction) to the life of Jesus. He was opposed to all of the supernatural elements in the Gospels. Like Baur, he roused a storm of criticism that led to his dismissal from Tübingen, where he was teaching. His influence, however, spread widely and subsequent German Protestant theology was marked by his stamp.

Albrecht Ritschl (1822–1889) was a disciple of Baur who taught at the universities of Bonn and Göttingen. At first he defended Baur's notion of a radical conflict between Pauline Hellenism and Petrine Judaism but later broke with that idea. He rejected metaphysics and was loath to accept doctrines that lay beyond verifiable history or true Christian faith. He denied the objective and historical notion of Christ's divinity as something that transcended knowledge. He denied that the death of Christ was in any sense penal and a propitiation of just judgment. He is known as the father of the Ritschlian School of theology and as such wielded an immense influence in Europe and America.

Julius Wellhausen (1844–1918) studied at Göttingen and taught there for several years before going to Greifswald. He resigned from that school in 1882 as a result of the furor created when he cast doubt on the inspiration of Scripture. He then taught at Halle, then Marburg, and finally at Göttingen in 1892. He is noted for his Documentary Hypothesis of the Pentateuch. He said that the Pentateuch was derived from several sources: the Jahweh strand, the Elohim strand, the Priestly strand, and the Deuteronomic strand (all together labeled JEPD). This viewpoint was adopted by virtually all of the Old Testament scholars in the West except for evangelicals and was widely taught and still is in most of the theological seminaries in the United States. Some scholars have asserted that his place in biblical studies is comparable to that of Darwin in evolution. His works in the New Testament field found less ready acceptance, yet he laid down many of the lines now common to form criticism (a scholarly discipline that held that much of Scripture was orally communicated before it took on written form. It led to speculation on how the form we now have was developed and led to the view that what we now have is different from what Jesus, for example, actually said), which also has undercut the Bible and hastened the decline of the church.

Long before Wellhausen was born, Jean Astruc (1684–1766), who lived during the age of the philosophes, had advanced views about the Pentateuch somewhat similar to those of Wellhausen. He was the son of a Protestant pastor (and many of the German higher critics in a later age were sons of the manse) and converted to Catholicism at an early age. Astruc was a physician and Pentateuchal critic. He rose high in the established order of his day as physician to the king of Poland in 1729 and to Louis XV of France in 1730. He published his celebrated work on the Pentateuch anonymously, which in itself tells its own story. In that work, *Conjectures sur les memoires originaux dont il paroit que Moyse s'est servi pour composer le livre de la Genese*, he argued that the book of Genesis was the piecing together of earlier writings, a view based on the use of varying names for God such as Jehovah (Jahweh) and Elohim. Still, he did think it was Moses who brought them together. However, those who came later raised the most serious questions about the Mosaic authorship of the Pentateuch. In particular, later scholars were to suppose that Deuteronomy was written centuries after the death of Moses, even though some of them held that much of the material contained in the book dated back to Moses.

The last German we will mention is Adolph Harnack (1851–1930), son of a professor of pastoral theology. His last academic post was a full professorship at Berlin (1889–1921). His main area of research was in Patristics, which brought renown to him as perhaps the most outstanding scholar in that field. He was known to entertain a theological viewpoint allied to that of Ritschl. He thought that metaphysics in early Christian thought was an alien intrusion from Greek sources (Hellenization). He had doubts about the authorship of the Fourth Gospel and other New Testament books. But more importantly, he veered away from historic orthodoxy in his unconventional views about biblical miracles, the resurrection of Jesus Christ from the dead, and a denial of Christ's institution of baptism.

Harnack was certainly liberal in his theology, and late in his life he clashed with Karl Barth, who was one of his former students. In one regard he appeared to be quite conservative in his views about the synoptic Gospels and the Acts of the Apostles. He accepted the Lucan authorship of Acts and dated it from the time Paul was a prisoner in Rome. He also assigned an early date to the synoptic Gospels. All of this was far removed from much of contemporary liberal and radical scholarship, which was seriously undermined if his views were correct.

Our excursion now leads to a few scholars outside the German fold who carried on the tradition of the philosophes and who promoted and encouraged theological liberalism. The first was a Frenchman, Joseph Ernest Renan (1823–1892), a philospher, orientalist, and theologian. Renan was deeply indebted to the Germans, for it was his study of German theology and Semitic languages that drove him away from historic orthodoxy. Doubts about the truth of Christianity caused him to leave the seminary at San Sulpice and the Christian ministry.

Renan's classic work appeared in 1864, just two years after he had been appointed professor of Hebrew at the College de France. His *Life of Jesus* showed his use of the new German critical apparatus and was marked by a radical rationalistic skepticism. He said Jesus was a remarkable itinerant preacher but in no sense the Son of God. He denied the supernatural element in Jesus' life as well. The book created such a furor that it resulted in his removal from his professorship and marked the end of his academic career, for he held no further posts in any institution.

William Robertson Smith (1846–1894) was a Scottish theologian and Semitic scholar. He was educated first in Scottish universities and then at Bonn and Göttingen in Germany, where he imbibed the advanced thinking of the German rationalists. When his articles in the ninth edition of the *Encyclopaedia Britannica* appeared, he became the storm center of controversy over his higher criticism of the Old Testament. He was removed from his post at Aberdeen on the ground that his views undermined belief in the inspiration of the Bible.

Smith supported and popularized the views of Wellhausen concerning the authorship and structure of the Pentateuch and the development of Israelite religion. His denial of the propitiatory nature of Christ's atonement was widely received, even though it was contrary to orthodoxy. Again we must note that Smith undoubtedly received some of his liberal views from his stay in Germany, when he was under the tutelage of modern biblical critics.

Thomas Kelly Cheyne (1841–1915) was an Old Testament scholar and critic. He was trained at Worcester College, Oxford, and also received part of his education at Göttingen under the auspices of H. G. A. Ewald, who wrote against the Tübingen School of Baur. Nevertheless his stay at Göttingen led him to adopt a critical view of the Old Testament along the lines of the then common general theory of Pentateuchal sources. In the later years of his life he became rashly unconventional in his biblical criticism and ideas. He represented one of those who were markedly influenced by the Enlightenment mentality and who departed from traditional Christianity.

A second Englishman who succumbed to the advanced thinking of developing biblical criticism of a liberal bent was Samuel Rolles Driver (1846–1914). He was a Quaker by descent and studied at Oxford. He was a master of the Old Testament and a Hebrew scholar of vast learning. From 1883 until his death, he was Regius Professor of Hebrew and Canon of Christ Church, Oxford, succeeding E. B. Pusey. This was the largest college in the Oxford University, founded in 1525 as Cardinal College.

Driver became noted for his acceptance of and the spread of the critical view of the Old Testament in England. He collaborated with Francis Brown and Charles Augustus Briggs in the well-known *Oxford Hebrew Lexicon*[2] and contributed widely to the *Dictionary of the Bible*[3] edited by James Hastings. But that he departed from historic orthodoxy and promoted the advance of rational liberalism cannot be denied.

In the advance of German liberalism in the United States Charles Augustus Briggs (1841–1913) was one of the key spokesmen for liberal theology. He graduated from Union Theological Seminary in New York City and then studied in the University of Berlin, where he encountered radical German thought. He taught virtually all of his ministerial life at Union Seminary and in 1874 he was appointed to the chair of Hebrew and Cognate Languages there. In 1890 he became professor of Biblical Theology, a new chair, and one in which he launched his severest attack against the Bible.

Briggs chose to begin his crusade in his inaugural address in the new chair at Union. He succeeded admirably, for in that address he hit hard against the doctrine of the verbal inspiration of the Bible. He was wildly cheered by the students, and the consequent fallout was an almost perennial appearance of his name and activities in the *New York Times*. The presbytery of New York acquitted him of heresy in 1892, but when the case was appealed to the courts of the church and then to the general assembly he was condemned and suspended from the ministry in 1893. He was later admitted to the ministry in the Episcopal church.

Briggs constantly struck out against the views of Benjamin Warfield and Charles Hodge of Princeton Theological Seminary. These two were the most learned and constant proponents of an inerrant Bible. They were just as much opposed to the view of Briggs as Briggs was opposed to theirs. It was a war to the finish and in the long run Briggs was the victor, even though neither he nor they lived long enough to see how great was the victory for the one and how dismal the defeat for the other two.

When Briggs was under attack in the Presbyterian church, Henry Preserved Smith rose to his defense. Like Briggs he had studied at the University of Berlin and like him he had imbibed some of the German viewpoints. His conservatism declined after 1882 and he stated in that year that textual corruption implied noninfallibility. Like Briggs he was tried for heresy and was suspended from the ministry by the Cincinnati presbytery, a decision that was sustained by the general assembly of the church. He was forced out of Lane Seminary and subsequently taught at Amherst, then at Meadville (a Unitarian school), and finally at Union Theological Seminary in New York City.

The Enlightenment can be dated from the last half of the eighteenth century. Since then any number of scholars have supported and advanced the radical viewpoints. We have mentioned a number of those who defected from orthodoxy. Now we need to retrace our steps to analyze what was at the center of the vast theological struggle and how it affected the church through its educational processes.

THE DEPARTURE OF INSTITUTIONS FROM ORTHODOXY

To trace the rise and fall of educational institutions involved in the struggle of orthodoxy against German rationalism and unbelief we must begin with Johann Salomo Semler (1725–1791). Semler's father was a Pietist but Semler departed quite early from his father's stance in favor of a rationalistic position he called *liberalis theologia*. He was one of the first German theologians to embrace the historical-critical methodology. He taught first at Coburg and then at Altdorf. After this he went to Halle, where he finally became the head of the theological faculty. Professor Eugene F. Klug writes of his work as follows:

The historical-critical approach to the Bible has its history, of course. Johann Salomo Semler is usually designated as father of the technique, which not only handled the Bible as an object for historical scrutiny, but also as a book little different from and no more holy than any other, and surely not to be equated with the Word of God. Very plainly he was saying that he rejected the divine inspiration of the text. This was but a symptom of his total theological stance, a tip of the iceberg so to speak. His was really a revolt against miracles and the supernatural in general, and against heaven in particular. God's supernatural activity in history simply was not in Semler's "book." Not unexpectedly, under his and others' hand, the Bible text and content suffered deliberate vivisection. The surgery was quite often radical and overt, and without benefit of anaesthesia for those directly affected by it in the churches.[4]

It was obvious that Semler had little use for the traditional view that the Bible was a joint product of human authors and the divine author, the Holy Spirit. Gerhard Maier, from whose book we quoted Klug, also draws attention to a key component of Semler's bibliology and indeed the bibliology of most of those who followed in his track. Semler said, "The root of the evil (in theology) is the interchangeable use of the terms 'Scripture' and the 'Word of God.' "[5] Semler meant that the Bible contains the Word of God but not all Scripture is the Word of God. This meant that all who read the Bible must determine which parts of it are the Word of God and which parts are not. This constitutes the task of finding the canon in the canon, a subjective, not to say impossible task.

It is safe and fair to say that at last this question raised by Semler has been and still is central to all theology down to this very hour. And Semler's view was reproduced all over Europe in the educational institutions. Of course there were academicians and institutions that opposed this view of Semler's, but in the long run his view prevailed. It has resulted in the paganization of those institutions, that is, they became secular rather than religious and Christian. And the paganization of the institutions that educated the clergy resulted in the paganization of the pulpit and the decline of the churches themselves.

The effect of the Enlightenment on the German churches in the early nineteenth century was disastrous. The pulpits in Hamburg for instance, were decimated and only one evangelical pastor could be found in the entire town. The German churches were generally empty, indicating how deep the rejection of the Christian faith was. In Kiel around 1815 there were ten empty churches for every full one. In Mannheim one church with ten thousand members on its roster had fewer than eight men and fifty women coming to public worship on any given Sunday.

The decline in church attendance reflected a waning emphasis on morality as well as an abandonment of the faith to the new rationalism. Because the clergy by and large had no faith, their contact with the people was contaminated. The secularity of the age was said to be the chief cause for the skepticism in the pulpits that plunged the parish members into the same swamp and quicksand of unbelief.

There were times of spiritual quickening and evidences of awakenings in Germany, but they did not last. The universities were not reformed and the students in those institutions were apt to change their views and conform to the liberalism of their professors. Over the years the situation worsened and led eventually to the rise of Adolph Hitler in the land of the Reformation. No one can fail to see that Hitler's regime rested on the firm support of the majority of the nation. They had departed from the faith of their forebears. Right now the religious situation in Germany is dismal. Not more than 5 percent of the people can be found in the churches on any Sunday morning. Germany has become a vast mission field. The Germans are pagans and there are no evidences that the situation is about to be corrected or that the Christian faith will once again become a majority position of the German people.

What has been said about Germany can be said about all of Europe. At best there is no nation in Europe where the people in church on any Sunday morning number as much as 10 percent of the population. The possible exception to this is Poland, which is 90 percent Roman Catholic. To be sure Britain did not collapse as quickly as did other parts of Europe. Gradually, however, Britain has been overcome and now stands as a classic example of a secular nation. And like the rest of Europe, its institutions of higher learning are as pagan as any elsewhere.

THE AMERICAN SCENE

Europe was ahead of the United States in the race to paganize the culture, destroy the Christian uniqueness of the educational institutions, and denude the churches of their membership. Quantitatively, the situation of the American churches still looks better on paper than does that of the Europeans. But the unhappy fact is that America has been won over by the forces of the Enlightenment, even though more of its people remain evangelical than in Europe.

A vast host of American colleges and universities were started as Christian institutions. They, like the European schools, were infiltrated by aberrant theological viewpoints and capitulated to secularism or paganism. Harvard, Yale, Princeton, Dartmouth, Wellesley, Mount Holyoke, Bryn Mawr, Smith, and other institutions have now departed from their original moorings and make no profession whatever of being genuinely Christian. Virtually every private college in the land had Christian beginnings. At this moment no collegiate institutions that once were Christian have maintained their commitment for more than a hundred years. One exception is Wheaton College in Illinois, but outside of that school one searches in vain for others like it. When it comes to public colleges and universities that had their beginnings in the Land Grant Act of 1862, there isn't a single one of them that is Christian in any sense of that term. Many, if not most of them, are loaded with professors who are anti-Christian, neutral, or seriously pro-Marxist. Those who are dynamically Christian constitute a small minority and rarely make the media.

What is said about the colleges and universities can also be said about the theological seminaries. Except for a few institutions such as Meadville, which was founded after the Unitarian defection in New England, the theological seminaries were all orthodox when first established. Most of them that existed at the turn of the twentieth century were infiltrated by German antisupernatural rationalism, as were the Christian colleges and universities. During the fundamentalist-modernist controversy of the 1920s, most of the theological seminaries capitulated to modernism.

There were exceptions, of course. The Southern Baptist seminaries at this time remained orthodox. The Lutheran Church, Missouri Synod, escaped the liberal invasion and new conservative seminaries were created to offset the loss of the older institutions to liberalism. Northern Baptist Theological Seminary and Eastern Baptist Theological Seminary were created during the course of this struggle. But even schools such as these were to feel the encroachment of theological liberalism later on. Most of the seminaries crossed the Rubicon, moving from orthodoxy to liberalism. And liberalism's strength was of such a nature that few of the institutions had or wanted to have conservative or evangelical representatives on their faculties.

The Good News movement in contemporary United Methodist circles came into being to promote historic orthodoxy in a denomination that had strayed far from its early roots. In the May/June 1986 issue of *Good News,* it was stated that "United Methodist seminaries have for the most part remained bastions of theological liberalism. In spite of our church's avowed commitment to theological pluralism, scholars with orthodox-evangelical beliefs have been largely frozen out of the teaching posts of our seminaries."[6] The statement is revealing. Liberalism has shown itself to be illiberal. Rarely do seminaries that have become liberal open their doors to conservative scholars for faculty appointments. And evangelicals have been placed in a position where the faith they profess has lost currency and they have to beg for the freedom to teach in their institutions.

LIBERAL VERSUS ORTHODOX THEOLOGY

It is indubitably true that liberalism realizes that orthodox theology does present an ever-present threat to its hegemony and that the two groups hold antithetical viewpoints that are logically irreconcilable. How true this is may be seen from the perspective of orthodoxy. J. I. Packer says that today "Preaching is hazy; heads are muddled; hearts fret; doubts drain our strength. . . . We stand under the divine judgment. For us, too, the Word of God is in a real sense *lost.*" He amplifies this in another way:

Liberal theology, in its pride, has long insisted that we are wiser than our fathers about the Bible, and must not read it as they did, but must base our approach to it on the "assured results" of criticism, making due allowances for the human imperfections and errors of its authors. This insistence has a threefold effect. (1) It produces a new papalism—the infallibility of the scholars, from whom we learn what the "assured results" are. (2) It raises a doubt about every single Bible passage, as to whether it truly embodies revelation or not. (3) And it destroys the reverent, receptive, self-distrusting attitude of approach to the Bible, without which it cannot be known to be "God's Word written." . . . The result? The spiritual famine of which Amos spoke. God judges our pride by leaving us to the barrenness, hunger, and discomfort which flow from our self-induced inability to hear His Word.[7]

C. S. Lewis was also concerned about the methodology that strikes at the truthfulness of the Bible. As a literary critic he was fully aware of the dangers of that discipline. He said:

The undermining of the old orthodoxy (Biblical authority) has been mainly the work of divines engaged in New Testament criticism. The authority of experts in that discipline is the authority in deference to whom we are asked to give up a huge mass of beliefs shared in common by the early Church, the Fathers, the Middle Ages, the Reformers, and even in the nineteenth century.[8]

Lewis went on from there to say:

I want to explain what it is that makes me skeptical about this authority. . . . First whatever these men may be as Biblical critics, I distrust them as critics. They seem to me to lack literary judgment, to be imperceptive about the very quality of the texts they are reading. . . . These men ask me to believe they can read between the lines of the old texts; the evidence is their obvious inability to read (in any sense worth discussing) the lines themselves. They claim to see Fernseed and can't see an elephant ten yards away in broad daylight.[9]

About Rudolph Bultmann and his work Lewis said:

Dr. Bultmann never wrote a Gospel. Has the experience of his learned, specialized, and no doubt meritorious life really given him any power of seeing into the minds of those long dead men who were caught up in what, on any view, must be regarded as the central religious experience of the whole human race?[10]

Lewis also had a word to say about the dismissal of miracles by those engaged in higher criticism:

If one is speaking of authority, the united authority of all the Biblical critics in the world counts for nothing here. On this they speak simply as men; men who are obviously influenced by, and perhaps insufficiently critical of, the spirit of the age they grew up in.[11]

In a concluding observation about what literary critics said of his own writings he added what might be the best postscript for any discussion of the historical-critical methodology:

My impression is that in the whole of my experience not one of these guesses has on any point been right; that the method (literary criticism) shows a record of 100 percent failure.[12]

The mainline theological seminaries today stand in the forefront of the opposition to theological orthodoxy. These institutions are not pluralistic, as we have already stated, for thoroughgoing evangelicals are unwelcome on their faculties. We need to understand how these faculties function in their criticism of the Bible and how they undermine the faith of the apostles in this ongoing struggle between them and evangelicals.

BIBLE CRITICISM

The best of those in the seminaries go no further than to say that the Bible is the only rule of faith and practice. By this limitation they mean that the Bible has errors in it in matters of fact, science, cosmology, and the like. But most of the academicians go far beyond this and boldly proclaim that the Bible is not correct in many theological matters as well. Some deny the deity of Jesus Christ. Some do not accept the doctrine of Jesus' vicarious atonement. Some do not believe there will be a Second Advent of Jesus Christ. Some are universalists. This list is easily expandable in the writings and lectures of numerous professors in all denominations. And there are other ways in which the faith is reduced, ways that are more sophisticated and appear to be more digestible to those who cling to orthodoxy.

In today's scholarly world redaction criticism of the New Testament is having a field day. This methodology is widely used and has reached an interesting point of no return. Basically, *avant garde* redaction critics begin with the assumption that the writers of the four Gospels were writing theology. In doing this the Gospel writers put into the mouth of Jesus things He never said and attributed to Him acts He never performed. Thus the critics pursue the task of discovering the historical Jesus, that is, the real Jesus, the words He actually spoke, and the acts He really performed. The leaders of this movement have set up a committee whose business it is to determine which of the sayings of Jesus were His and which were redacted back into the Gospels by the writers who used later church traditions. For example, most of them are convinced that the great "I am" sayings of Jesus in the Gospel of John (and some of them do not believe that John was the author of what they all the Fourth Gospel) were never spoken by Him. It is interesting that the panel of voters are by no means agreed and that in most instances there is a division of the house. If the scholars themselves cannot agree, that leaves poor nonscholarly readers of the Gospels with a sense of despair. The point at stake, however, is that the critics are saying that parts of the four Gospels are false. Thus readers are always at a loss to know whether what they read can be trusted. And the pulpiteer must be careful to preface his or her remarks by saying that what is preached about may not be true, leaving listeners perplexed and uncertain about that part of the Word of God. This opens the dike to doubt about all of the Word of God, for the next generation of redaction critics may well destroy the views of its predecessors and emasculate all of the Gospels instead of just parts of them.

Another area where the Bible is being severely damaged is in the field of hermeneutics. The word itself is neutral; it simply means "the study of the methodological principles of interpretation" of the Bible. Whoever reads and studies the Bible must, of necessity, engage in the use of hermeneutics. It is therefore a legitimate tool for all who read the Bible. But hermeneutics can be used constructively or destructively. And it is the latter use of this methodology that bears evil fruit.

A few examples of hermeneutical practices will show what the misuse of the methodology can result in. One of the leading questions today has to do with the historicity of Adam and Eve. Virtually all liberal scholars deny the historicity of this original pair, and a number of those who profess to be evangelicals do too. The latter usually argue that one must ask what the intention of the writer was. And they respond to this question by asserting that whoever wrote the opening section of Genesis (for many of these evangelicals also do not think the Pentateuch was written by Moses as the Scriptures claim) did not intend to write history. And since it was not the intention of the writer to speak literally, the notion that Adam and Eve were two actual human beings is incorrect; the writer never intended that the reader should suppose they were real people. When this principle is adduced for Adam and Eve, it literally opens a Pandora's box. If Adam and Eve were not real people, they could not have had children. Therefore the early accounts of Cain and Abel and so on are also unhistoric. This generally leads to the conclusion that the first eleven chapters of Genesis are not to be understood literally. Real history begins with Abraham. There are other implications. Jesus and the New Testament writers leave us with the impression that they believed in a literal Adam. They too were wrong. And so were the great scholars of past ages who all believed in the historicity of Adam and Eve.

The same sort of hermeneutics are used in connection with the creation of human beings among those who believe that God is the author of human life. What is at stake here, especially from the viewpoint of theistic evolutionists, is whether Adam was an immediate creation of God or whether he was derived from lower and simpler forms of life according to evolutionary theory. By using this kind of hermeneutic, modern scientific opinions and biblical data are thought to be harmonized. One can accept the judgments of science and accept the Bible at the same time, since the offense against science has been removed by denying special and immediate creation. Since it is thought by some that the Bible must be interpreted in the light of modern scientific findings, then science has the last word and a hermeneutical device is employed to make the Scripture say what it does not say. It would be far more rational simply to say the Bible is wrong and let it go at that. But whoever believes the Bible says that science is wrong and the Bible is right. And this is the unpardonable sin in this pagan age.

Another hermeneutical dodge employed by concessive evangelicals who practice redaction criticism of a negative type is to misuse the role of the Holy Spirit in the authorship of the Scripture. This type of critic agrees with modern redaction criticism and approves the notion that the Gospel writers put into the mouth of Jesus words He never spoke and attributed to Him acts He never performed. But this was done under the aegis of the Holy Spirit, who thereby certifies this as Scripture. This implies that what is attributed to Jesus can be thought of as being from Jesus and this becomes Scripture and truth. This hermeneutical dodge smacks of gross deception and does violence to the truthfulness of the Holy Spirit and the divine purity of God. It is far easier to take the Gospels literally and believe Jesus said and did all reported therein than to resort to such an explanation in order to sustain the validity of negative redaction criticism.

The conclusion of the matter with regard to educational institutions should be plain enough. The secular institutions are pagan and therefore constitute a challenge to historic orthodoxy. And the theological seminaries that function within the orbit of the churches have generally accepted the views of the pagan institutions outside of the churches. Thus the churches face challenges from within their own/spheres of influence as well from those forces outside their boundaries. The seminaries are heavily tilted away from orthodoxy and the churches themselves reflect this condition, as we shall see, for the churches of today are the result of what the seminaries were yesterday and what the churches of the future will be like can be seen from what the seminaries are today. The picture is therefore dismal.

THE DECLINE OF THE AMERICAN CHURCHES

The decline of the American seminaries was followed by the decline of the churches, which came to reflect the influence and effect of the Enlightenment. The seminaries declined first, however, and this decline precipitated the decline of the churches, even though it took more time and came about more slowly than it did in the seminaries.

Two things happened to the churches. The first is that they lost their commitment to the world and life view they had enjoyed from the time of their beginnings. They moved to the left theologically and took over the modern views of their institutions. The second change marked their departure from their traditional life-style and the adoption of one quite similar to that of the paganism around them. These changes on the part of the churches brought about other consequences of a very practical sort. The churches lost members, their Sunday School enrollments plummeted, and their missionary outreach shrank considerably. The churches were no longer able to influence society as they had previously. And they did little about evangelism on the home front so that, as their people went out the back door by death or estrangement, fewer people were coming in the front door via Sunday Schools and direct evangelizing. We must now consider these factors.

MEMBERSHIP LOSSES

The *Yearbook of American and Canadian Churches*[13] documents the numerical decline of membership in most of the major denominations. Using 1965 as the base, the study compared the membership figures of virtually all of the denominations, large and small, up to 1982–1984 depending on which statistics were available. I had made a similar survey for the years 1962 to 1979, which was then published in *Christianity Today*.[14] The results varied only because of the starting and stopping dates. But the story was the same—substantial losses were suffered by the mainline denominations.

The Episcopal church lost almost 650,000 numbers during this time. The Presbyterian church (USA) lost 862,000, the United Methodist 1,662,000, and the United Church of Christ 368,900. The Reformed Church in America dropped from 385,000 to 344,000, the Lutheran Church in America dropped from 3,142,000 to 2,925,000, and the American Lutheran Church went from 2,541,000 to 2,343,00.

While the mainline denominations that had fallen into the liberal orbit with theological pluralism declined, the denominations that remained conservative increased by leaps and bounds. The Church of the Nazarene went from 343,000 to 507,000. The Baptist General Conference increased from 86,000 to 129,000. The Assemblies of God leaped from 572,000 to 1,153,000. The Wisconsin Evangelical Lutheran Synod went up from 358,000 to 414,000. The Christian and Missionary Alliance went up from 64,000 to 215,000.

SUNDAY SCHOOLS AND MISSIONS

At the same time the number of members of the major denominations shrank, so did the Sunday School enrollments and the number of missionaries sent abroad. Virtually all of the mainline denominations lost half of their former numbers of pupils in their Sunday Schools. Since the Sunday School traditionally had been a main source of new members, this factor alone accounted for a large part of the declining church member statistics.

The number of missionaries sent abroad declined sharply. The Division of Overseas Ministries of the National Council of Churches had in its membership virtually all of the major denominations except for the Southern Baptist Convention and the Lutheran Church, Missouri Synod and Wisconsin Synod. The number of missionaries declined between 70 and 80 percent.

While this was happening, the conservative groups were increasing the number of missionaries they sent into the world and their Sunday School enrollments were rising. The difference was the result of conservative theology versus liberal theology, the latter of which showed little desire for evangelism but strong attachments to the kind of theology that had its roots in the Enlightenment. The situation in the mainline denominations was not as grim as it would have been, had there not been numbers of evangelicals whose local congregations moved against the liberal trends in their denominations.

THE EFFECTS OF LIBERALISM

The mainline denominations are presently in a state of morbidity according to the research and opinions of some careful scholars. In July 1985 the American Academy of Political and Social Science devoted one issue of its *Annals* to "Religion in America Today." Benton Johnson, professor of sociology at the University of Oregon in Eugene, surveyed liberal Protestantism. In that survey the following statements appeared:

Theology had turned critical and destructive and was undermining the very foundations of the Christian faith. . . . By the early seventies, it was clear that all the liberal denominations were losing members. By the middle of the decade the losses numbered in the millions. . . . Now, 10 years later . . . the liberal Protestant community remains mired in depression, a depression far deeper and more longlasting than it suffered earlier in the century. Moreover, this time the conservative, or evangelical, wing of Protestantism has been spared from decline. . . . As the liberal wing lost numbers and influence, the conservative wing achieved high public visibility and made greater strides toward claiming the leadership of the Protestant community than anyone would have thought possible even fifteen years ago. Meanwhile no Reinhold Niebuhr has come forward with new theological resources to energize the liberal wing. No wonder a note of sadness and defeat has recently crept into the writings of many Protestant intellectuals. No wonder many of them have little hope that their community can regain its former preeminence in American religion. What went wrong? ...

Kelley, a liberal Protestant with a record of involvement in the civil rights movement, argued that the reason the liberal churches were declining was that they failed to provide their members with a clear-cut vision of the meaning of life and with a moral code to govern their conduct. . . . Some of them substituted social action programs for the real business of religion. . . . Liberal Protestant churches were indeed uncertain about the theological issues, were reluctant to sell themselves, and had long ago given up any formal effort to oversee their members' moral conduct. Moreover, Kelley's observation that social action is no substitute for religion in church life seemed to pinpoint the really decisive factor in the decline of the liberal denominations. . . .

Broadly speaking, liberalism was an effort to assimilate the new intellectual climate of science, history, and philosophy. . . . In the process, the liberals gave up traditional Protestant views of the Bible and greatly modified their conception of human nature as sinful and in need of supernatural redemption. . . . Theirs was an optimistic world view in which vibrant, self-fulfilled Christians would, by social reform and the example of their own lives, bring history to a triumphant climax. . . .

All the various theological reconstructions of the so-called neo-orthodox period were therefore highly vulnerable to intellectual assault. That assault came in the 1960s, revealing, as Ahlstrom lamented in 1970, that neo-orthodoxy had, after all, only managed to place a "layer of dogmatic asphalt" over "the old claims of scientific and historical investigations." Once this layer had cracked, theology went into a steep decline, thus depriving the liberal churches of any living roots for spiritual nourishment. . . .

Can the liberal churches recover from their current slump and resume their former position of senior partner among the nation's leading religious communities? A consideration of this question must begin with the frank acknowledgement that serious obstacles lie in the way of such a recovery. . . .

In my opinion there is no ready remedy for liberal Protestantism's tired spiritual blood. A spiritual renewal on a really large scale would require a new theological perspective that is both intellectually sound and psychologically provocative. Such a renewal is not on the horizon. . . .

Unless the liberal churches can fashion new ideas to launch a third epoch in their history, the end of their long road as a powerful presence in American culture will soon be in sight.[15]

Another writer in the same issue of the *Annals,* Phillip E. Hammond, wrote about "The Curious Path of Conservative Protestantism." He said:

Sometime after the Civil War, and for the next several decades, there developed within Protestantism two camps regarding this question of modernity—of just how to contend with it. As Peter Berger reminds us, then as now there were basically two religious choices: accommodate religion to the worldly circumstances [i.e., to the Enlightenment—my addition], meeting changes with all available resources; or hold firm to the religious convictions, insisting that worldly changes do not alter supernatural truths. The first choice created liberals, the second conservatives.

The evangelicalism that had been mainline evangelicalism throughout most of the nineteenth century thus became conservative Protestantism by 1920, not so much because its tenets changed but because the surrounding world changed. Many Protestants not only did not change with it but also elaborated a theology that defended their decision not to change. About this time, indeed, there appeared a series of pamphlets proclaiming the fundamentals of Christian doctrine, from which came the label "Fundamentalist," a title used by friend and foe alike. Evangelicalism was still firmly entrenched in some sectors, but now it was defensive, locked in a struggle with its accommodative counterpart over control of Protestant institutions in America—local churches certainly, but more strategically the seminaries, church-related colleges, denominational headquarters, the church media, and thus the public face of Protestantism.

Conservatism lost that struggle, with the Scopes trial of 1925 being the publicized scene of surrender. . . .

What exactly was the battle about? The forces of modernity . . . may be conveniently grouped into three areas: (1) immigration . . ; (2) industrialization . . ; and (3) education, especially in the form of Darwinism and biblical higher criticism, thus evoking new understanding of the Scriptures. . . .

They [Fundamentalists/evangelicals/conservatives] and their predecessors, having chosen not to engage in and address the forces of modern social life, retrenched through most of the twentieth century, only to burst now onto the national scene—via the media and the political arena—espousing a religious viewpoint that was common enough 100 years ago but was long ago judged naive by most literate Americans. Theologically that viewpoint is still naive, as pathetic attempts to defend biblical literalism, especially creationism, illustrate.[16]

Thus Professor Hammond cast his vote against conservative theology and in favor of liberal theology, but he saw exactly what the differences were between them and how the Enlightenment had won the day. The resurgence of conservative theology to him represents a nonviable option, even though it is apparent that liberal theology is hardly an answer.

The foregoing statements do not constitute something new to observers of the contemporary scene. They reflect what was well known more than fifty years ago. J. Gresham Machen in his book *Christianity and Liberalism*, published in 1923, said that the issues rending the mainline denominations were clear-cut. Modernism or theological liberalism was not simply a variation of traditional Christianity—it was essentially a new religion. It forsook the supernatural element of true Christianity. It maintained much of the traditional language of the faith but substituted and promoted the worship of humanity. He thought that honest liberals should peacefully withdraw from the Presbyterian church, of which he was a member, and start their own organizations. But a separation between the two disparate groups was the crying need of the hour. But in 1923 the full flowering of the Enlightenment had not yet come, nor had the new Weltanschauung and Zeitgeist characteristic of the Enlightenment fallen into place. In fact, there are still battles going on over the matter Machen addressed in his book. The Southern Baptist Convention illustrates this.

Among the mainline denominations, the Southern Baptist Convention and the Lutheran Church, Missouri Synod, represent two groups that have resisted and continue to resist the New Paganism. The recent history of the Southern Baptist Convention is a case in point.

THE SOUTHERN BAPTIST CONVENTION

For the last ten years a critical battle has been waged by the conservatives (call them fundamentalists, for the two terms mean the same thing except that the word "fundamentalist" is a pejorative word widely employed by the opponents of historic orthodoxy and by the press) in the Southern Baptist Convention. The conservatives represent a large majority of these Baptists. They organized to do battle against the liberalism in their denomination. The opponents opted to call themselves the moderates, which was nothing more than a slogan designed to make their views more palatable; the underlying difference was there in any event.

When the struggle began, the conservatives elected a conservative to be president of the convention and they have continued to do just that year after year. In June of 1986 they elected Adrian Rogers of the Bellevue Baptist Church of Memphis, Tennessee, to be president. And the trustees of the six theological seminaries who are elected by the convention have been chosen from among the conservatives. They now represent approximately 50 percent of the membership of the seminary boards and it appears that the balance will increasingly fall into the hands of the conservatives.

The *Los Angeles Times* headlined the last election of Dr. Rogers as "Southern Baptists Once More Elect Fundamentalist as President." The other candidate, the Rev. Winfred Moore, was called the "moderate-conservative" candidate. The issue at stake in the election was the same old battle over whether the Bible is trustworthy in the whole and in all of its parts. Moore professed to trust the Bible, but he was the candidate of those who have adopted more liberal views. Rogers got 54.2 percent of the votes; Moore received 45.8. This raises questions about Rogers's judgment that 90 percent of the people in the pews believe the Bible to be wholly true. Clearly, the Southern Baptist Convention is as pluralistic as the other mainline denominations. The main difference is that there are fewer liberals among the Southern Baptists than there are in the other denominations.

The actions of the Southern Baptist Convention have occurred within the context of the pagan world and life view and a culture that stands in opposition to what most Southern Baptists believe. Whether this group can reverse this paganism and restore the Judeo-Christian tradition in America and the West remains to be seen. Perhaps this denomination will join the slide and become more closely identified with the other mainline denominations or else it will stand aloof and be a small minority in a sea of modernity.

The decline of the Judeo-Christian civilization in the West is apparent. We must now take a look at how present culture is pagan and anti-Christian from a moral and ethical viewpoint.

6. The Triumph of the New Pagan Weltanschauung

We have alleged that Western civilization in the Judeo-Christian tradition has collapsed and in its place the New Paganism has come and is dominant in the new culture of the present age. In this discussion it is important to define more narrowly what we mean by paganism or heathenism. The need for this is plain, since we have earlier talked about Christian pagans, which appears to be a contradiction in terms. We have meant by that term that there are those who appear to be identified with Christianity, indeed those who may even call themselves Christians, but who are really not Christian. And whoever is not Christian is pagan.

Webster's Third New International Dictionary (unabridged) defines a "heathen" as "an unconverted member of a people or nation that does not acknowledge the God of the Bible: pagan." This means that those who are members of the ethnic religions such as Buddhism, Shinto, Hinduism, Islam, and others are pagans even though they may profess to worship God in some form or another and with different names. The same is true about those who in America belong to certain sects such as Jehovah's Witnesses, Mormonism, Spiritism, Theosophy, and the like. This does not take from such people their right to believe as they choose, nor does it mean they cannot propagate what they believe. What separates such people from the Christian faith is that they do not believe in the God of the Old and New Testaments. They may even purport to accept the Bible while they alter and abridge what the Bible teaches and what the church of Jesus Christ has held to be true across the ages.

Moreover, there are those who do not believe in the God of the Bible or any god whatever—they are atheists. It is interesting that Charles Hartshorne in his book *The Divine Relativity* makes this statement: "The Russians have their forms of impiety, but is there not some truth in what Tillich, Niebuhr, Heimann, and the late Bishop Temple have told us that the Soviets are Christian heretics rather than pagans?"[1] Then he adds another sentence that identifies his own position: "The one thing that needs to be added is, *so are we.*" Surely if one is a heretic, that is, holds "an opinion or doctrine contrary to church dogma" (and here we mean the basics of the Christian faith), that person is not a Christian, and whoever is not a Christian is a pagan. So we are saying that the prevailing Weltanschauung today in America and in Europe is pagan. Are there adequate evidences to support this contention?

HARTSHORNE

Charles Hartshorne, whom we have just mentioned, is a case in point. He was influenced deeply in process theology by Alfred North Whitehead, who came to Harvard from England in 1924. Hartshorne in turn influenced Bernard Meland, John Cobb, Jr., Daniel Day Williams, and Schubert M. Ogden. Carl F. H. Henry says of their views: "In place of widely current antimetaphysical theories, but still in opposition to classic Christian theism, these men promoted schematic dipolar theism that denies miracle and for biblical supernaturalism substitutes a one-layer theory of reality."[2] In conclusion Henry states: "Whatever else may be said for the new theism, its god is not the God of the Bible."[3] And if its god is not the God of the Bible, these men are pagans. Hartshorne's book *The Divine Relativity* carries on the back cover enthusiastic blurbs from eminent scholars such as J. S. Bixler, Henry N. Wieman, and S. Paul Schilling:

One comes from this book with new confidence in the ability of philosophy to attack religious problems and, through careful analysis, to reveal what is alone conceivable must be true. [Bixler]

Hartshorne's work is a major achievement in religious thought because it strives to clear away errors that have been insuperable obstacles to religious search. [Wieman]

The position taken is described by Professor Hartshorne as surrelativism, or panentheism, and these terms indicate the two major emphases of the volume. . . . He who follows its precise logic with the alertness it demands will have a clarifying and enriching experience. [Schilling]⁴

These eminent scholars fall into the same pagan trap as Hartshorne and his coterie.

DEWEY

In the field of education, John Dewey, perhaps more than any other person, was responsible for supplying American school teachers with a pagan Weltanschauung that was to move them away from the Judeo-Christian tradition into secularization. He published many books, but none is more important than his volume titled *A Common Faith*. Curiously, this book, like Hartshorne's, was published by Yale University Press, the publishing arm of a university that is now wholly secular. The university itself is far removed from the Weltanschauung of its founding fathers: its divinity school and its religion department are open to any viewpoint and have no central frame of reference springing out of historic orthodoxy.

Yale published Dewey's book in 1934 and by 1980 the book had gone into its thirty-first printing. Its universal importance may be seen from the publisher's note that the book has also been distributed in Great Britain, Europe, Africa, Asia, Australia, and New Zealand.

Dewey received his Ph.D. from Johns Hopkins. He taught at the University of Minnesota, the University of Chicago, and finally at Columbia in New York City. He was president of the American Psychological Association, of the American Philosophical Association, and of the American Association of University Professors (which he helped to establish). This explains his widespread influence in America and around the world. He stated that, "Ultimately and philosophically science is the organ of general social progress."⁵ Philosophically he was a pragmatist, although he referred to himself as an instrumentalist or experimentalist. He denied that there are any ethical absolutes. He was one of paganism's greatest pagans. In any event he was a leader in the break away from traditional theism and is numbered among those who helped to bring about the defeat of the

Christian Weltanschauung and the ascendancy of the New Paganism.

As an empiricist wedded to scientism, Dewey was opposed to the supernatural. This, of course, lies at the heart of his basic inconsistency. He moved from empiricism to metaphysics when he made his opposition to supernaturalism an absolute that was not demonstrable empirically and amounted to a faith premise. In doing this he was refusing to accept the evidence God supplied in the resurrection of Jesus Christ from the dead. This is the classic event demonstrating the better and higher claims of the Christian faith over against the views of Dewey. (See John Dewey in Appendix I, pp. 233–34.)

Scientism's Defeat of the Christian Faith

Scientism, not science per se (because there are Christian scientists who have not departed from the Judeo-Christian tradition), is a strong enemy of the true faith and has been responsible in a large measure for the defeat of the church since the Enlightenment. At the heart of scientism lies its dismissal of the supernatural. And with the denial of the supernatural Christianity cannot be sustained and cannot be true.

There are many illustrations of outstanding scientists deeply opposed to the Christian faith. Hermann J. Muller, Nobel laureate from Indiana University, wrote an introduction to a speech delivered to university students by Anton J. Carlson, University of Chicago professor and one-time president of the American Association for the Advancement of Science. Both men denied the supernatural, and Carlson was one of the signers of the first Humanist Manifesto which opted for atheism. (See Herman J. Muller and Anton J. Carlson in Appendix I, pp. 234–35.)

Gordon Haddon Clark responded to the challenge presented by this sort of pagan Weltanschauung. He pointed out their commitment to the empirical and their opposition to nonobservational and nonexperimental authority in the field of experience. (See Gordon Haddon Clark in Appendix I, pp. 235–36.)

One of the classic instances of professorial attack of traditional Christianity involved the work of Immanuel Velikovsky. When his book *Worlds in Collision* was published, he and the publisher were harassed because Velikovsky offered evidence supporting the Old Testament account of Joshua's long day. To accept this account would require acceptance of the supernatural. The response from some scientists was unbelievable. They saw in his work a formidable attack on their basic presuppositions and sought to suppress publication of Velikovsky's book (See The Velikovsky Case in Appendix I, pp. 236–37.)

In more recent years one of the three most popular professors at Harvard University gave further testimony to the thesis that scientism has won a victory over the church. Eric J. Chaisson published his article "The Scenario of Cosmic Evolution" in the November–December 1977 issue of *Harvard Magazine*. The editor of the magazine said: "To make new discoveries about the origins of matter and life, modern science is synthesizing research from many disciplines"—except, of course, anything metaphysical or pertaining to a Creator.

Chaisson thinks humans have no special place in the universe. To him, humans are simply combinations of chemical elements originating from the cosmos. It is the opinion of some that Professor Chaisson operates only in the field of science based on the empirical. If what he says is correct, there is no room for theism or for the church or for religion as known and championed by historic orthodoxy.

Fortunately well-known figures, such as Paul Tournier and Aleksandr Solzhenitsyn, seriously question men like Chaisson and offer different viewpoints.

Tournier argues that the modern world has abandoned the religious and supplanted it with reason and common sense. He laments the repression of religion from life in the West. (See Paul Tournier in Appendix I, p. 237–38.)

Aleksandr Solzhenitsyn believes that Russia, his beloved homeland, has forgotten God, as has the West. He bemoans the drying up of religious consciousness and attacks the modern pursuit of happiness. Science alone does not have the answer; repentance and a quest to be enfolded in the warm hands of God is humanity's only hope. (See Aleksandr Solzhenitsyn in Appendix I, pp. 238–39.)

Before leaving scientism and going on to evolutionism, a word of genuine appreciation must be expressed for scientists, both Christian and non-Christian, for their contribution to the advance of learning. They have served humankind loyally and have done much to make living easier and better. Even pagan musicians, painters, biologists, chemists, and physicists must be lauded for the help they have been to all of us. We regret that they are not Christians yet acknowledge that God has gifted them and has used them in ways that through His common grace bring glory to His name. Whatever the differences are between those of us who are supernaturalists and those who are not, we can appreciate their contributions and urge them to continue their quest for the advance of knowledge. We are just as interested in truth as they are, but there are limits to science beyond which they cannot go without divine revelation.

EVOLUTIONISM

It would be amiss to overlook the great power of evolution as propounded by Charles Darwin in his *Origin of the Species* and by those who have followed closely in his footsteps. This theory of how things came into being and how humanoids have developed from lower forms of primate life and ultimately from the first cell has been a part of the Enlightenment heritage that has destroyed the Judeo-Christian Weltanschauung in the West. In the scientific fraternity today the theory of evolution has reached a status where it is proclaimed to be fact, not theory, and its proponents move heaven and earth to destroy the views of any who oppose it.

In August of 1986 the *Los Angeles Times* ran a story on the front page of the paper titled: "72 Nobel Winners Urge Rejection of Creationism Law." The protest was occasioned by a Louisiana law that called for "balanced treatment" of evolution and creationism in public schools. The Nobel laureates urged the Supreme Court to reject this law. By and large the scientists who issued the statement are people of international fame who teach and engage in technical research in leading universities in the United States.

The statement claimed that the case before the court is crucial for American science. The brief said that "teaching religious ideas mislabeled as science is detrimental to science education."[6] Stephen J. Gould, a professor of paleontology at Harvard, said that " 'Creation science' is a meaningless phrase, a whitewash" designed as a cover for injecting "a minority religious view—biblical literalism—into public schools."

The Louisiana law, according to Louisiana officials, is not based on religious convictions. " 'Creation science is scientific and non-religious,' their brief asserts. 'In fact, (it) is as scientific as evolution.' " Nothing in the brief of the scientists who oppose the Louisiana law indicates that evolution is simply a theory and definitely not a proven fact. The scientists are saying that evolution is true, that is, it is scientifically demonstrable. Their statement "It misleads our youth about the nature of scientific inquiry . . . and strips our citizens of the power to distinguish between the phenomena of nature and the supernatural articles of faith" tells us all we need to know.

It is fair to say that evolutionism is indeed believed by a vast majority of scholars in America precisely because they reject the supernatural or miracles. It is fascinating to note that some who claim to be in the evangelical tradition fully support the idea of evolution from lower to higher forms of life under the umbrella of "theistic evolution," by which term they mean that God is behind evolution and used it to bring humanoids into existence. A few illustrations will make this trend plain.

THEISTIC EVOLUTIONISTS

Dale Moody was a professor at the Southern Baptist Theological Seminary in Louisville, Kentucky, for many years. As a theologian, he was fully aware of the implications of evolution and considered himself sufficiently educated to speak about it with confidence. In an article he endorsed the theory of evolution and found fault with the Genesis account of Adam and Eve, saying that Adam, Eve, Cain, and Abel were no more than representative human beings among many other unnamed contemporaries. He favored a symbolic interpretation of the Adam and Eve story and found himself in agreement with modern scientific anthropologists. (See Dale Moody in Appendix I, pp. 239–40.)

Dr. Moody's views are of such a nature that to accept them would be to throw out the Bible as a reliable witness to history. After all, if Adam and Eve were not historical then they could not have had children. Even a cursory examination of the genealogical tables in the Old and New Testaments witness to the historicity of Adam and Eve and of their immediate offspring. The chronological tables in Chronicles bear witness to the historicity of Adam. And so does the account given in Luke 3. Moody's mistake springs in part from his failure to read the Genesis account carefully. Genesis 5:4 says that Adam had other sons and daughters. This statement alone indicates two important facts. The first is that in the early days of the human race sisters and brothers intermarried. The second is that Adam and Eve had other children not named specifically in Genesis and the number of those children is not specified. Moreover the account of the conversation of Cain and God is misunderstood by Moody. Commentators such as Matthew Henry and more recently Gleason L. Archer *(Encyclopedia of Bible Difficulties)*[7] have given adequate information to answer the queries of Moody. Moreover Moody's thesis seems to deny the Mosaic authorship of the Pentateuch, which is clearly affirmed in the New Testament by the apostles and Jesus.

Another supporter of theistic evolution is George Marsden who taught at Calvin College in Grand Rapids, Michigan, for some years. He is a professor of history and author of a number of books. At a colloquium at the Graham Center in Wheaton, Illinois, where the subject of evolution was under discussion and all sorts of opposing views were presented, Marsden contributed to the dialogue in favor of theistic evolution.

Marsden, according to the Religious News Service dispatch,[8] supported a third option. He spoke of those who regard the theory of evolution and the theory of creation as mutually exclusive beliefs. In place of this schema he presented "a case for the excluded middle." By this he meant that he accepted evolution but that God had the divine hand in it. Evolution was God's way of bringing humans into existence. Like Moody, he claims that Genesis is to be understood as a metaphor, not as real history.

The *RNS* said that Dr. Marsden "cited examples of highly respected evangelicals who, soon after Charles Darwin announced his theory of evolution, proclaimed that this theory did not necessarily refute their theology." Moreover, Marsden said that "the tendency to interpret the Bible literally on future events fuels the notion that the Bible should be read literally when it speaks of past history." One finds it hard to avoid response to this sort of reasoning. The New Testament is replete with statements saying that what happened then was a fulfillment of what was prophesied in the Old Testament. In fact there are more than forty such Old Testament prophecies that are said to have been fulfilled in the life of Jesus. How, then, can anyone suppose that past history in the Old Testament is not to be looked upon as literal?

In his lecture Marsden went on to say it is improper to view the Bible "as a book filled with scientific statements that have essentially the same precision as might be found in 20th century scientific journals." This claim that science is precise is quite false. It is not precise. For example, a yard is only a yard or an inch is only an inch under highly controlled laboratory conditions—there is no precise yard or inch outside the laboratory. One example of the inexactitude of science is the use of pi (3.14) to find the area of a circle. Pi is the ratio of the circumference to the radius. When a numerical value for it is attempted, division goes on forever; no exact value is ever reached. Therefore whoever uses pi for a compilation always ends up with a conclusion that is not genuinely exact. But more will be said about the exactitude of science in another connection.

Indeed some so-called evangelicals wonder whether the issue of evolution and the struggle between scientism and biblical orthodoxy is really important. One is Karl K. Turekian, professor and chairman of the department of geology and geophysics at Yale University. He graduated from Wheaton College in Illinois. Dr. Turekian's current work involves him in marine geochemistry, earth processes, and "planetary evolution." Dr. Turekian said, "Evangelicals should not be hung up on the creation/evolution dispute. It is no more an issue than the shroud of Turin."[9]

Dr. Turekian is evidently one who accepts the evolutionary theory but does not see that the issue is pivotal and ultimately dynamically related to one's theology. The college from which he graduated thought it was a question that required attention and in recent times added an addendum to its doctrinal statement of Christian beliefs. The original statement said:

We believe that man was created in the image of God; that he sinned and thereby incurred not only physical death but also that spiritual death which is separation from God, and that all human beings are born with a sinful nature and that those who reach moral responsibility become sinners in thought, word, and deed.

This statement was amended to include the following provision:

By this statement we affirm our belief that man was created by a direct act of God in his image, not from previously existing creatures, and that all mankind sinned in Adam and Eve, the historical parents of the entire human race.

By this statement the college was saying that the dispute over evolution versus creation was an important question and the college was going on record in support of the biblical account of creation. This viewpoint, of course, is unpopular and there can be no doubt that evolutionism has undermined the Christian faith for multitudes. And the educational institutions of the West have, for the most part, cast their lot on the side of evolution.

To say that the Enlightenment through evolution has given the church a bad time is true. But there is another side to the story. Despite the popularity of evolution and the support it has garnered from millions of people, there have been some voices raised against this theory, voices that have asked tough questions that most of the evolutionists pay no attention to. It so happens that most evolutionists say in effect, "My mind is made up; don't bother me with the facts." What are these facts that should be of concern to the evolutionists?

EVOLUTION: FACT VERSUS THEORY

M. D. Aeschliman wrote a review article about two books: *Angels, Apes, and Men*,[10] written by Professor Stanley L. Jaki, a historian of science who thinks evolution to be untrue; and *Is God a Creationist?*[11] edited by Roland M. Frye and carrying the subtitle, "The Religious Case Against Creation Science," which means he is in favor of evolutionism. Readers can read these books themselves, but what Aeschliman wrote is something of an eye-opener.

Aeschliman first took exception to the scientific naturalism of the type held by Jacob Bronowski in his book *The Identity of Man*,[12] in which Bronowski blandly says: "Man is a part of nature, in the same sense that a stone is, or a cactus, or a camel." People who make such statements, Aeschliman said, saw off the branch of rationality on which they sit when arguing in favor of human purposelessness. He claimed that promoters of Darwinism lack scientific integrity, noting how little attention evolutionists give to splendid books challenging their views. He documented the failure of scholars even to include in their extensive bibliographies any mention of books written by nonevolutionists. He also offered evidence against the notion of blind forces operating in nature. (See M. D. Aeschliman in Appendix I, pp. 240–42.)

Aeschliman is not alone, but he is only a part of a small minority of first-rate thinkers who question the ultimacy of empiricism. Another one of this small group is Sir John Eccles, an eminent neurobiologist whose visit to Harvard University is mentioned in Walter Percy's book *Lost in the Cosmos: The Last Self-Help Book*. In reviewing this book, Robert Royal made clear that Harvard students were quite at home with empiricism and opposed to the supernatural. Royal said:

A few years ago, the eminent neurobiologist Sir John Eccles ended a lecture at Harvard by asserting courageously that evolution could account for the brain, but not for the quintessentially human things— mind, consciousness, and thought. Only something transcendent, he judged could account for them. The Harvard students, predictably, hissed.

Closed minds in Cambridge and an odd array of other contemporary phenomena have convinced Walker Percy that our chief intellectual error and the principal cause of our modern malaise is scientism, the unscientific prejudice that knowledge consists solely in empirical observation.[13]

To further clarify the viewpoint that science does not have answers to ultimate questions and that these answers lie beyond the reach of science is a statement made by Sir Peter Medawar. He was the 1960 Nobel Prize winner in medicine and as "the theoretical father of cloning" is nothing if not pro-science. He made the following statement in his book *The Limits of Science:*

That there is indeed a limit upon science is made very likely by the existence of questions that science cannot answer and that no conceivable advance in science would empower it to answer. These are the questions that children ask: How did everything begin? What are we all here for? What is the point of living?[14]

Before concluding our remarks about the success of Darwinism in breaking down the Judeo-Christian Weltanschauung and bringing us into the impasse of secularism without God, two points should be made. One has to do with those evolutionists who reject the notion of God and the transcendent and are at best nontheistic; the other has to do with theistic evolutionists who do start with the idea that there is a God who lies behind an unfolding universe.

ORIGIN OF THE COSMOS

All of nontheistic evolutionists are agreed that the cosmos is quite old. Usually they talk about billions of years. The fact that they use some figure about the age of the cosmos clearly indicates that if the cosmos is two billion years old then one must face the question, "What was there before the cosmos came into being?" If there was nothing, then the cosmos came into being from nothing. Did this happen by chance or by some intelligence at work to bring matter into being? Or is matter eternal? And whence can any scientist come to such a conclusion from the empirical methodology?

A number of scientists speak about the big bang theory for the beginning of the cosmos. We need not go into details familiar only to those in the field of physics, but we do know that the big bang theory is no longer accepted by some scientists. There has emerged in its place the unified field theory's version of the big bang, which was first propounded by Alan H. Guth of the Massachusetts Institute of Technology in 1980, and is called the inflationary universe theory. Daniel Lazich, an aerospace engineer, says that

the inflationary theory has literally opened the door of science, at least a crack, to consideration of the possibility that our universe originated by fiat. And if that is the case, then there is also the possibility that a creator was the one who issued that fiat. And if everything in the universe just may have been made by an intelligent being, who is to say that same intelligence did not also create the orderly forms of life we see on earth. . . . The questions have to do with the matter of causality—is there a cause for the existence of the universe? And is it an intelligent cause? Here again physicists exploring the microcosmic world of the atom are finding evidences that may shock some religionists who have consigned Genesis to the mythological dustbin.[15]

ADAM AND EVE

Theistic evolutionists differ in one regard from the non-theistic evolutionists: they say that God indeed is the Creator. In this they disagree with so many of the scientists today, but they do agree with the evolutionists generally who say that life began with the first atom and that all life has proceeded from that point onward and upward. Humans have sprung from lower forms of life.

The problem the theistic evolutionists face has to do with the biblical account of creation. They are saying that the Genesis account, when read literally, is at variance with the findings of science. To cut the Gordian knot they declare that the biblical account is mythical, figurative, not historical. By whatever name you call it they wipe out the Genesis statements and explain them away in agreement with science.

We have already referred to some like Daly Moody and George Marsden. Mention might also be made of the book *Old Testament Survey* by William LaSor, David Hubbard, and Frederic Bush from Fuller Theological Seminary. The writers say that the author (unnamed) of Genesis "is writing as an artist, a storyteller, who uses literary device and artifice. One must endeavor to distinguish what he intends to teach from the literary means employed." Before this they say: "Surely, when an author of a story names the principal characters (i.e., Adam and Eve) Mankind and Life, something is conveyed about the degree of literalness intended!"[16]

In an article titled "Biblical Authority and Interpretation," Randy Maddox of Sioux Falls College writes:

This is not to say that Scripture is full of false scientific statements, but rather that many of the statements treated as scientific claims by defenders and critics alike were not really intended that way in Scripture itself. A good example is the Genesis prologue. In its Hebrew form this chapter is an artfully crafted and highly stylistic literary piece. This fact, in conjunction with an analysis of its sevenfold structure and symbolic use of names (Adam = humanity, Eve = giver of life, etc.), makes it clear that the prologue is much more a theological account of the source and purpose of creation than a narrowly scientific or historical account of the details of creation. When this realization is related to the growing sensitivity to the differences between such theological reflection and modern scientific explanation, the basis is provided for a constructive integration of the authoritative teachings of the Genesis prologue and the findings of modern science.[17]

Apparently most of the theistic evolutionists who do not think there was a historic Adam and Eve assume that their names constitute evidence to warrant such a conclusion. Certainly the names of Adam and Eve actually express the truth of human creation. Adam was taken from the dust of the earth and was the first human being. And Eve was the mother of all living so that life proceeded from her womb. Naming human beings in this mode was common to Scripture. Samuel means "heard of God." Adonijah means "Jah is my Lord." Adoram means "high honor." Saul means "asked." David means "beloved." Joshua means "Jah saves." Reuben means "behold a son." Levi means "joined." Judah means "praise." Miriam means "thick, fat, strong." Obed means "serving." And Ruth means "friendship." With this by way of background and comparison, the names of Adam and Eve make excellent sense.

Making Adam nonhistorical also does violence to the remainder of the Bible. Scripture in other places, if we use the analogy of Scripture, requires that the Genesis statements about Adam be accepted as literal. In Romans the apostle Paul says: "Nevertheless death reigned from Adam to Moses, even over them that had not sinned after the similitude of Adam's transgression, who is the figure of him that was to come" (5:14). Paul strengthens the case still further by his statement "For as in Adam all die, even so in Christ shall all be made alive" (1 Cor. 15:22). But, if this is not sufficient, Paul's clearest statement leaves no doubt whatever as to what he believed and taught. In his Letter to Timothy he says: "For Adam was first formed, then Eve. And Adam was not deceived, but the woman being deceived was in the transgression" (1 Tim. 2:13, 14). Since Paul also wrote under the inspiration of the Holy Spirit, this is also the Holy Spirit's teaching. Those who hold that Adam and Eve were nonhistorical must, of necessity, say that the apostle Paul was wrong and the Holy Spirit erred. Since one part of Scripture cannot teach the opposite of other parts of Scripture and since the Pauline teaching is so clear and unambiguous, then it follows that one must understand the Genesis account in the light of Paul's teaching and accept the historicity of the Genesis account of the creation of the first man, Adam.

Those who deny the historicity of the early parts of Genesis have still other problems. Where does mythology leave off and historicity begin? With Abraham? But did not Abraham have a father? Who was Abraham's father? Moreover the genealogical tables in Chronicles and Luke seem to be speaking about a historical person when they refer to Adam. Are these tables partly true and partly false? And why should the so-called certainty of science, about which there are many questions, sit in judgment on Scripture rather than vice versa?

The biggest problem for those who are theistic evolutionists and who destroy the historicity of the early parts of Genesis has to do with the role of the Holy Spirit as the divine author of Scripture. Since the Holy Spirit is omniscient, why in the world would He tell us what He knows is not true and why would He hide from us the truth of how things actually happened? If the Holy Spirit told us things in Genesis that are not true, why should He not also tell us other things in the Bible that are also untrue? The answer to this question by those who are theistic evolutionists always turns out to be what we have just quoted: "the basis is provided for a constructive integration of the authoritative teachings of the Genesis prologue and the findings of modern science." This means that science is placed over Scripture and Scripture is relativized and reinterpreted in the light of science's so-called certainties. The theistic evolutionists have capitulated to the empiricism of science, have thrown their support to the founding fathers of the Enlightenment, and are part of the modern problem of secularism from within the boundaries of the church.

MARXISM, THE CHURCH'S DEADLY ENEMY

The triumph of the New Paganism has been aided in its victory by atheistic Marxism. More than one-third of the earth has fallen into the clutches of Marxism and its proponents continue to reach out day and night for further conquests all around the globe. While it is true that Marxism can be shown to be based on presuppositions that are untenable and that it does not do what it promises, this seems to make little difference to multitudes on the planet earth.

In one respect communism is not new. It is found in Plato's *Republic*. It is also found in the Bible in the Acts of the Apostles. In the latter case it should be emphasized that what some of the followers of Jesus did was done voluntarily. No one was coerced into following their pattern. They simply held all things in common. But when Ananias sold a piece of property and brought part of the sale to lay at the apostle's feet, he lied by saying that he had brought the full price. He dies as a result of his deceit. But the apostle made it clear that when Ananias had the property, it was his, and when he sold it, the money was his and he was free to do with it what he pleased. Thus the inalienable right to private property is taught there and elsewhere in the Bible. But nowhere does the Bible assert that Christians may not set up a communal enterprise with common ownership of property, so long as it is voluntary and no one is forced to join.

Behind Marxism lies the idea found in philosophy and religion that all people are brothers and sisters caught up in economic, political, and social systems that organize them into categories of masters and servants. All forms of socialism, whether utopian or Marxist, have in mind the desire to establish an egalitarian society in which economic and political distinctions are broken down so that all are equal.

Karl Marx, in his voluminous writings, introduced a philosophy the substance of which first, showed how the present order came into being; second, showed how the present situation could be improved by a better one, namely communism; and third, created a belief in the ultimate salvation of humans on earth on a scientific basis. The latter objective had in mind the creation of the New Person, which would make communism possible at last. Marxism became the largest mass movement since the days of early Christianity. It also became the greatest subversive force in the modern world.

Marxism aimed to bring into being a classless society in which the means of production would be owned by the community. The distribution and exchange of goods and commodities would be under the direction of the state. Under socialism, which is the last step before communism is attained, the state or government would be needed, but eventually the state as an instrument of coercion would disappear. The ultimate goal is "from each according to ability and to each according to need." The public ownership of the land and all of the means of production meant, in the simplest terms, state capitalism, (the Soviet Union is the most ruthless and consistent version of this today).

How was this ideal sort of world to be brought into existence? Utopian socialists hope to do this by the ballot box, that is, through the democratic process. Marxists, on the other hand, were and are committed to revolution and the use of force. Bullets, rather than ballots, is the Marxist choice. To the Marxist the private ownership of property is the worst of all evils. How did Marxism fare in the marketplace and how well did it succeed in bringing this bright future into being? What made the rise of Marxism possible?

Marx thought the revolution would come at the hands of the oppressed factory workers, the proletariat, in places like Britain and other technologically advanced nations. It came to Russia, which was by no means advanced in that regard and it did not come from the proletariat. Marxism advanced swiftly among the intelligentsia, who passed it on to the lower classes. A second key reason for the advance of Marxism was the vacuum created by the breakdown of organized religion, which was the result of the Enlightenment some years before Marx. The third important reason for the success of Marxism was the secularization of life in the West.

Atheism lies at the heart of Marxism and the destruction of religion, the churches, and the family sprang up like a weed from the atheistic presuppositions of Marx. In place of God and revelation as the foundation for a world and life view, Marxism affirms that its basic premises or fundamental beliefs are guaranteed by science, which they are not. But that is beside the point, for Marxism has a creed that is highly dogmatic, one surely no less dogmatic than what the Christian church holds about the existence of God. When people question their creeds, trouble is brewing. This happened in the Christian church as a result of Enlightenment thinking, but as yet the creed of Marxism has not been questioned seriously by those who have embraced it. In fact the continuing advance of Marxism around the globe suggests that there are millions of people who are willing to die for the Marxist faith.

Marxism has a Weltanschauung marked by a consistent philosophic, economic, political, and social body of dogma. Basically Marxists say that the present world and its system is doomed by its own internal contradictions. And a better world is being born in accordance with irresistible laws. People everywhere are called upon to choose either to collaborate with this wave of the future or oppose it. This Weltanschauung has its own Bible: the writings of Marx, Engels, Lenin, Stalin, and others.

When Marxism and the Christian faith are compared, it is easily demonstrable that they are wholly incompatible. Marxism starts with matter as the ultimate reality, Christianity with God or spirit. Marxism bases it entire world and life view on human reason; Christianity starts with revelation and the supernatural. Marxism promises what it has never been able to achieve. It has failed wherever it has been tried. Human freedom and especially religious freedom and the right to propagate one's faith is everywhere denied by the Marxists. The degradation of humankind, whether it be in Russia, Cuba, China, or Southeast Asia, is endemic to the system and demeaning, especially to those who do not buy into Marxism and are unwilling to sell their souls into slavery.

Marxism's so-called scientific foundation is pure myth. Neither Marxists nor anyone else can prove there is no God. Nor can anyone prove that matter is eternal. And the claim that Marxist dogma is guaranteed by science is to misuse science, defy rational thought, and propound a thesis that defies the laws of logic. Marxism is a leftist dictatorship and is just as bad and no different from a rightist dictatorship like Hitler's. Both are alien to the Christian faith and alien even to the better understanding of those who are outside the church and constitute a pagan mission field for the church.

LIBERATION THEOLOGY

Liberation theology, so widely employed in Latin America, is inextricably tied to Marxism even as it pretends to be Christian by so many of its advocates. No one can deny that the masses of people in Latin America have been oppressed for centuries. This oppression has its roots in rightist dictatorships. Nowhere in Latin America has there been any attempt or even a statement of commitment by the landholding minority who control most of the resources of those nations to make it possible for the masses to own their own lands by purchase or by long-term mortgage payments. Marxism has moved into the vacuum and has made exorbitant promises its advocates have no intention or even possibility of fulfilling. In their desire for freedom and for a stake in society the masses do not understand that Marxism, which promises them freedom from their oppressors, food for their bellies, and roofs over their heads, has a sorry track record wherever it has seized power.

Pope John Paul II has called for the world and for Roman Catholics to recognize and for the world's religions to collaborate to "eliminate hunger, poverty, ignorance, persecution, discrimination and every form of enslavement of the human spirit." At the same time the pope has warned the Brazilian bishops against those who profess to be Christians and yet who have adopted Marxist socioeconomic theory or who advocate violent revolutions. However, a number of leading Catholics have taken the very step the pope warned against. They have used the dialectic of Marxism to seek a synthesis of opposites, that is, some form of Christian Marxism.

In his book *The Theology of Liberation*, Gustavo Gutierrez, the widely acknowledged father of liberation theology argues passionately against the so-called reformation of capitalism. He advocates socialism and calls the Roman Catholic church capitalism's accomplice. He urges the Catholic church to place itself at the heart of the revolution. The capitalistic structures, not individuals, are the true enemies, and Christian love demands abolishment of these structures.

Gutierrez spoke at Harvard's divinity school in 1984. He was introduced by another noted Roman Catholic, Henri J. M. Nouwen, who lauded Gutierrez and clearly joined with him in approval of the theology of liberation. He spoke touchingly of Gutierrez's Christian love and his devotion to the poor. (See Henri J. M. Nouwen in Appendix I, pp. 242–43.)

No one can fault the many Catholics who have a genuine concern for the poor. Nor can it be argued that all of those who support the theology of liberation cannot be Christians. But what is clear is this: liberation theology with its Marxist components cannot be reconciled with the historic Christian faith. It is difficult to see how the term Christian Marxist can make sense. The term is intrinsically contradictory however sincere the people may be who use the term. (See Can Christian Marxists Remain Christian? in Appendix I, pp. 243–44.)

As well, there are many Protestant denominations boasting followers of liberation theology, though their total numbers are fewer than those of the Roman Catholic church. The World Council of Churches, to which many of the Protestant churches belong, has in it vocal and influential Protestant proponents of Marxism and the theology of liberation. Any review of the materials published by the major Protestant denominations and the World Council of Churches show how similar many of the Protestants are in their views to those of the Roman Catholics on this subject.

The Protestant counterpart to Gutierrez, José Miguez-Bonino, is an Argentinian, a Methodist, and a president of the World Council of Churches. He is one of the keenest advocates of the theology of liberation and Marxism. His views do not differ too substantially from those of Gutierrez.

Miguez-Bonino confesses the Christian faith and acknowledges Jesus Christ as Savior and Lord. He criticizes capitalism and opposes development or reform. Instead, he advocates capitalism's destruction, calls for basic and revolutionary change, and wishes to bring in socialism based on the Marxist analysis of the sociopolitical situation in the world.

Miguez-Bonino praises the accomplishments of Castro's Cuba and heartily endorses the notion that a Christian can and should be a Marxist too. For him socialism is the wave of the future and the only hope for humanity caught up in the tentacles of an oppressive, grasping, and unbiblical capitalism. He does not openly commit himself to violence as the means for making the change from capitalism to Marxist socialism, but nowhere has there been a peaceful transition to Marxist socialism. Nor can one escape the Leninist principle that force is the midwife that brings the new baby into existence.

There are, of course, those who are more or less radical than Miguez-Bonino. But he is the archetypal model among Protestant liberationists. (See José Miguez-Bonino in Appendix I, pp 244–46.)

All of this, of course, is only the briefest summary of Marxism and the theology of libertion which is its stepchild. There is a mountain of material available on both subjects and it is fair to conclude that both of these views entertain a Weltanschuung that is foreign to the Judeo-Christian one. These movements have included multitudes outside the church of Jesus Christ and a fair number of those who work in the church but whose views are incompatible with historic Christianity. They have had a powerful impact on the church and are in a substantial measure responsible for the triumph of what I have called the New Pagan Weltanschuung. The church has been a victim of these movements and has suffered a serious defeat, a setback that means it is a minority in the midst of a pagan majority. Until this fact is grasped one cannot know where the church is today. Still other movements in the West have helped to bring about the supremacy of the New Paganism.

HIGHER EDUCATION AND THE NEW PAGANISM

Colleges and universities have not only imbibed deeply from the well of the new Weltanschauung, they have also been prominent in the spread of paganism. At the heart of this movement are professors who use their classrooms for the purpose of propagating their beliefs. This can be seen in many different ways.

One organization has estimated there are ten thousand Marxist professors in the colleges and universities of the land. Some think this number is considerably higher. "The tilt of university faculties was revealed in a 1975 study by the Carnegie Commission on Higher Education. It found that 49 percent of professors surveyed called themselves liberal or left-wing and only 25 percent conservative. 'Since then,' says David Brock, a recent graduate from the University of California at Berkeley, 'traditional liberals have been overtaken by the radical left, a different breed entirely.' "[18] The same article says other equally important things:

But there is no disputing the fact that a host of radical organizations has emerged, publishing a growing number of academic journals.

Over two dozen of these journals are openly Marxist. And book sales by the Marxist Monthly Review Press are running at nearly half a million volumes a year. Bertell Ollman, a Marxist theorist and professor of politics, New York University, five years ago boasted that "A Marxist cultural revolution is taking place today in American universities." His textbook, *Alienation: Marxist Conception of Man in Capitalist Society*, is now in use in more than 100 universities. College curricula offer over 500 courses on the "philosophy" of Marxism, and professors openly espouse their ideological beliefs. Samuel Bowles, an economist at the University of Massachusetts at Amherst, writes in the book *Schooling in Capitalist America*, that Marxists believe "all of the glaring inadequacies of political democracy in the U.S. are attributable to the private ownership of the means of production."

Michael Wallace, a historian at John Jay College of the City University of New York, writes in *The Left Academy*, that "Marxism is a long-term historical movement of liberation, and Marxist scholars are those who contribute to the project of building a popular, democratic and socialist society." There are countless other such avowals from radicals who now hold tenure on today's faculties.[19]

The March–April 1986 issue of *Harvard Magazine* published the results of a survey conduct among graduates of Harvard and Stanford universities. The 3600 replies derived from a survey "systematically selected to form a cross section of the alumni bodies as a whole. Alumni of graduate schools as well as of the undergraduate colleges were included in the sample." The article said: "Few would deny that Harvard and Stanford alumni exemplify the American educational elite."[20] One section of the survey is particularly significant; it had to do with religion. One question was, "Have you ever had a born-again experience?" In order to relate this and other questions to the total population of the nation the Harvard survey used figures taken from Yankelovich, Skelly and White, a New York City firm that uses behavioral science research methods to analyze social change and help organizations manage it effectively. Florence Skelly the president is an alumna of Hunter College in New York City and has done postgraduate work at Columbia University. Using this data, 34 percent of the total population of the United States acknowledge having had a born-again experience. Eleven percent of the Stanford alumni said they had had such an experience. Eight percent of the Harvard alumni said they had a born-again experience. While 94 percent of Americans believe in a supreme being only 73 percent of the Harvard and Stanford alumni so believe. Whereas 63 percent of Americans generally hold that religion is a very important part of their lives, only 24 percent of the Harvard and Stanford alumni responded affirmatively.

Unfortunately the survey does not indicate what percentage of these people had a born-again experience before they attended college and how many had such an experience while they were in college. What it does tell is that neither college made any significant contribution to these students by way of helping them have a born-again experience. And when 90 percent of these graduates are obviously pagan, it says something about the state of education in two major private universities as it relates to religion.

Harvard differs from Stanford in that it has a divinity school attached to its complex. In the early 1900s Harvard became Unitarian. This has moderated, and today the divinity school is a theologically pluralistic institution. A former dean who recently left Harvard to become president of Rice University, George Rupp, was interviewed in the *Bulletin* of the divinity school.

Among other things, Dean Rupp said that many students, faculty, and alumni are not attracted to preaching the gospel and saving souls, for the *ethos* of Harvard is different from that of traditional Christianity. He regards the claims to absolute truth with skepticism and is confident that in the long run the temporary success of resurgent fundamentalism will die out. However, he does say there is a tense struggle between fundamentalism and what Harvard stands for. He is wholly unhappy with what he labels "outbursts of frenzied reassertions of authoritarian religion." It may take five hundred to seven hundred years to realize the objectives he sets forth for the divinity school but he has confidence that these will win the day at last. (See Dean Rupp in Appendix I, pp. 246–47.)

When this statement by Dean Rupp is weighed against the Harvard/Stanford survey in which 90 percent of those polled have never had a born-again experience, one can say that it will not take five hundred to seven hundred years to do what is envisioned by Dean Rupp. Paganism has won the day in the college and university realm.

This is further evidenced by a recent conclave of religion scholars at Claremont Graduate School. Leading Christian theologians came together and one of their spokesmen, John Hick, said "interfaith exchanges have contributed to a 'pluralistic vision' in which Christianity is perceived as 'not the one and only way of salvation but one among several.' "[21]

The Claremont Graduate School may be far outdone by the University of Chicago Divinity School. Faculty member James M. Gustafson is an ethicist who trained under H. Richard Niebuhr at Yale. Gustafson wrote a two-volume work titled *Ethics from a Theocentric Perspective*,[22] which was reviewed by Donald G. Bloesch, a professor of theology at the University of Dubuque Theological Seminary. In his review Bloesch makes it clear that Gustafson holds many views that are contrary to historic orthodoxy.

Gustafson is a naturalist. To him, God is not transcendent, and there are no absolute timeless truths. The Bible is no more than the aspirations of seeking people conditioned by their times and circumstances. When Gustafson comes to the New Testament he denies virtually all of the doctrinal claims regarding Jesus Christ, including his death and resurrection. Moreover he does not believe in any life after death and he has no gospel to preach. (See Donald G. Bloesch in Appendix I, pp. 247–48.)

Union Theological Seminary in New York City is another illustration of an educational institution that has been subverted by the Enlightenment mentality even as it professes a belief in God. Not so long ago Reinhold Niebuhr was on the faculty of the institution.

Niebuhr went through a series of changes that led toward a more middle-of-the-road position, but it never led to his becoming a full-fledged supporter of orthodoxy. He ran for Congress on the Socialist ticket but was not elected. He led the Pacifist Fellowship of Reconciliation. Later on he moved from these far left positions and came to accept the doctrine of the Fall as a telling myth, but certainly not a fact of history. *Time* said of him that "Although Niebuhr was thoroughly a modernist in theology and did not believe in the literal truth of Scripture" he did say the human race is "ineradicably given to self-deception."[23] Niebuhr influenced a generation of seminary students away from orthodoxy and from the Bible as the standard of reference for all theological beliefs.

Paul Tillich was another Union faculty member who exercised a great influence in the theological world and on students far and wide. He was by any standard wholly removed from theological orthodoxy and was thus a subverter of the Hebrew-Christian tradition. One can easily find this in his systematic theology when he talks about the cross of Christ. He writes:

The idea of the subjection of self is expressed by Paul in *mythical* terms in Philippians, chapter 2. The pre-existent Christ gave up his divine form, became a servant, and experienced the death of a slave. Pre-existence and self-surrender are combined in this *symbolism*. It corroborates the central symbol of the Cross, *but it cannot be taken literally as an event* which happened at some time in some heavenly place. The same idea is expressed in *legendary terms* in the stories of the birth of Christ in Bethlehem, his lying in a cradle, his flight to Egypt, and the early threat to his life by the political powers. . . .

This completes our discussion of the symbols which corroborate the central one of the Resurrection of the Christ. The symbols have been greatly distorted and consequently were rejected by man because of a literalism which makes them absurd and nonexistential.[24]

Union Theological Seminary is only one of a number of educational forces that have done their share in overturning the traditional Hebrew-Christian viewpoint. The Death of God school of theologians were institutionally based and played an important role in the further decline of orthodoxy. The leading exponents of this movement were delineated as the three high priests of the new cult by Allen Spraggett in the Canadian *Toronto Daily Star* in its April 2, 1966, interview with one of them. The trio mentioned were William Hamilton of the Colgate-Rochester Divinity School in Rochester, New York; Thomas J. J. Altizer of Atlanta's Methodist sponsored Emory University; and Paul Van Buren, an episcopal priest on the faculty of Nashville's Vanderbilt Divinity School.

Spraggett interviewed Hamilton, who said among other things: "We are atheists, but Christian atheists. We differ from classical atheism in that it says there never was a God, whereas we say that there once was a God but there isn't now. We do not know, we do not adore, we do not believe in God. We say it is possible to live as Christians, in obedience to Jesus without God. If prayer is construed as something addressed to a reality outside of oneself, there is no place for it. I see no way of affirming the life of the human community after death. Nor can I affirm the existence of Jesus after death. He, too, has ceased to exist."[25]

Another force demonstrating the defeat of the church in the West was and is atheistic existentialism. At the University at Freiburg in Germany Edmund Husserl led the way. He was succeeded by Martin Heidegger, whose avowed atheism marked a movement that was to include others of great note. One was Jean-Paul Sartre, who also studied under Husserl at Freiburg. Sartre, too, was openly atheistic. Albert Camus and Franz Kafka are also members of the same clan.

These figures were titans identified with leading educational institutions; their writings have influenced at least two generations of students in the West. It is impossible to underemphasize their importance and there is no way that their influence can be fully appraised. Multitudes have embraced their teachings and even those who profess to believe in some sort of God have often succumbed to their other views. Meaninglessness, which lies at the heart of their teaching, is a hallmark of millions who have no hope, see no future good, and regard death as a goal that is as good as life, for neither life nor death have any meaning.

The educational world has also been influenced by the objectivism of Ayn Rand. The *Los Angeles Times* ran a review of her biography *The Passion of Ayn Rand* by Barbara Branden. The reviewer, Carolyn See, said:

She would invent an entire school of philosophy called objectivism. Her novels would sell into the millions, and thousands of young people would join Ayn Rand clubs all across the nation. While the academic establishment would scorn her, her influence would defy that establishment and, in a sense, surpass it. Her biographer, in the last 20 or so pages of this book, lists all the Americans in high places who owe their accomplishments to an early reading of Rand's novels and an allegiance to her system of thought.[26]

The academic establishment could indeed scorn Rand, but somehow it missed the fact that she was a product of its own Weltanschauung carried to a different end and happening to endorse conclusions it found to be distasteful. Rand, herself an atheist, proclaimed what she believed. In later years she wrote:

I have held the same philosophy I now hold, for as far back as I can remember. I have learned a great deal through the years and expanded my knowledge of details, of specific issues, of definitions, of applications—and I intend to continue expanding it—but I have never had to change any of my fundamentals. My philosophy, in essence, is the concept of man as a heroic being, with his own happiness as the moral purpose of his life, with productive achievement as his noblest activity, and reason as his only absolute.[27]

Given the Weltanschauung of academia today it is difficult to see how its professors could fault Rand. Her basic commitment to reason as a metaphysical absolute is no different from theirs. Neither she nor they have any force, God, or reason outside of themselves against which to measure their own views or hers. Their distaste for her views is no less than an indictment against their own unverifiable parochialism.

SUMMARY

This discussion by no means exhausts the subject at hand. It simply makes clear that the New Paganism with its anti-Christian Weltanschauung has led to the defeat of the church in the West. It has furthered the decline of the church as a force in society and culture and made it a minority in a post-Christian and pagan world.

Most of the institutions of higher learning can no longer be considered to function within the orbit of the Hebrew-Christian tradition. And many of the theological seminaries that claim to be functioning within that orbit are only on the edge of it. Most of them are internally divided in a curious mishmash of viewpoints that are overtly in conflict with each other. This means that students are being taught in one class what is being denied in another. They are lacking any internal consistency by which a coherent system of thought is held and taught. This fragments the churches, weakens their witness, and furthers the decline of the Hebrew-Christian tradition.

7. The New Pagan Zeitgeist

We have traced the decline of the Judeo-Christian Weltanschauung and have seen how the New Paganism has supplanted the old biblical view. And we know that along with the loss of the Judeo-Christian viewpoint the West has lost its guidelines for life and conduct. The Zeitgeist has changed.

The laws of a nation are a mirror that reflects the world and life view of the people of that nation. When the world and life view changes, the laws that are in accord with the displaced world and life view change too over a period of time, long or short.

In the West, and for us in America more specifically, the New Paganism now may be seen in the laws and the life-style of its people. In some instances the laws have been altered specifically; in others they are left in the dustbin of history as their enforcement ceases. There are numerous examples of this process. For instance, America in past days had strict Sunday closing laws. In most states these prohibitions have been removed from the books or, if they still exist, they are unenforced. One of the victims of the New Paganism, then, is the Sabbath legislation of bygone years. Sunday has been thoroughly secularized—something quite understandable in the light of the controlling pagan world and life view.

Specific alienation of laws occurs when courts of law simply find these old laws to be unconstitutional. By legal fiat the courts without the consent of the lawmakers alter or abridge the existing laws of the land. Many laws enacted by state legislators forbidding such things as pornography or the limiting of the freedom of speech, or permitting prayer in the public schools have been overturned. The courts have also ruled that a statute can be legal in one state and a similar statute in another state unconstitutional on the basis of differing community mores. Judicial relativity reigns and is quite consistent with the New

Paganism, which has a decided distaste for moral absolutes and supports that form of human freedom in which all people are autonomous and can do as they please. Legitimate human rights have been so extended that license prevails and laws that restrict people from exercising their freedom in conduct once thought to be morally and ethically wrong are no longer acceptable.

All of this leads to the central issue of this discussion. Can it be shown that the present culture no longer follows principles consistent with the old Judeo-Christian moral and ethical standards? And can it be said that the current culture in the West is pagan and that what it stands for and how it lives is consistent with the prevailing pagan Weltanschauung? The answer to both questions is yes and the evidence needs to be presented. Let us start with human sexuality.

THE PAGANIZATION OF SEX

In the Christian tradition two ordinary forms of sexual intercourse have always been regarded as illegitimate: fornication and adultery. Associated with these forms of sex is what has been called the oldest profession: prostitution. In the Old and New Testaments this too was regarded as illegitimate.

Whoever has sex relations outside of a marriage is either committing fornication or adultery. For the unmarried it is fornication; for the married it constitutes a violation of the marital contract and is adultery. Both carried penalties in the Bible, not the least of which was and is the disfavor and condemnation by God. Aside from the use of prostitutes, whether male or female, fornication and adultery now are looked upon as accepted forms of conduct and are not regarded by many to be a sin against God.

The proportion of people who engage in sexual relations outside of marriage is quite high. Sometimes it leads to pregnancy and then to abortion (of which we shall speak later), and sometimes to marriage subsequent to the pregnancy. The number of children born out of wedlock is substantial. The *Los Angeles Times* reported that out of all births, twenty-five percent of the women were unmarried.[1] This means, of course, that for each of those women who gave birth out of wedlock, there is a man also responsible for the birth of the child. The difference in today's world is that few people regard these activities as sinful. They are looked upon as quite normal, and the chaste are regarded as strange and outdated. The Christian tradition that sex outside of marriage is wrong has yielded to the New Paganism, for which sin has little meaning; sin in the Christian tradition is obscurantist and passé.

Adultery is common, and conjugal faithfulness, even among some who call themselves evangelicals, is dying out. All of this is not surprising. A rather common attitude is that having an affair is the "in" thing to do. Affairs are so general, they are not looked upon as negative but positive. Indeed some flaunt their sexual freedom as in "open marriage." These newer attitudes are related to the paganization of marriage, a custom that formerly regarded the family as the basic unit of society and the glue that held the nation together.

MARRIAGE

In the Judeo-Christian heritage marriage was regarded as permanent and lasted till the death of one partner. The teaching stated that in the marriage of a woman and a man the two become one flesh. The two exception clauses, the two reasons for the breaking of the marital tie were adultery and desertion. Adultery was punishable by stoning, so that the surviving spouse was either a widow or a widower and could marry again. Some in the Christian tradition, notably the Roman Catholics, have regarded marriage as indissoluble even when adultery has occurred. But in general, Christian tradition has held the marital bond to be sacred and the union permanent.

Under the impact of the New Paganism marriage is no longer looked at from the Christian perspective. And when God is left out of the picture, the permanence of marriage is left suspended, with no enduring foundation. Freedom means that one can change partners for any or for no reason at all.

At one time marriages were protected by law, and divorce was difficult and in many cases impossible to obtain except for adultery, which was hard to prove. In New York state the law formerly allowed divorce only for adultery and the spouse had to be caught *in flagrante*. Gradually the grounds for divorce were extended until now it is possible in most states to obtain a divorce for almost any reason, although the length of time it takes differs widely.

Divorce has skyrocketed and shows no sign of a letup. In 1915 one out of every ten marriages ended in divorce. In 1983 five out of every ten marriages ended in divorce.[2] It is still true that bigamy generally remains illegal, but many practice serial polygamy, that is, one mate at a time but many different mates over a long period of time. These statistics do not include the large number of people who live together without the benefit of matrimony. For them no divorce is necessary, for they never married.

The Christian tradition about marriage no longer prevails; as an institution it has been paganized. Unfortunately, multitudes of those who profess to be Christians function in a way that is biblically impermissible. But what is difficult to comprehend is that the churches themselves have fallen for the pagan Zeitgeist and freely allow for divorce for virtually any reason whatsoever. In this sense paganism has infiltrated the churches and they have capitulated to it. Some inconsistently follow the pagan Zeitgeist while they continue to profess allegiance to a Christian Weltanschauung. The necessity for consistency of practice with theory is the need of the hour. But there is something worse yet.

Some churches with a pagan Zeitgeist also have a pagan Weltanschauung. The Unitarian-Universalist denomination in America is one of them. This church has gone as far from the Christian faith as can be done. Its view on such matters as marriage, sex, and divorce are wide open so that anything goes. Its pagan practices are quite in accord with its pagan world and life view. There are also some local congregations in major denominations whose world and life views and their daily practices are quite in accord with those of the Unitarian-Universalists. There even are congregations here and there who hold special services recognizing the divorces of their parish members. All of these views and practices mark the corruptions of the present age of which we have been speaking.

ILLEGITIMACY

We cannot talk about sex without talking about bastardy, although the word "bastardy" is rarely mentioned today. William

Buckley of *National Review* fame saw a relationship between the sexual revolution in America and the rapidly increasing number of bastards.[3] If bastardy is too strong a word, illegitimacy might do, but it is also fast coming into disuse. The reason is simple enough. That which is illegitimate is wrong. But few people regard illegitimacy as wrong because they have discarded the notion of wrongness. Historically, that which is regarded as wrong is punishable by some penalty. But today there are no penalties for producing children out of wedlock. No one should be surprised at this turn of events. Given the prevailing Weltanschauung and the Zeitgeist that conforms to it, producing illegitimate children is not regarded as evil; it is an acceptable mode of conduct not to be deplored or condemned.

One illustration will suffice to convey what is happening in this area of life today. The *International Herald Tribune* has a column titled "People." In the July 4, 1986 issue of the paper the following account appeared:

Farrah Fawcett says she and Ryan O'Neal, who have an 18-month-old son, will eventually marry. "He's had two marriages that didn't work out, and I had one," she told Parade magazine. "And I don't—and I know he doesn't—want another divorce." Fawcett said the baby, named Redmond after the character O'Neal played in the film "Barry Lyndon," was not planned. The actress said another unmarried mother, O'Neal's daughter, Tatum, was very content with her baby and its father, the tennis star John McEnroe. "She was ready for family life," Fawcett said. "I'm sure she'll go back to acting eventually."[4]

This is a commonplace story for those in the entertainment and sports industries, but their lead is being followed in every realm of human endeavor where people ape the actions of people of note. No social stigma is attached to such actions any longer, and this is a sign of decadence from the biblical perspective. Many years ago Charlie Chaplin was evicted from America and from the screen because of his sexual behavior. Later Ingrid Bergman committed adultery with an Italian movie director, bore his child, and suffered for it. But things are different now. Fawcett and O'Neal are fornicators, not to say adulterers, who have a bastard son. O'Neal's daughter, Tatum, has followed the example of her father and now has a son conceived out of wedlock by John McEnroe, with whom she lived without the benefit of marriage. Some months after the birth of the baby she was married to McEnroe in a Roman Catholic service. All of this simply shows that the Age of Paganism indeed has come and the old life-style based on biblical revelation has been discarded.

Not so long ago children conceived out of wedlock were bastards and there was stigma attached to having them; see, for example, the *Scarlet Letter* by Nathaniel Hawthorne. But the term "bastardy" is an unused, offensive word today because people who have children out of wedlock believe their conduct is licit. And what the Fawcetts, the O'Neals, and the McEnroes have done has not hurt their careers, in fact it may have given them extra publicity. America no longer rises up in arms against sex outside of marriage and babies conceived out of wedlock are no longer considered illegitimate. The media carrying stories like this say nothing derogatory; there is no suggestion whatever that such conduct is unacceptable.

What the Fawcetts, the O'Neals, and the McEnroes have done simply exemplifies the rising tide of these sort of actions. The number of babies conceived out of wedlock in the nation tells the story of the low estate of marriage. What it does not tell us is how grave the situation really is; that we see when the number of abortions secured by unmarried women is added to the figures for live births. If our thesis that people reap as they have sown is correct, then America is due for the coming of a payday someday when sinners who are pagans will discover that they cannot break the laws of God with impunity.

Mrs. Billy Graham observed on one occasion that if America does not come under the judgment of God, He owes an apology to Sodom and Gomorrah. The pulpits of America should be sounding forth warnings telling people that they should repent and come to God, and that if they do not repent, they will indeed reap the consequences of their wickedness in the life to come if not in the life here and now.

One further word needs to be said on this issue. The conduct of the pagans must be understood by Christians as quite consistent with their presuppositions. Viewed from the presuppositions of Christians, the conduct and the world and life view of the pagans are wrong. What is at stake is whose views and life-style will reign in society and culture. As a result of the Enlight-enment, Christianity today is running against the prevailing tide or current. If Christians who still remain faithful to historic orthodoxy are to count in the struggle of two opposing forces they must be countercultural, that is to say, steadfast in their judgments and activities.

ABORTION ON DEMAND

Surely one of the most obvious signs of a pagan society is the practice of aborting fetuses at any stage of pregnancy. Current practices even go beyond the limits set by some of the earlier pagan peoples. Hippocrates (fifth century B.C.) is known as the father of modern medicine. In the Hippocratic Oath, which until recently was taken by virtually all graduates of medical schools in America, the following statement appears: "I will give no deadly drug to any, though it be asked of me, nor will I counsel such, and especially I will not aid a woman to procure an abortion."[5] The *Britannica* does note that "The term 'oath' should not be interpreted too narrowly. It was, rather, an ethical code or ideal and in no sense a law. It is an appeal for correct conduct, but contains no threat of punishment. In one or other of its many versions, it has guided the practice of medicine for more than 2,000 years."[6]

It is true that some pagan societies practiced infanticide. The Romans did. But it was a custom that ended when the Christian church became a dominant force in society. In our age the conflict over this issue is being fought between two opposing viewpoints. Ultimately the choice for or against abortion on demand depends on which world and life view one accepts, a fact many people do not really comprehend. This means that those who claim to adhere to the Judeo-Christian tradition and still opt for such abortions are choosing something the tradition bears witness against. At best they are inconsistent. At worst their Christian commitment is just a veneer covering an intrinsic paganism they do not wish to face or at least to acknowledge openly.

A key issue in the abortion controversy is the question of human freedom. The claim is that any woman has the sole right to the use of her body; she is free to choose whether to give birth to the fetus or abort it. This notion of human autonomy is in line with the paganism of the Enlightenment; humans are not subject to the laws of God in the Bible, for God is either far off, or has left people to themselves, or does not exist. In the latter event we are left with what some call the laws of nature or a vacuum of nothingness, in which aborting a fetus has no transcendent consequences either in this life or the life to follow if there is one.

We must say as plainly as possible that once anyone accepts the Enlightenment perspective, that is, paganism, the issue is foreclosed and abortion on demand is quite understandable. Such a practice is consonant with its Weltanschauung.

The battle line focuses on the issue of whether the Christian viewpoint against abortion on demand will prevail in our society. And the point is made that Christians have no right to enforce their morality on those who do not follow their line of thought. Somebody, of course, is going to set the ground rules and whichever view prevails, the opposition will be unhappy. In any event it is plain that the Christian viewpoint no longer prevails. Pagans are in control and the Zeitgeist is their Zeitgeist, not that of the Christian faith.

Reportedly, in the view of the Supreme Court decision (*Roe v. Wade*) that legalizes abortion on demand, whatever the limitations added, the fetus at the time of conception is not to be regarded as human life. The court made a judicial decision based on sociological opinions about the beginning of human life. But apart from divine revelation there is no certain answer to this question. Indeed when humans presume to answer the question themselves, then they can also make decisions about euthanasia, infanticide, and even murder. The day well may come when all of these options will be legalized. One merely needs to read the platform of the Humanist Manifesto II[7] to see the point. It went beyond the first Humanist Manifesto and advocated the right to euthanasia for all. Already infants born with serious defects have been left to die, and euthanasia for the aged is more widely practiced than we sometimes suppose. Moreover, suicide is now considered by many to be a human right under the umbrella of human freedom. Henry Pitney Van

Dusen, retired president of Union Theological Seminary of New York, and his wife made a pact to commit suicide together. His wife died and he survived the dual attempt for a short time thereafter.

The Christian who holds that human life truly begins with conception insists that abortion on demand is murder. But this viewpoint is not only under attack outside the framework of the churches, it is also being challenged seriously by some within the churches who identify with the prevailing pagan viewpoint on this particular issue. Few seem to realize that human freedom is not an absolute, for when it is carried out to its logical conclusion it is anarchic. There are limitations to freedom, and unless there is a Supreme Power who has set the limitations, humans are left to themselves and to their own self-destruction.

Abortion on demand is one of the sure signs that our culture is pagan. The Christian who is countercultural, who feels "counter" to this culture, will always encounter fierce opposition to any effort designed to legislate against this evil. Without such legislation the practice will continue and will show that pagans are in control of the legislative halls of the nation and the courts as well.

HOMOSEXUALITY

Any consideration of sex must include the vexing homosexual revolution. More recently, this life-style has been exacerbated by the AIDS controversy, which has made media headlines and is the subject of discussion everywhere. The threat of a possible epidemic of AIDS has frightened millions of people; this contagious disease could sweep through America like the plagues of bygone days.

Homosexuality involves a number of imponderables. For example, we do not know for certain whether homosexuals are born this way or become so through environment, conditioning, and human choice. But homosexuality is by no means a modern phenomenon. It has been with us for centuries. The Old and the New Testaments witness to its existence among the Hebrews by the prohibition against homosexual practices. It is condemned everywhere in the Bible as a crime against nature and in the Old Testament it was punishable by death. According to

1 Corinthians 6:9, 10 in the New Testament "neither the immoral, nor idolators, nor adulterers, nor homosexuals, nor thieves, nor the greedy, nor drunkards, nor revilers, nor robbers will inherit the kingdom of God."

One homosexual with whom I have had conversation has suggested that sex may be wholly irrelevant and that what homosexuals desire is a working and harmonious relationship with members of the same sex without any sex acts. No one could object to two homosexuals living together in a celibate state any more than one could object to two heterosexuals living together without sex. Under such conditions there would be no fear of AIDS. Unfortunately the number of males or females, for that matter, who do not practice some sort of sexual activity is miniscule and therefore hardly worth our attention.

Today homosexuals have come out of the closet. They openly flaunt their life-style and engage in intensive efforts to legitimatize their form of behavior. As a result, in some cities in America, laws have been passed to stop employers from refusing to hire homosexuals because of their sexual preferences. Christian freedom to refuse to hire a homosexual has been abridged. And there are other provisions equally unsatisfactory to those who oppose this practice. It is fair to say that homosexuality has come to be accepted as an alternate life-style that is legitimate and protected by law. Even among some Christians, homosexual behavior is now endorsed, and ordination, for example, to the Christian ministry encouraged. Some who claim to be evangelicals are in the forefront of the battle to affirm that homosexuals should not be denied any of the rights now enjoyed by heterosexuals.

Dr. Ralph Blair, a psychologist in New York City, heads up an organization called Evangelicals Concerned, Inc. The organization publishes a quarterly review and a newsletter. The organization seeks to establish homosexual chapters around the country and is seriously engaged in the business of endorsing the notion that homosexuality is a gift of God, is normal, is good, is legitimate, and has the blessing of God on it. Conferences are held around the nation and the case favoring homosexuality is presented wherever possible before college and seminary groups. One theological seminary in Los Angeles is a

homosexual institution training people for the Christian ministry and especially for homosexual churches. Another seminary
in the same area has had and may still have a homosexual
conclave on its campus.

Karl Barth discussed homosexuality at its deepest level and
drew conclusions that are distinctly biblical and undoubtedly
distasteful to those who think there is some biblical warrant for
this style of life. He said:

But neither men nor women can seriously wish to be alone, as in clubs
and ladies' circles. Who commands or permits them to run away from
each other? That such an attitude is all wrong is shown symptomatically
in the fact that every artificially induced and maintained isolation of
the sexes tends as such—usually very quickly and certainly morosely
and blindly—to become philistinish in the case of men and precious
in that of women, and in both cases more or less inhuman. It is well to
pay heed even to the first steps in this direction.
These first steps may well be symptoms of the malady called homosexuality. This is the physical, psychological and social sickness, the
phenomenon of perversion, decadence and decay.... In Romans 1
Paul connected it with idolatry, with changing the truth of God into a
lie, with the adoration of the creature instead of the Creator ... in a
sexual union which is not and cannot be genuine—man thinks that he
must seek and can find in man, and woman in woman, a substitute for
the despised partner.... But the decisive word of Christian ethics must
consist in a warning against entering upon the whole way of life which
can only end in the tragedy of complete homosexuality. We know that
in its early stages it may have an appearance of particular beauty and
spirituality, and even be redolent of sanctity. Often it has not been the
worst people who have to some extent practiced it as a sort of wonderful esoteric of personal life.... The command of God shows him
irrefutably—in clear contradiction of his own theories—that as man
he can only be genuinely human with woman, or as a woman with
man. In proportion as he accepts this insight, homosexuality can have
no place in his life, whether in its more refined or cruder forms.[8]

Homosexual marriages are on the rise and legislation protects
homosexual rights to rent apartments without restrictions even
though the owners of the buildings may object to such occupa-
tion. The impression is spread abroad that "straights" have
nothing to fear from homosexuals, but this is far from the truth.
By far the greatest number of homosexuals are promiscuous.

They engage in sexual escapades with many different partners. Few, if any, are celibate and forego sexual encounters like heterosexual Roman Catholic priests and nuns who take a vow of chastity.

How bad the situation is may be seen from a San Francisco homosexual publication listing specific places to go for sexual gratification in the major and minor cities of the nation. A substantial number of places are listed as "cruising areas," areas that homosexuals seeking gratification can walk or cruise around to find others with the same intention and form liaisons for sexual purposes, not for harmless and sexless fellowship. In my community, Laguna Hills, California, a small, tightly knit and conventional town, the Laguna Hills Mall is listed as a cruising area.

The sexual practices of male homosexuals beggar the imagination. In an article in *National Review* Joseph Sobran talks about the life-style of homosexuals, something the average reader knows little about. He gives the facts about this from the *New York Native,* the city's leading gay newspaper. He says:

In a typical issue, the *Native* carries two tabloid-sized pages of personals. These are accompanied by a boxed list of abbreviations for standard, repeat *standard,* homosexual practices and partner specifications. GWM stands for "gay white male," GBM for "gay black male," GJM and GOM for their Jewish and Oriental counterparts. BB means "bodybuilder." Fr/AP means "French (oral) active/passive"; Gr/AP, "Greek (anal) active/passive." JO means masturbation, S/M sado-masochism, B/D bondage and discipline, FF fisting, and W/S "water sports (urine scenes)."

There are other variations; some abbreviations are not explained. Many of the ads are bluntly graphic—too graphic to quote here. Suffice it to say their authors are not seeking romance. Some boast of the size of their organs, or specify the size they seek. Others advertise for favorite physical features, such as hairlessness, or such prized deformities as mutilated genitals. Others seek to be dominated, offering themselves as "girlfriend" or "maid" to a "real man." Sordid and desperate, the ads make it impossible to idealize gay life. Just as revealing, in a way, is what is implied by those who insist on "safe sex," or the one who cautions, "I love women so U can't hate them." Some are married; one is a Catholic priest.[9]

Sobran observes that in New York City, "Such is the behavior gay-rights legislation protects. Or rather, such is the behavior gay-rights legislation forbids normal citizens to disapprove." The forms of sexual pleasure herein stated by Sobran are enough to make one cringe in disbelief. If there are worse forms of sexual behavior, as Sobran says are contained in the ads in this paper, they go beyond any decent person's imagination. In any event it is clear that the Zeitgeist portrayed by what is happening in New York City is pagan.

A recent Supreme Court decision on sodomy sheds further light on the subject and is helpful in understanding the shift from the Judeo-Christian tradition to the paganism of the Enlightenment. The facts themselves are of interest. At stake in the decision was an 1816 Georgia law that defines sodomy as "any sexual act involving the sex organs of one person and the mouth or anus of another." The Georgia law was not unusual. The original thirteen states all outlawed homosexual acts. So did *all* states until 1961. As paganism advanced, twenty-six states either by legislation or by judicial fiat "have made private homosexual acts between consenting adults no longer criminal."[10]

The Supreme Court ruled to retain the law, but the narrow five-to-four decision indicates that four justices are lined up in the pagan tradition. They were saying that the Georgia law was an infringement of a "fundamental" constitutional right. Since the Supreme Court for many years accepted the state laws against sodomy, it shows that the current shift derives from the acceptance of a different Weltanschauung than the one that prevailed when all of the states prohibited sodomy. The early laws were based on the Judeo-Christian tradition. The decision of the minority, the four judges, shows that they are saying that states have no right to prohibit acts that the Judeo-Christian viewpoint condemns.

QUESTIONS OF FREEDOM AND PRIVACY

Inconsistency and ambiguity continue as a result of this latest Georgia ruling. However distasteful and opprobrious homosexual activities are, they are not on the same level as murder. Abortion on demand is a far worse crime than sodomy, although both stand under the judgment of God and the Scriptures. Beyond homosexual activity some states still have laws making it a crime for two unmarried people to have sexual relations. If such laws were enforced, a very large segment of the population would have engaged in criminal acts. This leaves open the question about the right of privacy for individuals.

In response to the Georgia decision *The New York Times* said that the five-to-four decision upholding the Georgia law was a travesty. The author of the editorial called Justice Harry Blackmun's dissent eloquent. He said that "Appealing to a calmer time, a high wisdom, and a broader grasp of liberty, [Blackmun] hopes, as all Americans should, for a court that will consider and conclude that legislation for the bedroom 'poses a far greater threat' to constitutional values than toleration of nonconformity could ever do."[11] The *Times* stands for a paganism that allows for actions the Bible condemns and appears to be saying that sodomy is not deviant. Of course, if sodomy is not deviant, then there should be no legislation making it a crime. But if sodomy is deviant, the *Times* adduces no adequate explanation why it should be tolerated externally in public view or internally in the bedroom to which the public has no access. Ultimately what is at stake are the questions of values, freedom, and privacy, and the outcome will be determined by whether the Judeo-Christian tradition or the tradition of paganism reigns in society.

Justice Blackmun's statement that "we should be especially sensitive to the rights of those whose choices upset the majority" is a two-way street. Paganism is rarely, if ever, sensitive to the Christian minority. And at every point where Christians contend against the values of the pagan majority, they are ridiculed, called obscurantist, and deigned to be behind the times of a more enlightened age.

Richard John Neuhaus, a well-known Lutheran minister and scholar, took a hard look at Justice Blackmun's dissent and made some important observations:

Yet more revolting is the hubris of judges who declare the people's wise affirmation to be a blind imitation, and who conform the law to "current values" as defined, of course, by themselves.

But the full force of Blackmun's animus is saved for religion. . . . Blackmun says he is not impressed by the "invocation" of Leviticus, Romans and St. Thomas Aquinas to the effect that sodomy is gravely wrong. . . . However, he overlooks the fact that Georgia and other states do advance justifications beyond religious doctrine. Such justifications have to do with the common good, but we have seen what Justice Blackmun thinks of the common good.[12]

Neuhaus clearly sees that Blackmun writes as he does because he is a pagan who starts with different presuppositions than do Christians. Blackmun supports freedom, or individualism, or the right of choice, or privacy that has no limitations. Surely the right to privacy, that is, what people do at home and in their private thought lives, opens a Pandora's box for theologians as well as for jurists and politicians. Few will argue that public acts cannot be regulated by law. But the trend in the new paganism is to make the home safe against all claims of criminal acts punishable by legislative action. If there are no moral absolutes and if the Enlightenment viewpoint is carried to its logical conclusion, anarchic conditions will be the outcome.

Oddly, there is one area in which the Enlightenment mentality has both succeeded and failed; this is in connection with its stepchild, Marxism. However much privacy, that is to say human rights, are extended by the new paganism, no place are they more denied than in atheistic Marxist states. The omniscient and omnipresent Marxist state has no regard for the privacy of the home or the rights of individuals in their own homes. Paradoxically, human freedom unrestrained by biblical revelation releases people from the commandments of God they don't like and delivers them into the hands of tyrants who make them slaves. A biblically oriented society is paradisaical when compared to this.

The fact that more than half of the states make sodomy legal and all of America makes abortion on demand legal confirms the notion that the Zeitgeist indeed is pagan.

BREAKING KNOWN LAWS

The AIDS development has raised another question we should not dodge. Some Christian clergymen have said that AIDS is the judgment of God against malefactors. This has distressed not only the homosexual community but others who have felt a certain compassion for AIDS victims. How should a Christian address those who object to the idea that AIDS is a judgment of God?

The true Christian asserts that we live in a moral universe governed by moral laws; those who violate them must face the consequences of such violation. The Bible proclaims that people reap as they sow, that those who perform the deed shall eat the fruit of it. Those who object to the statement that AIDS is the judgment of God tend to overlook several important points. Even atheists, empiricists, and scientists possess knowledge that generally cannot be gainsaid. We know, for example, that certain diseases are transmitted by sexual intercourse. Herpes, gonorrhea, and syphilis are among these diseases. People who have contracted these diseases have died from them. Furthermore we know that no one will become an alcoholic who does not imbibe alcohol. And cigarette smoking causes a higher incidence of lung cancer; a nonsmoker has less chance of getting this form of cancer.

There are laws of cause and effect, whether mandated directly by God or, from even a pagan perspective, existing for whatever unknown reason. Those who violate these laws must consider the price they may have to pay as a consequence of their deed or, if you please, their misdeed. No one is screaming for the tens of thousands who die each year as a result of diseases contracted by violating known laws. AIDS contracted through sexual misconduct properly belongs in this category.

Is it not also interesting that the adverse effects of certain activities happen to coincide with things that are forbidden in the Bible? Is it not the path of wisdom to suppose that what God forbids is designed to protect people from the adverse effects of breaking the divine commands? It is less likely that the diseases talked about here will come to those who obey the mandates of the Bible.

This is also true for abortion. Pregnancy occurs as a result of the sexual act. Any person who remains chaste and who does not indulge in the sex act will not be responsible for a pregnancy. But when two people engage in sexual relations (we are not talking about pregnancy resulting from rape—this is quite a different matter), they know that pregnancy may result and they should be prepared for the consequences. Abortion is a refusal to accept responsibility for one's conduct. The Enlightenment, of course, has altered all of this, for its humanism negates God and theism and refuses to take the divine absolutes seriously.

Whoever steps outside the boundaries of the laws of cause and effect, however they have come into being, must pay the price. AIDS contracted through sexual misconduct and unwanted pregnancies fall into this category. It is foolish, not to say homicidal, to engage in actions the consequences of which will be hurtful. Those who do this have no one to blame but themselves and are hardly to be pitied as one would pity an innocent someone who has been infected by a disease passed on by the guilty. Compassion for the guiltless is indeed the proper response.

Young People and Sexual Aberrations

Young people are liable to sexual exploitation by adults, both by people they know—parents, relatives, friends—and by strangers. There are no adequate statistics available to supply us with the total number of the victims of this form of vice. From what we do know, however, this form of sexual license is on the increase.

Today the victims of sexual perversion are increasingly making their woes known to the police, pastors, or to organizations that exist to assist in such cases. This perversion is sometimes found in so-called Christian homes. I can recall one missionary child caught up in this problem. A highly honored senior missionary made wrongful approaches to her, but when she confided in her father, he was loath to believe her. The experience affected her deeply; she found it difficult to understand. She did not know how to handle such a situation and there was no professional help available for her.

I can recall another girl, a college student in a Christian institution, who had been sexually violated many times by her own father. It was a scorching experience, the memories of which led her to a Christian counselor to whom she unburdened her soul. With time and patience she found deliverance from her burden of guilt and managed to regain her sense of self-respect and the ability to function more normally. But even with the deliverance, the memory remains and her personhood will never be what it would have been had she not been sexually abused by one she knew as her father, one who should have been her protector.

From my own daughter, who has been a probate officer for the courts, what I have gleaned about such evil practices suggests that for all the cases that come to the knowledge of the courts there are tens of thousands that remain undisclosed for fear and shame. In some cases mothers know what their husbands are doing but remain silent in the face of these tragedies.

I know of a number of families in which daughters have been subjected to sexual approaches by uncles, grandfathers, and friends of the family. And what happens to girls also happens to boys, although in a somewhat different fashion. Every day young boys are being solicited by homosexuals to engage in unnatural sex acts. Any number of homosexuals seek service in schools or organizations and even in churches that have activities for boys. Hardly a day goes by that the newspapers do not report incidents of the sexual use of boys by homosexual men of every age.

Homosexuals seek to condition society to make it believe that unnatural sex between male adults and boys is not wrong. And given the pagan perspectives with which they function and their detachment from the Word of God as normative for behavior, they have no sense of guilt or even of impropriety. With their deliverance from the mores of the Judeo-Christian tradition, they think themselves freed from its so-called bondage so that they can do as they please. Anything that will give them sexual satisfaction is legitimate and may be pursued without fear.

Homosexuals do not hesitate to make their wares known to strangers. My own son was solicited by a homosexual in the Pennsylvania Railroad Station in New York City when he was a teenager. He was not taken in by this crudity and did report it to me. But for every teenager who does not fall into this trap there may be another who does. I can well remember my own grade-school experience. We had a teacher in the sixth grade who used some of us to squeeze his genitals while he supervised recess. I do not believe it went beyond this, but I do not know for sure.

The protection of the young against sexual abuse is, at best, difficult for governmental authorities. The failure of so many of the victims to report such incidents hinders society from effectively coping with the problem. It seems clear, however, that there are no signs of a diminution of these forms of obscenity that are evidences of the prevalence of the paganism by which we are surrounded.

PORNOGRAPHY

Fifty years ago pornography existed, but it was underground and under the counter. There were laws virtually everywhere defining pornography and making it illegal. The laws were strictly enforced and they were upheld by the Supreme Court. The movie industry was under constant surveillance and had to meet rating standards, which guaranteed that films shown did not violate the standards. Both language and sex were carefully screened.

Books and magazines were also included in the legally mandated limitations against the obscene, explicit sex, and all forms of indecency. There were no magazines on the stands such as *Playboy, Penthouse,* or *Hustler.* And more offensive publications than these were absolutely taboo. Book publishers also functioned under the same or similar statutes. Books that were prurient, sex oriented, or otherwise offensive did not see the light of day. In short, the mores that governed the nation were those consonant with the Judeo-Christian tradition. But change was in the air and the legions of decency were to be defeated as an open and uncontrolled use of the constitutional guarantee of freedom of speech was expanded to the point where virtually nothing was forbidden. Acts and writing and pictures that were forbidden for two hundred years under the American constitution and legal system were now guaranteed protection under the law. The Enlightenment heritage at last led to the paganization of the culture.

The advent of television signaled a new advance in the movement away from traditional morality. It has become a wasteland that enters virtually every home in America. The children of the nation have been exposed to its pagan views directly and indirectly. It comes to children before their ethical development can handle this medium and resist its hedonism. Years ago

Edward John Carnell wrote a book, *Television: Servant or Master?*[13] He foresaw and indeed prophesied that TV would become the master rather than the servant. Certainly TV as a medium is like atomic energy. Both are neutral in themselves; what people do with them makes the difference. Since people without God are not governed by the law of God and are actively opposed to that law, TV has come to reflect the views of those who are pagan. This can be shown in many ways.

One need only look at a few of the most popular telecasts of recent days—"Dallas," "Falcon Crest," and "Dynasty." All constantly show men and women who violate many of the laws of God with impunity. Fornication, adultery, divorce, and remarriage are common. Lying, cheating, stealing, avarice, covetousness, hate, and violence are omnipresent. In the sexual area it only remains for programs to show frontal nakedness as in England or actual copulation. Even these can be seen in theaters, on TV shows in hotel rooms, and in some of the many stores that merchandise wares for VCR use.

This is not the end of the pitiful story. All sorts of movies are made and sold that display sado-masochistic themes and lesbian and homosexual affairs. Bestiality, whippings for kicks, and the most degrading practices, including the use of children in pornographic ways, only begin to depict the depravity that abounds. They all tell a twofold story. Much of the pornography industry is controlled by organized crime whose interest is in making money legally and illegally. The second side of the coin is that there are multitudes who buy these products, which would have no value whatever if no one purchased them. Organized crime caters to the sexual depravity of the masses, a depravity that is consistent with paganism.

The advance of pornography has been helped by the publication of scholarly works in defense of it. One would hardly expect that a professor from a Roman Catholic institution would be in the vanguard of an effort to endorse pornography and at the same time be a Marxist. Alan Soble has done all of this. He is listed in the Yale University Press bulletin (1986) as an assistant professor of philosophy at St. John's University in Minnesota. He is also the founder and president of The Society for the Philosophy of Sex and Love. This is the way Yale University

Press characterizes his book *Marxism, Feminism, and the Future of Sexuality:*[14]

In this book Soble provides the first in-depth defense of pornography from a Marxist perspective. In addition, he examines feminine thinking on contemporary pornography and reaches some controversial conclusions. Soble links the increasing consumption of mass-produced pornographic material to men's feelings of decreasing sexual power—feelings related to the nature of social and political life in our capitalist society and to the changes in the character of heterosexual relationships brought about by the women's movement. He compares men's use of pornographic material with women's consumption of romantic novels, theorizing that in each case the reader or viewer is using fantasy to compensate for a disappointing reality. Taking issue with feminists such as Susan Brownmiller, Andrea Dworkin, and Susan Griffin, Soble argues that pornography is not nearly as harmful and degrading as is often claimed. He further asserts that pornography need not be either sexist or dehumanizing if it is produced by collectives of freely associated workers who together decide its content, and that it might very well have a place in a communist society, becoming a positive aspect of human sexuality.[14]

This work was endorsed by Paul Robinson, author of *The Modernization of Sex,* who called Soble's work "a deeply scholarly work, with remarkable control of the philosophical, polemical, and popular literature on the subject." Alison M. Jaggar, author of *Feminist Politics and Human Nature,* said: "Alan Soble is a leading analytic philosopher in this field. He has read widely and reflected deeply on these topics and his book is a major contribution to the debate."

This leaves open the question why Yale University Press would publish a work that runs counter to its original purposes. The explanation, quite obviously, flows from the fact that Yale is now clearly secular and has abandoned any sort of commitment to the Hebrew-Christian Weltanschauung. We have also mentioned that Yale University Press published works by John Dewey and promoted his antisupernaturalism in the widest possible manner.

It is safe to predict that this revolution in morals has not yet come to its end. America still lags behind Europe in this regard. So it is likely to continue on this downward path, barring some form of spiritual awakening, which is not yet in the offing. The churches in Europe have done little to change the picture, and there is no reason to suppose that the churches in America will reverse the trend either. Both in Europe and America the mainline churches have not been in the forefront of the battle to make the old Judeo-Christian morality regnant in culture and society. Nor are the mainline churches in either Europe or America leading the vanguard for world evangelization.

In this struggle between two antithetical ways, one should note the aggressive and purposeful activities on the part of those who have no use for the Christian faith. Norman Lear is one of those key leaders. He founded the organization People for the American Way, which is vigorously opposed to anything Jerry Falwell, Tim LaHaye, Jim Kennedy, and others stand for, those who seek to turn the tide of hedonism. Lear's influence in the production of TV programs gives him access to the hearts and minds of millions of TV viewers. They are being infiltrated, brainwashed, and enlisted in a crusade that falsely identifies the American way with a viewpoint that negates what the Bible affirms. Presently there is no way by which such activities are subject to legislative prohibitions. Lear is legally free to pursue these activities unless one of two things take place. Either people like him will turn to Jesus Christ, be converted, and then adopt a Christian life-style, or they will have to be muzzled one way or another. There is nothing in sight that gives reason to hope that the latter will take place in the immediate future, and the former will surely come about only if God intervenes sovereignly and brings about a great awakening. And this will not take place until the people of God turn from their own neutral or careless ways. When they are filled with the Spirit and when they turn to God on their knees in ceaseless intercession and practical outreach with the gospel, then what is desperately needed will take place.

DRUGS IN AMERICAN SOCIETY

The use of drugs and the addiction that follows is another sign of the process of secularization and the decline of the Hebrew-Christian world and life view. Drugs are a hallmark of a pagan society, of a people bereft of guiding moral and ethical principles. It should occasion no surprise that a nation that has lost its bearings would fall into hurtful habits and experiment with anything that promises release from the tedium of life. A society so highly developed that free time equals and often exceeds the time spent in gainful labor opens itself widely to such things as drug abuse.

The National Institute on Drug Abuse has published materials on drug abuse and has supplied useful information that should keep any thoughtful and concerned person from experimenting with chemicals that are dangerous to health and lead to addictions that are difficult to break. The drug problem is aggravated by the fact that much of the manufacture and sale of harmful substances is controlled by organized crime in the United States and by foreign groups interested in the financial returns from their labors. So great are the monetary rewards that a deliberate program to promote the use of drugs is being executed in virtually all of the United States twenty-four hours a day.

Once hooked on drugs, those addicted will steal or even murder to gain the money to purchase more. The drug merchants use their victims to entice still others by the simple process of giving free or low-cost drugs to addicts to solicit others to start using them. It is a spiraling and ever increasing problem for the nation.

The number of drugs used by people is legion. Alcohol, marijuana ("grass," "pot," "weed"), hallucinogens (LSD, phencyclidine—"angel dust"), amphetamines, cocaine, morphine, opium, and heroin are constantly used, among others. There isn't one of them that is without adverse effects—none can be used safely as though addiction will never take place.

When those addicted to heroin stop taking the drug the immediate consequences are substantial. Within twelve hours after the addicted person stops using the drug there is sweating, shaking, chills, vomiting, running nose and eyes, muscle aches, abdominal pains, and diarrhea. The intensity of the reactions depends, in part, on the degree of addiction to the drug. Even sleeping pills can be hazardous. It has been reported that barbiturate overdose is implicated in approximately one-third of all drug-related deaths. When barbiturates are taken along with alcohol the results are often devastating.

A recent survey by the Institute for Social Research at the

University of Michigan indicates that there has been some minor drop in the use of some drugs but the results are still ominous. "Thirty percent of all college students will have used cocaine at least once by the end of their fourth year in college. . . . By their mid-20s, 'some 75 percent to 80 percent of today's young adults have tried an illicit drug.' More than half have tried an illicit drug other than marijuana."[15]

In August of 1986 President Ronald Reagan called for a national crusade against drugs. He emphasized the need for drug-free schools, better treatment facilities for those addicted, and severe punishment for "the big guys and little guys" who peddle the drugs. The key to the drug problem is a matter of education only in part. The most certain cure for stopping drug use is a return to the moral standards and ethical principles enunciated in the Bible and by the churches in bygone days. But to a Post-Christian society such standards no longer apply, nor do they appeal greatly to people freed from their "bondage" to the antiquated morality of yesteryear.

THE PAGANIZATION OF EDUCATION

A nation whose common life is marked lawlessness, materialism, gambling, and permissiveness can be influenced by educational institutions that militate against these evils. But the removal of God and the commandments of God from education has left a moral vacuum, so that even the question of what a value system should include is left open. Moreover, education has no way of arriving at values without a transcendent frame of reference, but the freedom brought about by the Enlightenment has delivered people from any absolute. This does not mean that there are no values taught in public education, but they are taught incidentally and by osmosis, and they are pagan values, not Christian ones. They are more in line with what the humanists believe and teach.

John Dunphy says his piece in *The Humanist* that there is a great battle being waged for the future of mankind and that that battle must be fought in the schools of America from the lowest to the highest levels by teachers who are proselytizers of a new faith. They know that there is a spark of divinity in everyone. These teachers must be as selfless and dedicated as the most rabid fundamentalist. The classroom will be their pulpit. They will be waging a struggle for humanist values in all of their classes. The battle must be fought and won by the humanist advocate.

If what the humanists want is not promoted overtly, they have attained their objectives by a deadly silence. There is a textbook bias against Christianity and religion in general. Kerby Anderson, a columnist with Probe, a Christian think tank in Dallas, wrote the following in one of his columns:

Although the "religious right" is often charged with censoring textbooks, a recent study found that public school textbooks are significantly biased against religious values.

The study, funded by the National Institute of Education and directed by Dr. Paul Vitz (Professor of Psychology, New York University) examined 60 major social studies textbooks and found they virtually ignore religion and traditional family values.

In social studies textbooks for grades first through fourth, not one word referred to a child or adult who prayed, or who ever went to church or temple.

Students were often told about Thanksgiving without mentioning the religious motivation behind it. Although one textbook said the Pilgrims "wanted to give thanks for all they had," it made no mention of God, to whom the thanks was given.

Dr. Vitz concluded that in these introductory texts, "The Pueblos can pray to Mother Earth, but Pilgrims can't be described as praying to God—and never are Christians described as praying to Jesus either in the United States or elsewhere, in the present or even in the past, at least as far as these forty books are concerned."

Fifth-grade textbooks dealing with American history ignored the role religion played in the history of the United States even though observers since de Tocqueville have seen religion as fundamental to American life.

The researchers found: "There is not one reference in any of these books to such important religious events as: the Salem Witch Trials; the Great Awakening of the 1740s; the great revivals of the 1830s and 1840s; the great urban revivals of 1870–1890 period; the important Holiness and Pentecostal movements around 1880–1910; the liberal and conservative Protestant split in the early 20th century; or the Born-Again movement of the 1960s and '70s."

Sixth-grade textbooks dealing with religion and culture in world history displayed a consistent bias against Christianity.

The report stated that "In several books Mohammed's life gets much more coverage than that of Jesus."

In fact, some books didn't even mention Jesus, leading Dr. Vitz to conclude, "In these books it is not as though great religious figures are totally avoided—it is rather that Jesus is."

The textbooks virtually ignore the first thousand years of Christianity and skip over important landmarks like the Protestant Reformation.

One textbook that had 20 pages on Tanzania and 19 pages on Crete made no mention of Martin Luther or John Calvin. And though it spent 19 pages covering the history of the Netherlands, the textbook completely ignored Protestantism's profound influence on that country's history.

Such omissions are not incidental nor accidental, but instead demonstrate a consistent and deliberate bias against religious values.

Dr. Vitz and his colleagues concluded that "those responsible for these books appear to have a deep-seated fear of any form of active contemporary Christianity, especially serious, committed Protestantism. This fear has led the authors to deny and repress the importance of this kind of religion in American life."

This textbook research study demolishes two cherished myths about public school textbooks.

First, it destroys the cliché that public education is pluralistic. All values are not being taught. In fact, religious values are being systematically excluded. Second, the study demolishes the canard that the "religious right" are censoring textbooks.[16]

It is fair to conclude that the public schools either attack the Christian faith overtly or by failing to deal with it at all or in such brevity that no student has a fair chance to know anything about the roots of this nation or to appreciate and understand what its progenitors thought and believed. Students may indeed and certainly do have a right not to follow what the founding fathers believed and taught. But at least they ought to have fair representation of the role of religion in the past history of the nation, so that they can consider this when they do make choices for themselves. Paganism has secured a great victory in American life.

8. Karl Barth, a Via Media?

Bernard Ramm has aligned himself with the theology of Karl Barth, as have many other scholars and institutions. He adduces his reasons for taking this step and traces his pilgrimage from an unadulterated evangelicalism to Barthianism. The center-piece of his current stance is the Englightenment, a movement he has come to perceive, as I have, as central to understanding where the church is today and how it got there.

Dr. Ramm makes it clear that he stands in opposition to such evangelicals as Carl F. H. Henry, Gordon Haddon Clark, Cornelius Van Til, and myself. He argues that these evangelicals are obscurantists who have refused to take the Enlightenment seriously. He uses the word "glosses" especially as it relates to modern biblical criticism, which was one of the most important contributions of the Enlightenment.

Concerning Carl F. H. Henry he says: "In *God, Revelation and Authority*, [Henry] sets out his views of revelation, inspiration, and authority against all other options, but his monumental effort stumbles because he glosses biblical criticism."[1] The word "gloss" can be used several ways. We will assume that he does not mean that Dr. Henry is guilty of a false and willfully mis-leading interpretation. Rather Henry, to use one of the diction-ary's usages, "glosses over scholarly controversies rather than confronting them head-on." In other words, Dr. Henry has passed by the problem and has not grappled with it. Therefore he is guilty of obscurantism. Thus Ramm says: "I learned that to ignore the Enlightenment and gloss over the problems it raised is to engage in obscurantism. Furthermore, I learned that obscurantism is a losing strategy in the modern world. I learned that those evangelicals who do not feel the shock of the Enlightenment gloss over its problems."[2] So it is with this, by way of general background, that we make our study of Dr. Ramm's thesis.

We will begin by indicating those points with which we are in agreement:

First, the Enlightenment, as we have argued, marked a crucial turning point in the history of the church. It led to dramatic change and its assault on the Christian faith was disastrous for the church.

Second, the Enlightenment did result in the overthrow of the Hebrew-Christian Weltanschauung and Zeitgeist.

Third, the Enlightenment introduced theological liberalism into the church in force, a fact that Dr. Ramm and I heartily agree on. And Dr. Ramm is no supporter of theological liberalism.

Fourth, we both agree that we live in the age of modern paganism, a term used extensively by Peter Gay in his two-volume work *The Enlightenment*. Dr. Ramm writes: "This character [modern paganism] is seen clearly in university education today. Education in the Middle Ages and at the time of the Reformation was based on Christian presuppositions, Christian revelation, Christian theology. Modern universities are based on modern paganism (sometimes disguised by the more tempered word *humanism*) that emerged from the Enlightenment."[3]

Starting from this vantage point Ramm goes on to define, in effect, three camps found in the church today. The first includes those who are theologically liberal. They have succumbed to the anti-Christian, antisupernatural emphasis of the Enlightenment. Ramm is not one of them and argues that neither is Karl Barth.

The second wing of the church is made up of those who are evangelicals or fundamentalists. These people are obscurantists. They have failed to address the issues raised by the Enlightenment. They have not even come to grips with this movement. They avoid confrontation like the plague and rest contented with a theology that is passé because it is not modern and they still embrace views that are no longer valid because of the great advances made by science and its methodology.

The third group represents the synthesis (my word, not Dr. Ramm's). These people acknowledge the claims of the Enlightenment and the problems it produced, but they refuse to become liberals in theology and they also decry the current stance of the evangelical/fundamentalist viewpoint and mind-set.

Ramm goes on to present what I choose to call the *via media*, the "middle way," of Karl Barth, who is looked upon as the hero who has delivered the church from its impasse and provided a way out. Barth has accepted the new Enlightenment understanding of the Bible as filled with errors, mythology, and the like. Yet he has retained confidence in the Bible and finds the Word of God in parts of the Bible but not in all of it.

Barth has been labeled, libeled, and deplored by the liberals and by the evangelicals/fundamentalists. But Barth is closer in his basic theological viewpoints to the evangelicals/fundamentalists than he is to the liberals. Thus Dr. Ramm is stalwart in his advocacy of a Barth who holds to the great fundamentals of the Christian faith. Ramm realizes that the liberals offer no hope and claims that the evangelicals/fundamentalists are obscurantists because they will not accept the assured results of modern science. So Ramm finds himself between the devil and the deep blue sea. He has found deliverance in the theology of Karl Barth and wants the evangelicals/fundamentalists to buy his option, enter the modern world, become a witness to those who rest their case on modern science, and embrace Karl Barth.

OPPONENTS OF KARL BARTH

Dr. Ramm candidly concedes that many modern scholars are in disagreement with important aspects of Barth's theology and this fact must be taken into account before one decides to commit oneself to his theology. What is at stake, of course, is whether the critics have scored hits against Barth proving that Barth is not the kind of evangelical theologian Ramm believes him to be. The list of Barth's critics is substantial.

Lutheran Gustav Wingren warns us that Barth's theology destroys the proper relationship between creation and redemption, and between law and Gospel.

The Scandinavian theologians (for example, Gustaf Aulen and Anders Nygren) warn us that, while Barth's theology is not existentialist in the narrow sense of being built on one existentialist's philosophy, it is existentialist in its largest sense.

Cornelius Van Til warns us very energetically that for all Barth's pretensions to orthodoxy his version of orthodox doctrines is radically off base.

Roman Catholic scholars such as Hans Balthasar and Henri Bouillard warn us that Barth is wrong on his view of natural theology and his interpretation of Thomas Aquinas.

Gordon Haddon Clark warns us of serious departures from historic Reformed faith in Barth's methodology.

Sytse Zuidema warns us that Barth reduced theology to existential prescripts and so robs it of its contact with creation and history.

Herman Dooyeweerd warns us that Barth makes a fateful division of nature and grace.

Carl F. H. Henry warns us that Barth's view of inspiration and revelation are defective.

Donald Bloesch warns us of the weak spots in Barth's theology of salvation.

Gerrit Berkouwer warns us that Barth's overpowering doctrine of grace has the power to eliminate the reality of our Christian faith.

R. H. Roberts warns us that for all Barth's denials, he nevertheless has created a vast metaphysical system and in his attack on natural theology virtually annihilates the natural order.

S. W. Sykes warns us that Barth does not recognize the many Christologies in the New Testament and the importance of that nonrecognition for any Christology.

And Helmut Thielicke—and a number of other theologians with him—believe that, for all of Barth's greatness in rethinking theological topics, there is something fundamentally eccentric about his theology.[4]

In addition to these, which Dr. Ramm mentions, we might add the name of Charles Hartshorne. In his book *Insights and Oversights of Great Thinkers* he says:

After all there are only three, not infinite, doctrinal possibilities: no God, a simply and wholly immutable God, a God not wholly immutable. . . . For four centuries now the third view has been more and more seriously considered (e.g., . . . Karl Barth, and others). . . .

Even so conservative a writer as Karl Barth rejects classical theism, and declares for "a new kind of holy change in God."[5]

In the light of what these scholars have said about the theology of Barth, it is clear that they read him quite differently from the way Ramm reads him. And if so many of them then apparently misread Barth, why should we accept Ramm's analysis rather than those of these other scholars? Is it not curious that he does not provide the names of an equal number of scholars who take Barth without the reservations?

Since Professor Ramm indicts scholars like Van Til, Clark, and Henry as obscurantists who gloss over the Enlightenment, are the others he mentions also obscurantists? But if some of them accept the historical-critical methodology as Barth does, why wouldn't they be better exponents to the question Ramm has posed about the need to come to terms with the Enlightenment?

Dr. Ramm says that Barth's "work is such a vast production, with so much rewriting of traditional topics, that it could well take a century of scholarship and scholarly reflection to assess it."[6] This can only mean that we do not yet really know what Barth did teach and we cannot properly assess it right now. Surely if Barth as he has been read cannot be understood, why should we think he is on target and why should we accept what we do not understand? And what gives us reason to believe that in a hundred years we will not find that Barth taught exactly the opposite of what some think he teaches as they read him today? But enough of that! Let us go on and raise two points that will enable us to reach some sort of decision as to the validity of Ramm's claim that Barth is orthodox.

TWO TESTS APPLIED TO BARTH'S POSITION

In the interest of brevity we can reduce the agenda on Barth and concentrate on two vital issues or particulars. They may be stated as follows:

First, is Barth orthodox in his theology as it relates to important doctrinal concerns of the Bible, or is he off base and not to be regarded as a reliable exponent of historical theological orthodoxy?

Second, since Barth, as Ramm agrees, bought into the Enlightenment methodology, that is, its empiricism as a principle for gaining knowledge, is it essential for evangelicalism/fundamentalism to do so in order to be saved from obscurantism and to rescue orthodoxy from the current plight Ramm addresses himself to?

BARTH'S BASIC THEOLOGICAL CONVICTIONS

Biblical Inerrancy

Dr. Ramm asserts that Karl Barth "stoutly defends the theological integrity of Holy Scripture as vigorously as any orthodox person would."[7] He also avers that Barth's "doctrine of inspiration is thus formed to preserve the spirituality of the Word of God. To note that Barth differs from such great ones in the theory of inspiration as Louis Gaussen or Benjamin Warfield or Charles Hodge does not really come to terms with Barth's doctrine."[8]

In response to these statements, which certainly appear to be inconsistent with the facts concerning the vigor with which Warfield and others defended biblical inerrancy, the following must be said. Ramm admits and testifies to the fact that Barth believed the Bible contains errors:

When Barth was asked in his appearance at the University of Chicago if his admission of errors in Scripture "sullied" the divine authority of Scripture, Barth objected. He objected to the verb "sullied." His argument was that if the Scriptures have a genuine humanity, then the presence of errors is part of the full humanity of the Scriptures and therefore does not sully the Scriptures. He also declared that, if God is not ashamed of errors in Scripture, why should we be? He also said that if we affirm the Scripture is without error because inspired by God, then God would be the cause of unbelief if we found errors in Scripture.[9]

In his *Church Dogmatics* Barth himself wrote: "The prophets and apostles as such, even in their office, . . . were real historical men as we are, and . . . actually guilty of error in their spoken and written word."[10]

There can be no doubt that Barth and Ramm hold there are errors in Scripture. This does violence to two facts. The first is that the Scriptures themselves declare the Bible to be free from all error in the whole and in the part. The second is that the church, at least until the Enlightenment, proclaimed its belief in the inerrancy of the Bible. This was true for the Roman Catholic church as well as for the founding fathers of the Reformation, John Calvin and Martin Luther. And the major confessions of the various churches assented to this same viewpoint.

The most recent encyclopedia of the Roman Catholic church in America, the *New Catholic Encyclopedia*, in its statement about the Bible says this: "The inerrancy of Scripture has been the constant teaching of the Fathers, the theologians, and recent Popes. . . . It is nonetheless obvious that many biblical statements are simply not true when judged according to modern knowledge of science and history."[11]

There may have been people in the churches before the Enlightenment who thought the Bible had errors in it. But they were few in number and none of them proclaimed their views in statements that bound their churches to that viewpoint. It is quite clear that the switch from inerrancy to errancy occurred *after* the Enlightenment and can be regarded as one of the consequences of the Enlightenment. Barth and Ramm have bought a viewpoint consistent with Enlightenment presuppositions. This they are entitled to do. But in the doing of it both of them have departed from historic orthodoxy. So as a beginning, with regard to bibliology, Barth does not stand within the circle of historic orthodoxy.

Christ's Bodily Resurrection from the Dead

Dr. Ramm argues that Barth believed in Jesus's bodily resurrection from the dead. Many evangelicals do not believe he did. Ramm says:

Some evangelicals have accused Barth of teaching that such events as the virgin birth and the bodily resurrection occurred in a special space and time divorced from our ordinary space and time. He is accused of teaching that such events of revelation occur in something like Kant's noumenal space and time, not in our empirical space and time. Such interpretations are eccentric.

Certainly Barth believes that Jesus Christ arose bodily in the Garden Tomb and in such a manner that one could touch his body, see his form, hear his voice and watch him eat food. All this is in our space and time, not in some noumenal realm. . . .

It [the resurrection] is an event that "actually happened among men like other events, and was experienced and later attested by them."[12]

Ramm says that Barth's writings are sprinkled with statements such as this. How then do we respond to the question?

In the *Theological Students Fellowship Bulletin,* May–June 1986, there appears a short article titled "My Encounter with Karl Barth" by Carl F. H. Henry. In it he says:

When Karl Barth came to America . . . George Washington University . . . invited 200 religious leaders to a luncheon honoring Barth, at which guests were invited to stand, identify themselves, and pose a question. A Jesuit scholar voiced the first question. . . . I asked the next question. . . . "The question, Dr. Barth, concerns the historical factuality of the resurrection of Jesus Christ." I pointed to the press table and noted the presence of leading religious editors or reporters representing the United Press, Religious News Service, *Washington Post, Washington Star,* and other media. If these journalists had their present duties in the time of Jesus, I asked, was the resurrection of such a nature that covering some aspects of it it would have fallen into their area of responsibility? "Was it news," I asked, "in the sense that the man in the street understands news?" . . . Barth took up the challenge: "And what of the virgin birth? Would the photographers come and take pictures of it?" he asked. Jesus, he continued, appeared only to believers and not to the world. Barth correlated the reality of the resurrection only with personal faith.

Later, UPI Religion reporter Lou Cassels remarked, "We got Barth's 'Nein!'" For Barth, the resurrection of Jesus did not occur in the kind of history accessible to historians. . . . Some years later when Barth wrote his *Evangelical Theology: An Introduction,* he commented in the preface that he could go neither the way of *Christian Century* nor the way of *Christianity Today.*[13]

It is important to observe that the resurrection of Lazarus from the dead was accessible to believers and unbelievers alike. And any daily newspaper could have written about it, for their reporters would have seen the risen Lazarus. Dr. Henry is therefore making it plain that the kind of resurrection Barth was talking about is not the kind of resurrection historic orthodoxy has talked about over the centuries. It should be plain, then, that Barth's resurrection with regard to Jesus is not the traditional resurrection and this is a marked change in theological perspective.

Universalism

Barth has been accused by many of being a universalist, that is, he believes that all people will be saved at last. Emil Brunner,

Ramm admits, thought that Barth was a universalist.[14] And so do many others familiar with Barth's writings.

Professor Ramm says that "Barth argues that no person can be a universalist, because only God knows whether all will be saved or not. To affirm that God will save all is to affirm something none of us can know. It is true the other way, too! To affirm that God will only save some is a bit of knowledge none of us have. But Barth says, wouldn't it be nice if on Judgment Day grace should surprise us and save all!"[15] One can agree with this argument only if there is no authority to which the Christian can go to settle the question definitively. Fortunately we have the Bible and it is quite plain. It teaches in many places that there is a separation of the saved from the lost and that the destinies of saved and lost are quite different.

We must emphasize the fact that there are many things we do not know and cannot know in and of ourselves. We can only know them from revelation, that is, from God's disclosure of them to us. None of the ordinary bystanders at the cross of Jesus could know what the difference was between the death of Jesus and the deaths of the two thieves on either side of him. The meaning of the atonement is known by revelation and no other way. So also is there no way we can know there is a life after death except by revelation.

The weakness of Barth's position is recognized by Ramm when he writes about the reaction of Gerrit C. Berkouwer to it. He says that Berkouwer holds that "Barth's view robs preaching of its seriousness, and the decision of faith of its meaningfulness. . . . However, the weight of Berkouwer's objection is not to be overlooked, for it reflects the spiritual weakness of all universalisms."[16]

It is in connection with universalism that Ramm makes clear a difference between Barth and orthodox theology about the atonement. Ramm says:

Barth believes that Christ was the Last or Second Adam. As such, in his saving work he is the substitute for every single human being who has ever lived, is now alive or will yet live. Christ died for all; he was buried for all; he arose as Victor for all. All people are *de jure* ("on the books of God") justified. This means that Jesus Christ is related to all people: Europeans, Asians, Africans, Muslims, Animists, Buddhists,

Hindus, Atheists. However, this relationship is secret—not obvious but nonetheless real. Jesus Christ is the secret meaning of every human life. Christians have experienced salvation and know this relationship. Non-Christians do not know it, but the fact remains unchanged.[17]

One might well ask the question where Barth got this information. Certainly he did not get it from the Scriptures. Has Barth received a special inspiration, a new revelation to add to the biblical revelation we now have? For centuries it has been stated that we have a back cover on the Bible and nothing can be added or taken from what we have. Barth's opinion is an addition to Holy Writ and it also happens to conflict with what we have in Holy Writ on this subject. Ramm says, "Whether or not his solution is correct it is courageous. He faces an issue that is so staggering that most of us gloss it over to avoid the uncomfortable experience of thinking about it."[18] Yet Ramm's statement is wholly inadequate. It is not courageous to affirm what Scripture denies; it is human reason over revelation. This sort of practice is, however, consonant with Enlightenment thinking for it places humans above the Bible rather than subject to it. And this cannot be.

By way of addition to the above, Kenneth Kantzer, who studied under Barth and who has read his *Church Dogmatics* seriously, wrote the following in *Christianity Today:*

Most serious of all is Barth's unorthodox doctrine of salvation. He rejected the penal substitutionary atonement in favor of Christ's overcoming of sin and evil. We who are sinners identify with this overcoming, therefore sharing in his victory. Coupled with this "Irvingite" theory of the Atonement is Barth's "hope-so universalism." He wrote that all humans are predestined to be saved in Christ. Indeed, belief in Christ is not so much the condition for our justification as for our becoming aware of what is true for all. So Barth felt we may confidently hope for the salvation of all, even including Judas and those who, throughout their entire lives, remained active opponents of the gospel.[19]

Jesus' Sinlessness

There are two Words of God, the Word of God written and the Word of God incarnate. Barth and Ramm are agreed that the Word of God written has errors in it. What does this mean in relation to the Word of God incarnate, Jesus Christ who became flesh and dwelt among us? It is here that Barth's emphasis on the full humanity of Scripture and of Jesus leads to the conclusion that Jesus, if truly human, also erred—sinned.

If, as Barth avers that the prophets and apostles were real historical people even as we are and that as historical people they were guilty of error in their written and spoken word, does this not apply to Jesus too? This question is reinforced by Ramm's assertion about Barth's view of the historical Jesus:

> I don't think that Barth is primarily worried at this point about the baying dogs of the Enlightenment, I think he is working in parallel to the incarnation. In both the humanity of Christ and the humanity of Scripture, the theologian must touch bottom. One must affirm that the Son of God took actual sinful humanity in the incarnation and also that the Scriptures are vulnerable to error. In doing so, Barth is able to come to terms with the critical heritage of the Enlightenment and the current state of biblical studies. . . .
>
> If to be human is to err, then it is a possibility that on the human side of Scripture there may be error. I don't recall that Barth anywhere says there *must* be error to be human . . . but only as a matter of fact there is error.[20]

We can only conclude that both Barth and Ramm are saying that because Jesus was human he erred. And this would be fully in agreement with the Enlightenment mentality, which went still further because its leading mentors did not believe that Jesus is God. What do the Scriptures say about Jesus in this regard?

Luke purports to give us the words of the angel who appeared to Mary and said among other things: "The Holy Ghost shall come upon thee, and the power of the Highest shall overshadow thee: therefore also that *holy* thing which shall be born of thee shall be called the Son of God" (1:35). The New Testament everywhere depicts Jesus as the Holy One (e.g., see 1 John 2:20; Mark 1:24; Luke 4:34; Acts 3:14).

Jesus was made after the likeness of the first Adam, that is, without original sin. And like Adam he was tempted in all points just as we are tempted. But the Scripture goes on from there to affirm that even though tempted he was without sin (Heb. 4:15). And there can be no doubt that only a sinless Christ could have offered himself as a vicarious substitute on Calvary for our sins and for our salvation.

Gordon H. Clark in his review of Ramm's book says that "the parallel between an erroneous Bible and a sinful Christ is not Christianity. . . . Ramm is such a fine gentleman. But Christ is sinless."[21] A refusal to accept the sinlessness of Christ marks a distinct departure from classical orthodoxy. And Christ's sinlessness is related to the written Word of God. The Scriptures declare that the Holy Spirit was the divine author of Scripture along with human instrumentalities. And He was also the One by whom the Virgin Mary conceived Jesus. In both instances we have a miracle. Even as the Holy Spirit rendered Jesus sinless in conception so He also rendered the Scriptures inerrant. Even as the human authors of Scripture could not have written an inerrant Word without the assistance of the Holy Spirit, so also Mary could not have given birth to a sinless son without the divine aid of the Holy Spirit. In both instances it is the Holy Spirit who made possible what was impossible for human instrumentalities to accomplish. Barth is to be faulted at this point and so is Ramm.

While we are talking about the Holy Spirit, we might well consider another observation made by Kantzer about the Trinity:

Even more serious was Barth's acceptance of a kind of modal trinity that sets forth the Godhead as a single person. ("Not three 'I's," he declares in his *Church Dogmatics*, but "one I thrice repeated"). Barth never really came to terms with the interpersonal relationship displayed in the Gospels between Jesus the Son and his heavenly Father. And even Rudolph Bultmann chided him for failing to delineate the person of the Holy Spirit.[22]

Dehistoricizing the Bible

Karl Barth and Bernard Ramm, who agrees with Barth, dehistoricize the Old Testament in part and by so doing make a mishmash of those parts they reconstruct according to what they call the assured results of modern scientific criticism. Ramm openly affirms that Barth accepts and uses the historical-critical methodology wherever and whenever it suits his purpose. No one will say that Barth denies history in the Bible in a fashion most people think of history. But he is choosy and does not look at certain parts of the Bible the same way he looks at other parts of the Word of God.

Dr. Ramm says that "Evangelicals cannot gloss over all that

the modern sciences say of the origin of the universe, the origin of life, and the origin of man. Francis Schaeffer stoutly defends his view of these matters in *Genesis in Space and Time*, but he glosses over the enormous amount of scientific information that bears on those topics."[23] He goes on to say later that "Barth knows well the development of scientific history from the time of the Enlightenment to the present."[24] Then he proceeds to dehistoricize along with Barth the early Genesis account of creation. He says:

For all Roman Catholic and Protestant scholars who still maintain that Holy Scripture is in some objective sense the Word of God, Genesis 1–3 pose a very difficult problem with reference to scientific history. These chapters mention the creation of the heavens and earth when there was obviously no human observer. They mention events at the beginning of human history when there was neither writing nor historians nor archives. No other documents or corroborative [sic] data enable the historian to double-check the historicity of these chapters. Yet these chapters are absolutely crucial to the biblical history that follows and to Christian theology. . . . Barth invokes the concept of saga for this history, which he borrows from old Icelandic and Norse stories. . . . Saga is a special kind of historical reporting. Saga deals with real events in real space and real time just as scientific history. But it deals with those kinds of events that elude scientific history.[25]

It is apparent that neither Barth nor Ramm think that Genesis 1–2 is history as we think of history. It is something different. It is real and true, but it is not the same kind of real and true thing we all call history. It is beyond the scope of the scientific historian, because no one was there and there are no available evidences. As to this two things should be said.

First, if this period has no empirical data from which to draw a conclusion, how then can scientific historians explain how humankind came into being and when this happened when they have no access to external corroborating evidences? Second, both Ramm and Barth, for whom he speaks, agree that to read Genesis 1 and 2 in a literal fashion and assume it to be straight history is to contradict "the story told by modern astronomy, geology, biology, paleontology, and physical anthropology."[26] Since this is so, they choose the modern scientific viewpoint and by doing this they place something above Scripture by which they interpret Scripture. They change the reading of Genesis 1 and 2 to something quite different from that done by anyone without the scientific background of Ramm and Barth. This means anyone faces a choice between what the Bible apparently says and what science says about the same subjects.

Ramm argues, and of course Barth would have to do the same, that whoever refuses to buy the scientific explanation is obscurantist. But might not the argument be reversed and those who take the science road be accused of being obscurantistic because they hide their heads in the sand and refuse to take the biblical evidences seriously? This, in turn, leads to the question of whether science is so certain that its conclusions are absolutes. If they are not, then the conclusions of the scientific fraternity are no more than provisional. They then are not facts but theories.

If evangelicals/fundamentalists have a problem with Genesis 1 and 2, Barth and Ramm have another problem they have not answered. When does actual history begin in Genesis? Stated another way, "When does that which is different from real history as we generally think of it start a new track and become the kind of history we all accept?" Does real history begin with Abraham as some suggest? If so, who was Abraham's father, grandfather, and so on? And who was the first human? And where did he or she come from? At best those who adopt the evolutionary hypothesis cannot call it a fact, because they have no empirical evidence, for, as Ramm says, no one was there when human life first began. Therefore, there can be no certitude from a scientific perspective as to what happened and when it happened.

This much is reasonably certain. Barth and Ramm do not accept the traditional liberal view, which means they do not follow the Enlightenment thesis to its logical conclusion. And they do not accept the traditional evangelical/fundamentalist view. Their *via media* is paradoxical, for it tries to blend into a new theory components that are antithetical and that makes logic stand on its head. This is a denial of the law of contradiction.

Gordon Haddon Clark mentions this in his review of Dr. Ramm's book. He says:

If Ramm in his present book has mentioned Barth's view of *paradox*, I missed it. Yet, Barth, when he first penetrated the American scene, was using the concept of paradox rather enthusiastically. This denial of the law of contradiction is Barth's first norm for doing theology. His involved sentence is, "The very minimum postulate of freedom from contradiction is acceptable only upon the very limited intepretation, by the scientific theorist upon the scarcely tolerable one, that theology will not assert an irremovability in principle of the *contradictions* which it is bound to make good."[27]

Lest anyone suppose that using the criticism of Clark, who is a strong defender of logic as well as an evangelical/fundamentalist, is incorrect, a word from one who is by no means associated with this viewpoint may help us understand the problem of Barth's notion of paradox. Princeton Theological Seminary held a conclave celebrating Barth's one-hundredth birthday. George Hunsinger replied to an article written by William Werpehowski titled "Narrative and Ethics in Barth," in which the name of James M. Gustafson of the divinity school of the University of Chicago appears. Hunsinger said of Gustafson:

Barth's argument about suicide, Gustafson stressed, is filled with ambiguities he does not resolve. Chief among these would be that while God's command confronts suicide with an unqualified No, suicide, says Barth, is not absolutely condemned and under exceptional circumstances might actually be obedience to divine command. "Karl Barth's assessment of suicide," comments Gustafson, "would be maddeningly equivocal to most philosophers." Although Gustafson does not fail to appreciate why such ambiguity reasonably follows from Barth's theology, he also makes it quite clear that dialectical to and fro are not for him. But why then should Barth himself seem to thrive on it? What was it that nourished his tolerance for paradox? What could have driven him again and again in his theology to fly in the face of the law of noncontradiction? Is he simply baptizing muddles and calling them mysteries?[28]

There are those who do not follow Clark or even know about Clark who also have trouble with Barth, paradox, and the obvious fact that Barth defied the law of noncontradiction. But this is quite consistent with Enlightenment viewpoints.

The most that can be said for Barth in relation to the acceptance of the scientific methodology is that he has endorsed it in principle but has not bought all of its conclusions. He certainly has not run against the prevailing tide of academic thought but has made enough concessions to it that one finds it difficult to suppose that he is a genuine evangelical.

Dr. Ramm has said again and again that those who do not accept the scientific methodology as Barth does simply gloss over the problem. It is interesting that Carl F. H. Henry, one of those Ramm includes in the charge of glossing over the Enlightenment, has himself used the word "gloss" about Karl Barth. Dr. Henry says:

But can one imply, as Barth does, that all philosophies can be serviceable in expounding Christian revelation, and therefore none destructive of it, unless he deprives revelation of normative content? On the one hand he declares that neither Aristotle, Descartes, Kant, Hegel, nor Heidegger may be permitted to place theology in bondage, while on the other he welcomes theology's eclectic use of "current ideas, concepts, images, and expressions" with the "greatest confidence" (*Evangelical Theology: An Introduction*, p. 12). To be sure, Barth inserts the qualification "as long as they prove themselves suitable," but are current ideas and expressions forged independently of revelation all that unbiased and neutral? Does not Barth simply *gloss* [my italics] over the adverse influence of certain philosophical elements upon theology in maintaining this stance? . . .

While our theological systems are assuredly not infallible, the inspired Scriptures convey the very Word of God in the form of divinely given truths. But since Barth depicts revelation of the Word as communicating no valid truths, and cheapens even Scripture into a "fallible pointer" to revelation, he can no longer discriminate infallible from fallible perspective on the basis of fidelity to revelation. Barth could therefore count even Feuerbach [a materialist and atheist from whom Karl Marx got some of his views—my addition] as standing serviceably within the church.[29]

The Conclusion

The answer to our first question, "Is Barth a reliable exponent of historical theological orthodoxy?" must be no. Barth differs radically from the traditional orthodoxy of Augustine, Calvin, and Luther. One cannot embrace Barth and stand firmly for these traditionalists. Thus if one stands up for Augustine, Calvin, and Luther, one cannot put them and Barth in the same category. This in no way diminishes the stature of this giant, nor does it suggest that he has nothing to contribute to the current dialogue rising out of the Enlightenment. It does mean that Barth's acceptance and use of the scientific methodology of the Enlightenment as applied to the Bible is unacceptable to evangelicals/fundamentalists for one simple reason. They would, if they accepted Barth's paradigm, no longer be evangelicals/fundamentalists. They would have to surrender what they have stood for over the centuries.

This means we have to take a hard look at the Enlightenment and develop some sort of apologetic by which we can sustain historic orthodoxy and yet live and function in this radically changed world. But before we do this, one point should be made plain. With or without Karl Barth and the Enlightenment, the church of Jesus Christ will go on to the end of the age. And so will the preaching of the old-fashioned gospel.

Most of us who have been regenerated came into this relationship with God without the benefit of the Enlightenment or Karl Barth. I suspect that Bernard Ramm became a Christian long before he knew much or anything about Karl Barth. And countless millions of people who lived before Karl Barth was born came into the kingdom without Barth or even Calvin, Luther, or Augustine. I teach a Bible class of several hundred people. I do not know of one person in that class who could tell me virtually anything about Karl Barth and his theology, yet they are all Christians professing to have been regenerated ("born again").

I attended the Amsterdam 1986 conference for evangelists hosted by the Billy Graham Evangelistic Association. There were more than seven thousand evangelists from all around the globe. Most of them never heard of Karl Barth. And they have returned to their homelands where they will preach the same gospel that was preached before Karl Barth was born. Multitudes will come to a saving knowledge of Jesus Christ without benefit of Barth. I have watched Billy Graham carefully over the years and I do not recall a single sermon he preached that had in it Barthian theology or was indebted to Barth in any way. Yet tens of thousands of people have been regenerated by personal faith in Jesus Christ as a result of these evangelistic meetings.

All of this does not mean we should not face the negative fallout of the Enlightenment or the effort of Barth and others to respond to it. Nor should we deny that the West is now pagan and that there is a crying need to do something to halt the onward march of this paganism. Nor should we shirk the church's responsibility to call people back to the Bible and to its primary mission to evangelize the world.

What then should the attitude of evangelicals/fundamentalists be toward what the Enlightenment stood for and what modern science stands for vis-à-vis the Christian faith?

BARTH'S ENLIGHTENMENT METHODOLOGY

In all fairness to Bernard Ramm, the time has come for us to consider the Enlightenment without "glossing" over it, as he suggests leading evangelical scholars have done. In doing this the defense will include two major considerations requiring separate treatment. They are: first, a statement about the various Enlightenment philosophical viewpoints, all of which can be shown to be at the very least less desirable than that which underlies historic orthodoxy; and second, a statement about the historical-critical methodology that was used by Karl Barth and that lies right in the center of the current impasse.

ENLIGHTENMENT PHILOSOPHICAL POSITIONS

Before discussing the various philosophical positions that either had their beginnings in the Enlightenment or were resurrected from the distant past and enlarged and expanded upon during the Enlightenment, we must first indicate some of the common presuppositions of the Enlightenment that had to do with the Christian faith directly. The Enlightenment was antisupernatural and antirevelation. Reason was placed over revelation and humans over the Bible. It was also antichurch and anti-God. It was from these things that Barth was supposed to have delivered us by accepting the historical-critical methodology, which was also an Enlightenment gift. This is not to say that Barth accepted or endorsed many of the philosophical positions of which I shall now speak.

Among the ideas current in the Enlightenment or deriving

from it are atheism, agnosticism, empiricism, scientism, naturalism, materialism, rationalism, evolutionism, deism, humanism, and logical positivism. We will not here include other more recent options such as process theology, liberation theology, or atheistic existentialism, all of which are partakers of elements common to the above list. None of these or any other options, for that matter, come close to that of the Judeo-Christian alternative.

Atheism

Atheism according to the dictionary means "the doctrine that there is neither God nor any other deity." This view, of course, is common to Marxism and is held by humanists and others in one form or another. Great numbers of people talk about their belief in the existence of God but they are functional atheists. So far as their thought lives and their life-styles are concerned, God might just as well not exist.

Atheism begins with an unprovable presupposition. There is simply no way that anyone can prove that God does not exist. Atheism also denies the supernatural and again there is no way the supernatural can be shown not to exist. Anyone is free to base a philosophy on an unproved and unprovable supposition. But why an atheist should hate theism and theists is not necessarily a mystery. One can properly assume that the nature of the Christian faith and its teaching concerning an afterlife of a heaven and a hell is enough to threaten an atheist, whose eternal estate will be one of everlasting conscious separation from the living God in what the Bible describes as the Lake of Fire. Indeed this is an offensive view to atheists and a reason for such people to hate those who hold these views. And since atheism has no basis for any credible system of ethics, there is no reason why the Christian law of love should find support with them.

In short, atheism has nothing to offer people in this life or in the life to come, if there is one. At the very least the Christian faith does provide some attractive answers to those questions. If atheists are wrong, they have lost everything. If Christians are wrong, they still haven't lost nearly as much as atheists.

There are positive external corroborative evidences for the truth of theism as to the existence of God and of eternal life.

These will be adduced when we have come to the end of the list.

Agnosticism

The agnostic might just as well be an atheist so far as the end is concerned. But agnosticism is defined as an "unwillingness on available evidence to affirm or deny the existence of God, or subscribe to tenets that presuppose such existence."

Clearly the so-called lack of evidence for the existence of deity carries in it notions that mark this viewpoint as hardly desirable. It has in it the same kind of defect contained in atheism. It says that there is no available evidence to prove God's existence. And it implies that there can be none. The only way atheists or agnostics could pronounce definitively against the existence of God is for them to be ominiscient. And in that event whoever is omniscient is God. Certainly whoever is not omniscient is incapable of making any assertions against the nonexistence of anything, for anything might exist outside the boundaries of his or her knowledge.

The argument that an agnostic cannot subscribe to tenets that presuppose the existence of God is rather senseless. This is true in view of the many arguments for the existence of deity. It is here that some reference should be made to David Hume and his so-called skepticism, which is more like agnosticism or atheism. His classic work against the evidences given for a belief in the supernatural are impressive, until we realize that he starts with the presupposition that there can be no miracles and he then goes on to prove what he has already decided before he offers the evidences.

Hume does not hesitate to set up an absolute for which there is and can be no foundation. He says:

I flatter myself that I have discovered an argument of a like nature, which, if just, will, with the wise and learned, be an everlasting check to all kinds of superstitious delusion, and consequently will be useful as long as the world endures; for so long, I presume, will the accounts of miracles and prodigies be found in all history, sacred and profane.[30]

Hume's presupposition against miracles can be seen in the following statement:

But suppose that all the historians who treat of England should agree, that on the first of January, 1600, Queen Elizabeth died; that both before and after her death, she was seen by her physicians and the whole court, as is usual with persons of her rank; that her successor was acknowledged and proclaimed by the Parliament; and that, after being interred for a month she again appeared, resumed her throne, and governed England for three years; I must confess that I should be surprised at the concurrence of so many odd circumstances, but should not have the least inclination to believe so miraculous an event. I should not doubt of her pretended death and of those other public circumstances that followed it: I should only assert it to have been pretended, and that it neither was, nor possibly could be, real.[31]

Hume concludes that "I should rather believe the most extraordinary events to arise from their concurrence, than admit of so signal a violation of the laws of nature."[32]

Empiricism

Empiricism can be defined as "the theory associated especially with the British philosophers John Locke, George Berkeley, and David Hume that all knowledge originates in experience." Empirical means "originating in or relying or based on factual information, observation, and direct sense experience."

Quite obviously, if empiricism is true, then there can be no supernatural and no special revelation by God. The denial of such possibilities because those who hold this viewpoint make such an assertion is no proof at all that such things cannot happen, unless, of course, such people are omniscient, which they are not. They are also saying something else.

Unless they can through sense perception experience what I claim to have experienced, they cannot and will not believe it. Who then is to judge whose sense experience is true and whose is false? To say that there can be nothing that goes beyond sense experience is an absolute for which they can adduce no proof. This viewpoint also leads its exponents to deny anything they have not experienced. And even if I have experienced something that can be empirically verified, it means nothing to such people unless and until they experience it too. But until that happens they must deny it unless they accept what I say by faith. But they are short on faith, for they do not consider that worthy of acceptance that something has really happened.

This surely does not mean that we are to accept anything and everything people claim to have experienced. But this does not mean that there cannot be some things that are true even if I offer no evidence for what happened. And, as we shall see, there are happenings for which there is demonstrable evidence that empiricists will not accept in any event.

It is quite true that in the fields of science we do and should use the empirical methodology so long as we are aware of its limitations and deficiencies. If empiricists will accept the metaphysical, there can be peace and progress, but so long as they refuse to do so, the system is closed and the supernatural is ruled out arbitrarily by their basic presuppositions.

Scientism

There is a difference between science and scientism. The latter term is designed to advance empiricism to an absolute that denies the supernatural and thus becomes at best irrational. The term may be defined as follows: "the view that the method of the natural sciences should be applied in all areas of investigations, including philosophy, the humanities, and the social sciences and that this is the only [sic] fruitful method in the pursuit of knowledge."

The claim that the empiricism of the natural sciences is the only fruitful method of gaining knowledge automatically rules out biblical revelation, metaphysics, and the supernatural. To do this emasculates the Christian faith so that it becomes useless. This is one of the reasons why the Enlightenment has dealt such a severe blow to Christianity and unless that defeat is reversed, the New Paganism will reign supreme over American life and culture.

From the perspective of the rational one must argue forcefully that the presupposition of scientism constitutes an absolute that cannot be proved empirically. It must be taken by faith and thus it becomes a substitute religion in place of Christianity. In scientism God is no longer needed and is nothing more than a cultural lag, so that those who continue to believe in God are behind the times. Given the presupposition of scientism, these conclusions about Christians and their beliefs are correct, but it arrives at this standpoint by refusing to accept empirical data in favor of the Christian faith. And of this we shall speak shortly.

Naturalism

This view is defined as "a theory that expands conceptions drawn from the natural sciences into a worldview and that denies that anything in reality has a supernatural or more than natural significance; specifically that the doctrine that cause and effect laws (as of physics and chemistry) are adequate to account for all phenomena and that teleological conceptions of nature are invalid."

It is clear that if there is an effect there is a cause. But that leaves open the ultimate question science cannot answer: whence came matter or energy that constitute the working materials of science? If naturalists say that matter is eternal they can only posit that, not prove it. It is at best only a guess or a theory and there is no way out from there. The Christian view that matter is not eternal and was created by God in the beginning of the cosmos is offensive to the scientific mind that entertains this viewpoint. It cannot stand for a God who made things and who stands over them in history as sovereign and purposeful.

Astrophysicists have grappled long and hard with the question dealing with the origin of the universe. One current theory says that there was a time when the cosmos was not. If that be true, what was there before the cosmos came into being? The answer is matter or energy and that there was a great big bang that produced the universe. But where did the matter or energy that was the cause of the universe's creation come from? Science cannot answer that question. The notion that there is a God who did it is at least as good an answer. And the evidences for this are stronger than the guesses of the physicists.

Again, as in virtually all of these philosophical systems there is the denial of the supernatural. We have already stated that no one can be a good scientist and deny that there can be a supernatural, unless of course the one who makes this assertion is omniscient and is therefore God. And whoever claims there can be no supernatural has entered the field of metaphysics and abandoned the field of science or the empirical. No scientist has a right to do this; it is inconsistent.

Materialism

Materialism is defined as "a doctrine, theory, or principle according to which physical matter is the only reality and the reality through which all being and processes and phenomena can be explained." This notion lies at the heart of Marxism and means very simply that one chooses either God (i.e., Spirit) or matter as the ultimate source of all things. This choice of matter over Spirit cannot be proven. But it is true that where one begins determines where one will come out at the end.

The materialist does not believe in a life after death, or the supernatural, or God, or salvation, or even a final judgment. Materialism certainly cannot tell us how mind, consciousness, and animation spring from the inanimate. Thus it has its own unprovable presuppositions that belong to the realm of faith. Human reason unaided by faith in God cannot understand the hidden things that can only be known by revelation. Wherever reason reigns alone without the benefit of divine revelation given in and through the Bible there will be error. The choice here, as in all the other cases we are examining, is between God and something else that is less than God.

Interestingly, Marxism has the worst possible things to say about those who are theists. Lenin went far beyond even Marx and Engels in his diatribes against any form of religion. He said: "Every religious idea, every idea of god, even every flirtation with the idea of god, is unutterable vileness. . . . Any person who engages in building a god, or who even tolerates the idea of god-building, *disparages himself* in the worst possible fashion."[33]

As a result of this approach toward God, ethics and morality were repudiated by Lenin as indissolubly linked to the Judeo-Christian faith. In their place he proposed a theory of ethics and morality tied to the class struggle. Judeo-Christian ethics and morality were bourgeois inventions. Ethics and morality had no absolutes; all is relative and what is done is good or bad as it helps or hurts the progress of Marxist advance. Therefore lying, cheating, stealing are good if they help the Marxist cause, and bad if they hurt that cause. This is situationalism at its worst. But it is certainly correct in the light of the Marxist presuppositions once they are bought. So we can understand why Marxism is what it is because of the materialism that lies at its heart.

Rationalism

Rationalism is definable as "a view that an appeal to reason and experience rather than to the nonrational (as emotion, intuition, faith, revelation, or authority) is to be employed as the fundamental criterion in the solution of problems."

Rationalism, like some of the other options we have already mentioned, continues the denial of revelation, the supernatural, and the Bible as applicable to life and to its problems. One of the gifts of the Enlightenment was the placing of reason over revelation and humans over the Bible. This produced a human-centered situation in which there was nothing outside or above humans to which to appeal; it was thus a complete repudiation of the Judeo-Christian tradition. Humans were now alone in the vast sea of life and had no one to look to and could expect no help of any kind beyond themselves.

The Hebrew-Christian tradition did not rule out reason, but it did subordinate it to biblical revelation. The Bible was over humanity and humanity's conformity to its demands was recognized as essential to reason and to happiness. This meant that people were not to question or deny divine revelation. Rather revelation was the standard against which people were to measure their reason and use it profitably. There was to be no autonomous humanity lying at the center of rationalism.

Rationalism was simply another viewpoint that shared with others its dislike of the basic prescriptions of the Bible and its determination to be free from anything or any system that curtailed its freedom to think, decide, and act as it pleased.

Evolution

We have already discussed evolution at some length earlier, so that we need not say a great deal more about this option. Yet it should be made plain that Darwin and evolution has its roots in the Enlightenment and it is thoroughly in accord with the principles consonant with it. Its standpoint is colored by that fact and even though it has more recently suffered greatly from criticism directed against its basic presuppositions, it continues to be the choice of many in academia today.

Basically, evolution is the theory that all known life derives from an original first cell (DNA) and through mutations and survival of the fittest were produced the life forms we now see. Human ancestry can be traced back through lower forms of animal life and ultimately back to the beginning of things when the inanimate first became the animate. Evolution in general has assumed two forms: nontheistic evolution, which has no use for God, and theistic evolution, which assumes that God worked through the process generally accepted by evolutionists. The latter form is held by those who cling to the Christian faith but hold that the claims of science tell us about "how" life came into being; they then interpret the early chapters of Genesis on the basis of the so-called assured results of the scientific method.

Whichever way we go one fact emerges quite clearly. There is no way anyone in the scientific world can prove the truth of the theory of evolution. No one was there to observe the process and since this is a necessary article of empirical faith, evolution can be no more than a theory. If those who hold to evolution would say this and go on with their work, current tensions would be lessened considerably. In any event most evolutionists, with the exception of theistic evolutionists, are in full accord with the Enlightenment principles and have long ago forsaken any commitment to the supernatural. In line with their evolutionary hypothesis they can be found and numbered among those who hold to options like the ones we have talked about so far. They are advocates of the New Paganism.

Deism

Deism is really no longer an option acceptable to very many people in the West. Thinkers have seen its weaknesses and moved over to other options more in keeping with their current views. It has been defined as "a rationalistic movement in the seventeenth and eighteenth centuries whose adherents generally subscribed to a natural religion based on human reason and morality, on the belief in one God who after creating the world and the laws governing it refrained from interfering with the operation of these laws, and on the rejection of every kind of supernatural intervention in human affairs."

Deism may be defined as a halfway station between genuine and orthodox Christianity and the New Paganism. It allowed for God but divorced Him from the world He created. He is absent from His creation and is in no sense immanent, although He may be regarded as transcendent. This kind of God is no God at all, for this theory takes away the divine attributes that are everywhere attested to in the Bible.

The denial of the supernatural and the appeal to human reason identify the deists with some or all of the options we have talked about. It must be considered one of the Enlightenment viewpoints that has resulted in the defeat of the Judeo-Christian faith or of the church in the West. It is by no means Christian.

Humanism

The *New Encyclopedia Britannica* says of humanism:

In recent years the term "humanism" has often been used to refer to value systems that emphasize the personal worth of each individual but that do not include a belief in God. There is a certain segment of the Unitarian Universalist Association that is nontheistic and yet uses religious forms to promote distinctive human values. In the same vein the 19th-century French positivist Auguste Comte established a nontheistic religion of humanity designed to promote social reform. The American Humanist Association publishes a quarterly magazine, *The Humanist,* and propagates the humanist point of view.[34]

This viewpoint suffers from problems similar to those associated with some of the other systems we have already mentioned. It assumes the nonexistence of God, which cannot be proved. It puts humans at the center of things and assumes that there is nothing superior to or over them. This, too, cannot be proved. Moreover humanism assumes the personal worth of the individual. Its advocates can supply no good answers to the questions, "Where did I come from?" "Who am I?" "What purpose is there in life?" and, of course, "Is there no life in the hereafter?"

Humanism has no transcendental frame of reference. Humans alone devise their own answers to all questions. But since there is and there can be no general consensus to the various questions, humanism has no substantial ground on which to rest any of its dogmas. And it has its own dogmas, most of which are wholly opposed to what is taught in the Bible. Like oil and water, humanism and the Christian faith cannot be mixed. They are antithetical to each other.

Logical Positivism

Logical positivism as such cannot be said to have been a part of Enlightenment thinking. It is introduced here because it is a stepchild of the Enlightenment and has its origins in the same sort of effort to destroy the Christian faith. It has been defined as "a twentieth-century philosophical movement that holds characteristically that all meaningful statements are either analytic or conclusively verifiable or at least confirmable by observation and experiment and that metaphysical theories are themselves strictly meaningless."

The definition means more simply that spiritual truths that are outside the boundaries of the empirical (i.e., beyond the scope of microscope or observation) constitute nonsense, are meaningless. Only those propositions that belong to the world of the natural sciences present to us the real world. The effort of the logical positivists was to destroy metaphysics, that is, those spiritual realities that are neither falsifiable nor verifiable. Since metaphysics are intrinsic to the Christian faith, such destruction would of necessity destroy the Christian faith. Moreover, as Carl F. H. Henry says, logical positivism is a "bold attempt to discredit Christian supernaturalism."[35]

The point we are making here is that there have been a number of theological systems spawned by the Enlightenment that have come to the forefront in more recent years, but they all have something in common with those systems directly related to the Enlightenment. They have shared the Enlightenment's denial of the supernatural, its distaste for a fully trustworthy revelation, its belief that the Bible is filled with errors, and its determined effort to destroy the traditional Judeo-Christian faith.

The objections to logical positivism have come not only from those in the tradition of orthodoxy but also other scholars who have been deeply influenced by the Enlightenment but reject this particular system. Nevertheless it has had a powerful influence among the educated and has helped to undermine and erode still further the confidence Christians formerly had in the Bible as the Word of God.

Concluding Observations

We have looked at some of the options opposed in principle to the Christian faith. All of them are based on the assumption that people can discover truth by the use of the scientific method, a method that lay at the heart of the Enlightenment. Humans could arrive at the truth by observation and through the use of the laboratory. Thus Science (note the capital S because there is a proper use of the term "science" with a lowercase s) can arrive at ultimates and in the process destroy old-fashioned orthodoxy, which the assured results of Science demonstrate to be untrue or at the very least unprovable. There is one hitch to this approach and what is about to be said will probably send shock waves to those who have placed their trust in Science.

Gordon Haddon Clark in his book *The Philosophy of Science and Belief in God*[36] says that all the laws of physics, the most advanced of all the sciences, are false! And that is enough to shake the academic world to its foundations. Indeed Dr. Clark devoted almost a hundred pages of that book to the arguments demonstrating the truth of his statement. John W. Robbins in the *Trinity Review* said:

Clark wrote: "Instead of being the sole gateway to all knowledge, science is not a way to any knowledge." Now this view of science is quite different from the view held by the common man and by many Christian scientists. It takes decades, sometimes a century, for the opinions of philosophers to become the common opinions of mankind, and Americans in 1985 still believe, by and large, what was taught in the 19th century, that science discovers truth. It is not simply the intellectual inertia in this case, for the science teachers in our high schools and college have a dim understanding that there is a religious issue involved here, and that if they were to admit that science does not discover truth, indeed cannot discover truth, the battle between

Christianity and science would be over. So they have a vested interest in perpetuating the myth that science discovers truth. It is not until graduate school, if then, that the student is told about the limitations of science. Until then, he is intimidated by the modern equivalent of "Thus saith the Lord": "It has been scientifically proved." The high-school and college student is not told that it is impossible to prove anything scientifically and that the phrase "scientific truth" is a contradiction in terms. He is, in fact, told the opposite, that nothing is to be accepted unless it has been scientifically proved, and that nothing has the claim to be called true unless science acknowledges that claim.[37]

The remarks of Clark and Robbins lead logically to the question of whether what they say is true. We will now hear the testimony of non-Christian scientists who have said the same thing. And some of them are among the keenest opponents of Christianity and revelational truth from the Bible.

Surely no one would accuse Bertrand Russell of being addicted to Christianity. He said in 1927 that "There is one very serious defect to my mind in Christ's moral character, and that is that he believed in hell." At least he must have believed that there was a historical Jesus and that He said there is a hell. This is a real improvement over those who use redaction criticism to forego the notion that Jesus said anything like this at all, that it was a later church addition. Bertrand Russell was an English mathematician and philosopher. He recognized the limitations of science, that is, according to that definition of science given in the *Oxford Dictionary* under section 5b where it says that science is "synonymous with 'Natural and Physical science,' and thus restricted to those branches of study that relate to phenomena of the material universe and their laws." And this was the contribution of the Enlightenment which made the change in meaning from *knowledge* to *natural science*.

John Robbins asserts that Russell understood some of the limitations of the scientific method:

By *limitations* I do not mean to imply that science is capable of discovering some truths but not others, that through science we can discover truths of astronomy, physics, or botany, but that we must rely on the Bible for theology. This is a fundamentally wrong view of the limitations of science, and Russell had no such delusions about science.

Science is based on observation and experiment. But induction, Russell admitted a little reluctantly, "remains an unsolved problem of logic." Put more bluntly, induction is a logical fallacy. Just because one observes a thousand white swans, one cannot conclude that all swans are white. Number 1001 may be black. Just because the sun has come up every morning for the past one hundred years does not imply that it will come up tomorrow. Or to give you a more theological example, non-Christian archaeologists used to claim that there was no evidence whatsoever for the existence of the Hittite nation; therefore the Bible must be mistaken. Today there are more Hittite documents in our museums than the archaeologists have had time to translate. Induction is *always* fallacious, yet science is based on induction.

A second problem with science that Russell saw is the problem of experimentation. Science proceeds by testing hypotheses through experiments. From a hypothesis a scientist deduces that if X is done, Y will occur. He then proceeds to perform an experiment, Y occurs, and therefore, he concludes, the hypothesis is confirmed. This form of argument is another logical fallacy, and *all* experimentation commits this fallacy. Its formal name is asserting the consequent: If p, then q; q, therefore p. If Einstein's theory of relativity is true, then light will bend in the presence of massive objects; light bends passing the sun, therefore Einstein's theory of relativity is true. Or to put it less scientifically, if it is raining, the streets are wet; the streets are wet, therefore it is raining. Russell wrote:

All inductive arguments in the last resort reduce themselves to the following form: "If this is true, that is true: now that is true, therefore this is true." This argument is, of course formally fallacious. Suppose I were to say: "If bread is a stone, and stones nourishing, then this bread will nourish me; therefore it is a stone, and stones are nourishing." If I were to advance such an argument, I should certainly be thought foolish, yet it would not be fundamentally different from the arguments upon which all scientific laws are based.[38]

Robbins also refers to Albert Einstein who, in a conversation with Chaim Tschernowitz, said "We know nothing about it (i.e., how nature really works) at all. Our knowledge is but the knowledge of schoolchildren. . . . We shall know a little more than we do now. But the real nature of things—that we shall never know, never."[39]

Karl Popper is a renowned scientist-philosopher with honorary degrees from the most prestigious universities in the world. He also has made statements about the truth and falsity of science. In his book *Conjectures and Refutations: The Growth of Scientific Knowledge,* Popper says:

The way in which knowledge progresses, and equally our scientific knowledge, is by unjustified (and unjustifiable) anticipations, by guesses, by tentative solutions to our problems, by conjectures. . . . They can never be positively justified; they can neither be established as certainly true nor even as "probable."[40]

He also says:

All scientific statements are hypotheses, or guesses, or conjectures, and the vast majority of these conjectures . . . have turned out to be false. . . .
  Our attempts to see and to find the truth are not final, but open to improvement . . . our knowledge, our doctrine, is conjectural; . . . it consists of guesses, of hypotheses, rather than of final and certain truths.[41]

Robbins, in his article, goes on to answer what is the almost certain question to be asked by those who would like to think science arrives at truth:

Some may be inclined to argue that even if all the laws of physics are false, they are still highly probable. In response to that, I quote from the words of Karl Popper, the British philosopher of science: "all theories, including the best, have the same probability, namely zero." Why does Popper say such an outrageous thing? The argument is simple: a scientist, after he has performed a number of experiments and made a number of measures, plots a graph. How many lines can pass through the points of a graph? An infinite number, of course. The nice smooth slopes we put in our science textbooks, even our Christian science textbooks, are but one line out of an infinite number that might have been drawn. The scientist has *chosen* the line he draws, he has not discovered it. But if it is possible that there is an infinite number of slopes, it follows that the probability of the slope that is chosen and the equation it represents being the right ones is one out of infinity, or zero. Therefore, "all theories, even the best, have the same probability, namely zero." Q.E.D. Popper repeated that statement many times in his books, and I wish some Christian theologians and scientists would read them.
  But there is a fourth reason for believing that the scientific method is a tissue of logical fallacies. It is quite easy to grasp, as are the first three reasons. Science, especially physics, does not deal with the world we live in. It deals with an imaginary world where there are absolute

vacuums, frictionless surfaces, bodies whose masses are concentrated at a geometrical point, and tensionless strings. The law of the pendulum, for example, applies to such an imaginary world; it describes no actual pendulum. The law of freely falling bodies applies in such an imaginary world; it describes no actually falling bodies. Science does not describe the behavior of things we see, but of the things scientists imagine, including electrons, protons, and quarks. . . .

Science, then, is not a way of discovering truth. What is its function? Well, it can have at least two legitimate functions. Science is not true but it can be useful. The thousands of inventions scientists have made in the past two centuries are nothing if not useful. Chemistry, physics, medicine, mechanics—all have made our lives much more comfortable than they were for our grandparents or even our parents. But these inventions can also be misused, and science cannot select the purposes which are legitimate and those which are not. The guidance must come from some other source. Nuclear energy can be used to light cities or reduce them to ashes. Chemistry can improve nutrition or make nerve gas. Biology can make vaccinations or germ weapons. Science furnishes neither truth nor moral values. But guided by the right nonscientific ethical principles, it can be a great benefit to man.

Science itself can be useful and science education can be useful in training people how to think. Physics is the most advanced science because it uses the most mathematics, and in math, unlike physics, conclusions follow necessarily from the premises. A course in physics can be a good training in rigorous thinking—or at least it should be. So science does have a function, but it is not what many people think it is.[42]

In an article "Natural Law and Natural Laws," David A. Forte (A.B. Harvard, M.A. the University of Manchester, Ph.D. the University of Toronto, J.D. Columbia University; professor of law at Cleveland State University College of Law) says:

In a forthcoming book, the philosopher Henry B. Veatch notes that modern revolutions in the theory of science have revealed its true epistemology. The destruction by Popper of the justificatory mechanisms of induction and verification, and the subsequent undermining of the theory of falsification by Kuhn, leave science quite incapable, as Quine points out, of discerning the nature of anything. Any theory, even one based on the Homeric gods, that seeks to describe why the physical universe appears as it does, is capable of an infinite amount of adjustments to contend with difficult counter-examples. We can never truly know which theory is correct. That means, of course, that we can never truly know what the nature of reality is. The only reason why we choose one model over another is merely pragmatic. Whatever model helps us to manipulate the appearance of reality to accomplish what we, for some reason or other, wish to accomplish is the one we opt for, until another more efficient model appears, or until our objectives change. In any case, the truth of it all evades us. The modern theory of science is not even materialistic, for it cannot tell what the material nature of things is. Nor, certainly, can it provide any moral or spiritual content to the universe.

Thus in the end the traditional method of hypothesis, deduction, and application continues to be accepted by science, not for its truth-seeking capabilities, but only because of its pragmatic effectiveness. . . . We can only know and manipulate our ideas about the appearance of things. We can never truly find out the nature of reality.[43]

We have presented the case against the Enlightenment philosophical viewpoints, all of which are based upon some sort of scientific methodology, and have shown them to be defective and deficient. The methodology itself cannot lead to truth. If this is true in the scientific world of chemistry, physics, and so on, it is also true in the world of the theological. Scientific methodology can never demonstrate that Christianity and faith in the Word of God as free from error are untrue. So this brings us to the second point about Barth's Enlightenment methodology.

THE USE OF THE HISTORICAL-CRITICAL METHODOLOGY

Dr. Ramm has argued passionately that Karl Barth has wedded orthodoxy with the assured results of the scientific method applied to the Bible and rescued orthodoxy from its greatest dilemma. He believes that if we do not follow this procedure, we are obscurantists and at best are guilty of "glossing over" the facts inherent in the Enlightenment. He has stated that evangelicals/fundamentalists have not provided a response to the Enlightenment.

We grant that the acceptance of the Enlightenment viewpoint is fatal to orthodox Christianity. Why do we say this? Because the methodology of the Enlightenment when applied to the Bible leaves us with only one of two choices: we either accept the notion that the Bible is a hodgepodge of truth and error or the Enlightenment itself is wrong. If we accept the former we must be prepared to say that the church through the ages has relied on a book that cannot be trusted. But if, as we have shown, the scientific method that came out of the Enlightenment and cannot establish any law as absolute is the same as that underlying the historical-critical method, then we need not be overly concerned. We will be able to conclude that Barth's acceptance of that methodology has hurt orthodoxy and has impaired the doctrine of the inerrancy of the Bible so that, logically, it is no longer what the church has said it is through the ages. We will be able to reject the Barthian view of the Bible and retain the so-called old-fashioned notion of an inerrant Scripture, a view that science cannot annul and that the Enlightenment has not really succeeded in disproving.

First of all, we need to define what we mean by the historical-critical methodology. We might start by simply speaking about *criticism*. The dictionary (*Webster's Third New International*) says that criticism is "the scientific investigation of documents (as the Bible) in regard to such matters as origin, text, composition, character, or history." Note carefully the use of the word "scientific," which came into use around 1589; the derivative term "scientific method" came into use around 1854. The latter term is defined as "principles and procedures for the systematic pursuit of knowledge involving the recognition and formulation of a problem, the collection of data through observation and experiment, and the formulation and testing of hypotheses."

For our purposes two forms of criticism should be mentioned: lower criticism and higher criticism. The former has to do with the text of Scripture itself. The latter has to do with our understanding of what the Scripture says and means. Edward J. Young, speaking of Old Testament higher criticism said: "Higher criticism . . . occupies itself with the study of the date, authorship, place and circumstances of composition as well as the purpose and nature of the individual biblical books. In popular parlance, however, the term 'higher criticism' has come to designate an approach to the Old Testament (and also the New Testament) that discards its absolute trustworthiness and in the study of the above mentioned questions feels free to set itself in conflict with express statements of the Bible."[44]

For our purposes we can think of the historical-critical method at two levels, that is, there is a good form of this methodology and a bad one. Whether the one we choose is good or bad depends upon the presupposition from which we begin. At stake is the source of my religious knowledge. Stated another way, "Do I get my religious knowledge from a human or a divine source, from humans or from God?"

The Enlightenment and science as we have described them refuse to accept anything that is not apparent to perception and subject to testing and experimentation. It is this aspect of the Enlightenment and of science that has found its way into the circles of the Christian church. The Bible has become the subject of scientific scrutiny. But this study depends on where you start. And here there are two possibilities. Dr. Roger Nicole of Gordon-Conwell Theological Seminary in an unpublished address to some alumni of the institution spoke about one's approach to the Bible as being "from below or from above."

Criticism from "Below"

The Bible has suffered at the hands of those who approach the Word of God from "below." This approach is based on the assumption that the Bible is a human book. As such it is subject to all of the frailties of human nature. Thus it, of necessity, has errors in it. Beginning with its presupposition from below, its practitioners go on to find all sorts of errors and reasons to make the Bible say what it does not actually say. As a result of form, source, and redaction criticism, the Bible has been shredded in such a manner that any belief that it is free from error is impossible to accept.

A word of caution is required here. The extent to which those who start from below varies widely among scholars. Some go very far and others stop short. Karl Barth has stopped short; he has accepted in principle the notion of the Enlightenment and the historical-critical methodology, but he has rebuked some of those who have gone too far and has himself accepted some things that are accepted and endorsed by evangelicals/fundamentalists such as the supernatural. But even though he has stopped short in his endorsement of the methodology starting from below, he has stated that the Bible contains all kinds of errors. And this cannot be as we shall see.

We can point to any number of statements that will make plain the fact that this methodology does great damage to the Bible. And some of those who have said these things are generally labeled as evangelicals, even as there are many who are not evangelicals/fundamentalists who have said even worse things. As we approach these illustrations it is important to remember that, like science as we have shown, its adherents by their use of the inductive method cannot establish that the Bible is in error at any point. This is the Achilles heel of the methodology.

In the November 25, 1987, issue of the *Los Angeles Times*, John Dart's story is titled, "Scholars Will Vote on Jesus' Sayings: Project Aimed at Deciding Which Are Most Likely Authentic." In the story itself Dart reports:

"What we are going to do is ask the question, 'What did Jesus really say?'" project organizer Robert W. Funk said in an interview. . . .

Harvard Divinity School's George W. MacRae, who has joined the group, said the scholars will be really asking the question, "What can we say after 60 years of form criticism, of analyzing individual miracle stories and sayings? . . . "

"I'm convinced we will come up with a Jesus that the church is unaccustomed to," said MacRae, looking ahead to a series of meetings expected to be held in the next few years.

Funk and MacRae agreed that the so-called "Great Commission" that Jesus gave his disciples to spread the gospel to all nations will be one of those sayings regarded by scholars as something put on Jesus' lips by later church tradition.

Also likely to face losing votes are practically all the sayings attributed to Jesus in the Gospel of John. The Fourth Gospel is replete with sayings of Jesus that have become favorites of Christians for centuries, such as the "I am" statements ("I am the door . . . the light . . . the way"). . . .

Some evangelical scholars will be added to the committee, but only those who use modern critical methods, MacRae said.[45]

The last sentence is significant. It means that these in the liberal tradition recognize that there are so-called evangelicals who use the same methodology and come out with the same conclusions as the liberal users of the method. It also means that these liberal scholars are using a methodology conservative or orthodox Christians cannot use without buying into the same conclusions that undermine and do away with any notion of biblical inerrancy.

One scholar who is a confessed evangelical wrote that Matthew embellished his Gospel, introducing events that did not actually occur and that he attributes to Jesus things the Savior never said. This is what he wrote:

Matthew now turns the visit of the local Jewish shepherds (Luke 2:8–20) into the adoration by Gentile magi from foreign parts. . . . Characteristically, Matthew gets the magi from the OT [Old Testament]. . . . The magi were astrologers. Matthew selects them as his substitute for shepherds in order to lead up to the star, which replaces the angel and heavenly host in one tradition.[46]

In the last chapter of the book the author adds these words:

Matthew's editing often goes beyond the bounds we nowadays want a historian to respect. It does not stop at selecting certain data and dressing them up with considerable interpretation. . . . Matthew's subtractions, additions, and revisions of order and phraseology often show changes in substance; i.e., they represent developments in the dominical tradition that result in different meanings and departures from the actuality of events.[47]

The author has fallen into the same old syndrome of supposing that "scientific precision" inheres in what scientists say. He wrote, "we do not demand scientific precision in a fairy tale or prosaic accuracy in poetry." And indeed we do not. And we would like mathematical precision in science but we do not get that either.

Another illustration has to do with the historicity of Adam and Eve, a very controversial subject. The critical methodology from below appears quite certain that there never was a historical Adam, or Eve for that matter. The authors of one book in which they make mention of Adam and Eve wrote the following:

The author [apparently not Moses] revels in naive but expressive anthropomorphisms. Yahweh appears as one of the dramatis personae. He is a potter (2:7, 19), a gardener (v. 8), surgeon (v. 21), and peaceful landowner (3:8). . . .

Literary device ["a scheme to deceive: strategem, trick" so says *Webster's Ninth*] also is found in the names used. The correspondence of the name with the person's function or role is striking in several instances. Adam means "mankind" and Eve is "(she who gives) life." Surely, when an author of a story names the principal characters Mankind and Life, something is conveyed about the literalism intended! . . . This suggests that the author is writing as an artist, a storyteller, who uses literary device and artifice. One must endeavor to distinguish what he intends to teach from the literary means employed. . . .

This is not to say that Gen. 1–11 conveys historical falsehood. That conclusion would follow only if it purported to convey objective descriptions. The clear evidence already reviewed shows that such was not the intent. . . . Put another way, the biblical author uses such literary traditions to describe primeval events that have no time-conditioned, experienced-based historical analogy and hence can be described only by symbol. The same problem arises at the end time: the biblical author there, in the book of Revelation, adopts the esoteric imagery and involved artifice of apocalyptic.[48]

The use of this critical methodology from below has enabled some scholars to become unitarians, to support the Documentary Hypothesis (JEPD) approach to Genesis, to say that the book of Daniel was written after the events occurred and is not a prophetic announcement of future events, that the virgin birth story is untrue, that Christ's atonement was not vicarious, that there are no miracles, no real Satan and no hell. Not all scholars who follow this line deny all of these things to be sure. But once the door is opened by denying some parts of the Bible, the way is made clear to deny any and all other parts of the Bible at the good pleasure of the scholar.

It is interesting that in some of the meetings of the scholars who were voting on what Jesus said and did not say and on what Jesus did and did not do in the Gospels, there was a division of the house. They did not have unanimous agreement on these matters. Who, then, is right and why? It leads to pick and choose and everything is up for grabs.

Criticism from "Above"

In contrast to the use of the critical methodology from below is the view from "above." Instead of presupposing that the Bible is simply a human book, the advocates of criticism from above start with the premise that the Bible is divine in that God is the author of the Scripture. To be sure God used human instrumentalities to do this, but He got written what He wanted written. The final product was a trustworthy book on whatever subject it chose to speak—whether it be theology, science, history, or fact. And this view does not employ devices that destroy the notion of God's inerrancy through strange hermeneutical twists.

Some argue for a limited inerrancy and this is a contradiction of terms. This could be said of any book, for all books can be said to have both truth and error in them. But to label such books under the rubric of limited errancy or limited inerrancy is meaningless. One scholar who calls himself an evangelical has asserted that while God is omniscient, there are some things He cannot know in advance of the happenings. His thesis is simple enough. Humans have free will and if God knew in advance what they would do, then they do not have free will. But he votes for human free will and decides that God cannot know before the fact what anyone will choose to do. Limited omniscience is surely not genuine omniscience and why say God is omniscient when in fact He does not know some things? The use of paradox here is not useful, for God cannot not know and also know at the same time. The law of contradiction operates and both cannot be true.

There are some questions science, the Enlightenment, or anybody of whatever persuasion cannot answer without help from above. "Where did I come from?" "Who am I?" "Why am I here?" and "What happens to me when I die?" are such basic questions. They are not susceptible to scientific inquiry and they involve some matters that must be accepted on the say-so of God who chooses to reveal the unknowable to humankind. But scientists revolt against this truism and in so doing establish metaphysical principles that belong to faith and cannot be shown to be true by the use of the scientific methodology. That is one reason why no believer in the truth of Bible need fear the Enlightenment mentality.

A. J. Carlson, onetime president of the American Association for the Advancement of Science said:

What is the method of science: In essence it is this—the rejection *in toto* of all nonobservational and nonexperimental authority in the field of experience. . . . When no evidence is produced [in favor of a pronouncement] other than personal dicta, past or present "revelations" in dreams, or "the voice of God," the scientist can pay no attention whatsoever, except to ask: How do they get that way?[49]

Again Clark quotes another very prominent scientist, Karl Pearson, who said:

The goal of science is clear. . . . it is nothing short of the complete interpretation of the universe. . . . Science does much more than demand that it shall be left in undisturbed possession of what the theologian and metaphysician please to term its "legitimate field." It claims that the whole range of phenomena, mental as well as physical—the entire universe—is its field. It asserts that the scientific method is the sole gateway to the whole region on knowledge.[50]

Teleology has to do with the end or purpose of things. Here we discover that the Enlightenment has failed signally. And this is true for the methodology that underlies science and also that form of critical methodology employed by modern biblical critics, a methodology that starts from below and not from above. It cannot arrive at ultimate truth. This can only be done by starting with biblical revelation, in which God speaks truly and authoritatively from above to humans below.

Does this mean that there are no external, humanly observable phenomena that can point us to that which comes from above and which demands of us a verdict? Indeed there are witnesses to people, which makes their failure to come to God for knowledge and eternal life a sin against Deity. And this will provide us with the conclusion to Barth as a *via media* and to anything that is based upon the presupposition from below rather than from above.

CHRISTIANITY'S FIRM FOUNDATION

THE RESURRECTION

Central to the Christian faith is the bodily resurrection of Jesus Christ from the dead. The apostle Paul makes this clear in 1 Corinthians 15. His argument is relatively simple: if Christ did not rise from the dead, the Christian faith is false, people are still in their sins, and there is neither salvation nor hope in this life or in the life to come. Thus the resurrection becomes the touchstone of the Christian faith.

If one starts with the assumption that there can be no miracles (i.e., the supernatural), then of course there could be no resurrection of the dead. But we have already shown that this pivotal point of the Enlightenment cannot be demonstrated. The resurrection can be disbelieved, but it cannot be disproved.

God has not left us without outward, external, confirming evidence of the resurrection. Some have maintained that the risen Jesus was known only to the disciples and not people at large. Those who hold this view seem to be suggesting that the resurrection belonged only to the dimension of faith and not to history as we know it. We have already referred to Dr. Henry's encounter with Karl Barth and the question Henry asked Barth. Dr. Henry was certainly saying that the resurrection belonged to the observable realm of history.

The life and witness of Jesus Himself gives us good reason to suppose that the resurrection was outwardly visible to those of faith and to those of no faith. This was true in the case of Lazarus (John 11). His body had already been subject to corruption and it was known to all that he had been placed in a crypt. He was seen subsequent to the resurrection by many people. It was a visible event and could not be hidden.

Prior to the raising of Lazarus from the dead Jesus had spoken about His own words and His works. Here a distinction needs to be made. One can believe or disbelieve what a person says. There is nothing of an external nature to show whether or not the words are true. But actions or deeds can be a witness in a way that words cannot. Jesus said:

> If I am not doing the works of my Father, then do not believe me; but if I do them, even though you do not believe me, believe the works, that you may know and understand that the Father is in me and I am in the Father (John 10:37, 38).

Of what value would the works of Jesus have been if no one could have seen them? But they were visible to all and for all to respond to. This was not only true in the cases of Lazarus and of Jesus. There were many other times when miraculous works were known to all. Elijah on Mount Carmel demonstrated to the priests of Baal that Jahweh was God when fire fell from heaven and consumed his sacrifice. It was not something done in the dark.

The preaching of the apostles and of the church after the days of the apostles was marked by a constant repetition of the truth that Jesus was not dead but alive forevermore. The event lies at the heart of the Easter celebration, and when the Eucharist is commemorated daily and weekly around the world, the resurrection is the pivotal point around which the use of the bread and the wine centers.

It is true that none of us today was a witness who had seen the risen Christ in a resurrected body. But we have the testimony of those whose word we believe. That testimony is incorporated in the Bible and Christians who start from above rather than from below are convinced of two things. First, they believe that the Word of God is true in all of its parts. This is a testimony from God and from people who say the same thing. This is a presupposition from which we start. And that presupposition, in the second place, can be looked at in terms of the evidences that confirm our belief that God has spoken and has not stuttered in his speech. And there is more reason to accept the first presupposition than there is evidence for accepting any other presupposition contrary to that one.

All manner of books have been written on the subject of Christ's bodily resurrection and lawyers who employ evidence have shown that it bears up under any assault. Neither the Enlightenment nor the liberal biblical critics can disprove it, so that, in the end, it does become a matter of faith in terms of decision. And for honest doubters there ever remains the pragmatic test: taste and see that the Lord is good. Or as Calvin remarked, "the Word of God is sweet like sugar." But don't refuse it unless and until you have tried it.

We have now come to the end of a long journey in which we have developed the thesis that the Hebrew-Christian tradition on which Western civilization and culture stood for two thousand years has been eclipsed. And in its place we have seen the rise of the New Paganism. It is dominant in the West, so that the Christian church is now a minority factor and lives in a sea of secular modernity. Yet the Christian faith is not dead. It has survived and it will continue to survive. This means that one last task lies before us.

We must address the questions: What is the role of the church in a pagan world? How shall its people live? What should the church be doing? Is there any future for Christianity or has it outlived its usefulness? Is there any hope left that is based not on passing human fancies but on a transcendent God by whose sovereign power the church will triumph at last?

9. The Role of the Church in Pagan Society

We have stated that the church in the West has suffered a defeat of great magnitude and that its civilization based on Judeo-Christian foundations has collapsed. In its place the West without exception now lives and functions as a pagan world. A pagan Weltanschauung and a pagan Zeitgeist now prevail. Thus the church in the West and everywhere else in the world exists in the midst of pagan controlled surroundings and is called upon to live and witness to a hostile world that is opposed to all Christianity stands for and against which it wages unceasing war. How then should the church and its people live? What should the church's role be? And what about its long-range objectives? And how is this all related to biblical eschatalogy?

THE CHURCH AND SURVIVAL

A primary question the church faces is whether it can survive in a pagan world as the forces of darkness mount an attack against it. First, it is important to note that the Bible speaks of a personal devil who hates God the Creator and who works day and night to undo the church, which is God's own creation. He will stop short of nothing to accomplish his malign purposes. Second, we must never forget the example of the invasion of North Africa by the forces of Islam in the eighth century that wiped out a vigorous and healthy church. That region has never been reclaimed by the church after a passage of more than a thousand years. Of course, the passing of the church in one region or area does not mean the end of the church worldwide, but it does show what can happen.

For Christians the promise of God with regard to the elimination of the church in the world provides its own answer. The gates of hell will not and cannot prevail against the true church (Matt. 16:18). There will always be a church in this world until the end of history. It may be a ghetto church, circumscribed, lonely, harassed, and persecuted, but the blood of the martyrs is the seed of the church. It has grown rapidly and numerically in places where the soil appears least fertile and where persecution is the greatest. Christ did not speak hyperbolically when He said "In this world you will have trouble. But take heart! I have overcome the world" (John 16:33).

There will always be a people of God. There will always be a body of believers who are willing to lay down their lives for the faith. No Gulag Archipelago, no torture, no death can extinguish this body, for the soil fertilized by the death of the saints will produce an ever-increased harvest.

THE CHURCH AND ESCHATOLOGY

What we have just said refers to the church militant. What about the church triumphant? Augustine in his *City of God* looked for a church triumphant on earth through the preaching of the gospel to the whole world. There have always been those who, like Augustine, stand in the postmillennial tradition, believing that the church will usher in a thousand-year period of worldwide peace and tranquility. Today in America there has been a recrudescence of this view by theonomists who anticipate the victory of the church worldwide before the Second Advent of Jesus Christ. Gary North from Tyler, Texas, and the evangelicals associated with him are carrying on a crusade marked by a vigorous apologetic, an impressive publication program, and an increasing visibility. They look for a theocratic kingdom marked by a return to the laws of God found in the Old Testament Scriptures. They are coming on strong at a time when the major denominations appear to be in retreat and when their future looks somewhat bleak.

In the 1920s the liberal wing of the church in America thought that the millennium was about to dawn. The Paris Peace Pact of 1928, signed by virtually all the nations of the world, was looked upon as a harbinger that there would be war no more and that the swords of the nations would be turned into plowshares. This dream was rudely shattered by the rise of Adolph

Hitler and World War II. Liberal optimism went down the drain even as neo-orthodoxy seemingly supplanted a decadent and powerless modernism that had no gospel and no sure Word from God to guide it.

Evangelicals generally are not convinced that the postmillennial scheme is supported from Scripture. Most of them are premillennialists who foresee an unprecedented time of trouble marked by apostasy in the professing churches and leading to the Second Advent, at which time Jesus Christ will usher in the millennium, which will be followed by the final consummation of history and the beginning of eternity. This will mark the end of sin and of Satan.

Certainly the eschatological timetable of God is revealed with precision nowhere in Scripture, so that no one correct view of the future can be developed from the available data. But the Scripture is quite plain that there will always be a true church in the world, or else the parousia spoken of in the New Testament would have no meaning. Jesus Christ will not return to gather the elect from the earth if there are no elect to be gathered. The testimony of Jesus in one sense is profoundly simple. The wheat and the tares will grow together until the time of the harvest. Even the godly cannot know who all the true believers are and who the tares are in the church. This does not mean that no possibility exists for determining the true from the false. Obviously those who do not believe that Jesus is God and who deny the bodily resurrection of the Son of God from the dead are not regenerate. And there are some who believe all of the major teachings of the Word of God and are like the fallen angels, who believe there is one God, but they are lost and irrecoverable (James 2:19).

Jesus' words about the wheat and tares raise insuperable problems for postmillennialists. How the whole planet Earth can enjoy a thousand years of peace without the Second Advent seems impossible. Unless all people come to know God, those who are evil would need to be restrained by force. But this use of force, which would have to be exercised by Christians, that is, the church of churches, does not appear consonant with the teachings of Jesus. An enforced world peace would hardly be satisfactory to those who do not know God and are opposed to the Gospel. It would also deny the teaching of Jesus that the wheat and the tares will grow together to the end of the age, at which time the sheep will be separated from the goats.

Unless the number of Christians were such that in every nation in the world they would be able to introduce and sustain a Christian Weltanschauung and Zeitgeist, there would be no millennial age. The defeat and elimination of the Western Judeo-Christian tradition in the Enlightenment marks a backward step away from a millennial age. There is no evidence to show that there is a developing Judeo-Christian Weltanschauung and Zeitgeit in any of the nations today. Nothing in history or Scripture suggests a sudden and rapid success for evangelism worldwide, something that would of necessity precede the millennial age of peace. That leaves us with a gradual growth of the church and the infusing of righteousness over a period of time. This happened after Pentecost but it did not lead to a thousand-year millennial peace in Europe. Moreover sanctification will never lead to glorification until death or the personal advent of Jesus Christ. The lack of perfect sanctification in the here and now and the obvious movement away from orthodoxy in the mainline denominations, not to mention the disarray in the Roman Catholic church, means conflict not peace. And if the churches cannot enjoy peace, harmony, and theological agreement on the great fundamentals of the faith, there will be no reason for optimism that a millennial age is about to dawn.

The biblical evidence, sustained by the facts of history, must lead to the conclusion that a millennial age before the Second Advent will not occur. Thus the major mission of the church will be the evangelization of the pagan world and the ingathering of the harvest until the total number of God's elect known to an omniscient God have come into the kingdom. Even if a new Christian Era should come into being around the earth, it would still be imperfect, earthbound, and certainly less like the milennnium seen by the premillennialists. It would also be quite different from that projected by the amillennialists, who see no millennium in the future, only a torn world in which they await for the Second Advent of Jesus Christ. His coming will be followed by the divine judgment and the beginning of the everlasting kingdom for perfected, holy, and sinless saints who have been glorified.

THE CHURCH AND PLURALISM

THE PROTESTANT CHURCHES

Today we know that all of the major denominations are pluralistic. They have in them those who are theologically liberal and who deny many of the traditional teachings on which their denominations were founded. These churches are doing nothing of a serious nature to purify their bodies and return themselves to the orthodoxy that prevailed at the time of their founding. Several possibilities are open for those who have remained faithful to the teachings of the Word of God. The orthodox in the churches can excommunicate the unorthodox and thus purify their fellowships. Or the orthodox can leave the demoninations and go elsewhere. Or they can remain where they are and have some sort of continuing gospel witness, hoping against hope that a revival will return the churches to their original commitment and mission. Except perhaps for the Southern Baptist Convention, there are no signs of any crusade for orthodoxy, nor will there be any major ruptures that would separate the true believers from those who are not. It appears that most of the major denominations will maintain the status quo and continue to speak out of both sides of their mouths in the discernible future. Whether this then means they will ultimately become like the Unitarian-Universalist denomination remains to be seen.

A further word on the implications of maintaining theological pluralism in the mainline denominations is required. Pluralism constitutes a coalitional unity, which has in it a serious weakness evangelicals must think through carefully. The case of John Hick will illustrate the dilemma. He edited and wrote one chapter in the book titled *The Myth of God Incarnate*.[1] All of the contributors argued that Jesus is not God. Professor Hick, teaching at the Southern California School of Theology, applied for admission to the presbytery of the United Presbyterian Church in his area. The presbytery voted by a small majority to admit him to the presbytery. The decision was appealed to the courts of the church. The case was sent back to the presbytery for reconsideration on the grounds of a procedural error, not on the basis of Professor Hick's theology. Dr. Hick himself later stated publicly that this was a sort of smokescreen and the real issue involved in the situation should have been discussed. The underlying issue, Dr. Hick's unitarianism, was avoided by the church court. In any event one fact emerged clearly: the presbytery by a majority vote was saying that it is all right for one who denies the deity of Jesus Christ to be admitted to the church.

John Hick pursued the matter further and reintroduced his petition for admission to the San Gabriel Presbytery. The *Los Angeles Times* reported the result of that request. It was stated that Dr. Hick not only disbelieves that Jesus is God, he also made it plain that he thought the central issue was his "view of the other great world religions as (additional) spheres of salvation and his consequent diminution of the traditional absolute and exclusive claims of Christianity. He believes our contemporary experience of people of the other world faiths leads us to see those faiths as different but authentic parts of salvation".[2]

The committee on ministry voted eight to seven on February 20 to recommend against Hick's membership. This indicates how pluralistic the presbytery is on foundational truths. The Rev. James Angell, pastor of the Claremont Presbyterian Church, said "I think the Presbyterian church needs creative minds like John Hick. I think we are impoverishing ourselves by taking such a narrow view of what is orthodox." This statement again reveals the pluralism of those already *in* the denomination. It leaves wide open the question why Dr. Hick should not be admitted to a church that has in its midst and on its rolls those who hold similar or even more disparate views. If Dr. Hick's views are unacceptable, why does the presbytery allow such people to remain in good standing in the church? A basic inconsistency appears to exist.

We must repeat again that whoever denies the deity of Jesus Christ cannot be regenerate, that is, cannot be a Christian. In any denomination that has in it those who deny that Jesus is God (and all the mainline denominations have the same problem) a coalition in unity exists. Unbelief and belief function then in tandem. This offends God, defiles the church, and brings judgment at last by God as it did in the Old Testament church. And the evangelicals always seem to lose out. In recent years this unity has led to a decline in church membership, Sunday School enrollment, and the number of missionaries sent abroad with the gospel. Pagans in the churches are like termites in a house. If allowed to persist, the house will fall sooner or later and so will the church. The classic case of apostate Israel illustrates this truth. Israel has no priesthood, no altar for the sacrifices God required, and no high priest to enter the Holy of Holies once a year to make atonement for the sins of the people. Evangelicals must understand what the consequences are of electing a coalition in unity that allows for the existence and acceptance of what they deny. The purity, the peace, and the unity of the church make a seamless garment; the absence of any of the three threads has consequences that bode ill for the future. There are those who in good conscience choose to remain and accept the pluralism of their churches and do nothing to change things. They must give account to God for the choices they make.

In our discussion of pluralism in the Protestant churches (we shall speak more specifically about the Roman Catholics shortly) it is plain that the pews as well as the pulpits have been markedly influenced by the leadership in turning away from belief in some of the major doctrines of the faith. The *Los Angeles Times* conducted a poll of the people in the pews and reported its findings in its July 26, 1986, issue of the paper. Twenty-two percent of Lutherans say they are "born again"; 45 percent of Methodists and 69 percent of Baptists make this claim. Ninety-two percent of Baptists believe in Christ's deity; 81 percent of Lutherans believe it, as do 80 percent of Methodists. Only two-thirds of Presbyterians hold this view. Four-fifths of other Protestants hold that Christ is God.

Twenty-one percent of Lutherans, 22 percent of Presbyterians, 23 percent of Methodists, and 25 percent of Baptists do not believe there is a life after death. When it comes to the Bible and its truthfulness, that is, whether it can be taken literally, 45 percent of Baptists, 78 percent of Lutherans, and 81 percent of Presbyterians do not believe in a inerrant, literal Bible. Sixty percent of all other Protestants do not hold to an inerrant, literal Bible.[3]

These statistics indicate that the pulpits have influenced and affected the people in the pews. The pluralism of the pews is sufficiently pronounced that one can conclude that the non-Catholic churches in America are deeply divided over important theological issues. This means that the message of these churches has been diminished and that the right to membership has been broadened, so that anyone can believe almost anything and still be in good standing in most of the churches. The fact that 98 percent of those polled said they are religious and believe "in God or a universal spirit" reveals how inadequate is their knowledge of God and of who He is and what He does.

THE ROMAN CATHOLIC CHURCH

Along with our consideration of Protestant churches, we need to take a hard look at the Roman Catholic church, which is the largest church in America numerically. This church is, de facto, pluralistic also. The Enlightenment syndrome has fully penetrated this church in recent years. In the West particularly, many priests and scholars have employed a methodology that enables them to disbelieve many doctrines the church has taught as binding for hundreds of years. Even the Petrine infallibility of the pope, now more than a hundred years old in its formulation and acceptance, is being challenged and disregarded implicitly if not explicitly.

Hans Küng, who no longer has the approval of the church to teach, has criticized papal infallibility and no longer believes some of the important doctrines of the church. For every Hans Küng there are a hundred others who dissent from Catholicism's historic positions. The new Dutch cathechism reveals some of the departures from traditional dogma. Father Edward Schillebeeckx of the Dutch church is no less a problem to the Vatican than Hans Küng. This Belgian-born priest's problems relate to the immaculate conception of Mary and the deity of Jesus Christ as well as the notion that under some circumstances unordained lay people could consecrate the host and celebrate Mass. In 1983 Joseph Cardinal Ratzinger, obviously with the approval of Pope John Paul II, took issue with Schillebeeckx's views. He publicly rebuked Schillebeeckx.

In America the case of Charles Curran points up the fact that the Roman Catholic church is no different from the Protestant churches that have been caught up in the secularization process. True enough, the issues over which there is conflict differ at least in part from those experienced by the Protestant churches. But the central problem is the same. The Roman church has in it a goodly number of those who have abandoned major doctrines peculiar to the church, doctrines that were regarded by the Reformers as contrary to the Scripture.

The removal of Curran from his teaching post at the pontifical American Catholic University in Washington, D.C., produced a severe backlash from within and outside of the church. A number of Protestant scholars joined in criticizing the Vatican and its action. Arguments were heard from three schools of Catholic thought: the progressives, the conservatives, and the middle-of-the-roaders. The conservatives are the old-fashioned supporters of an outdated theology. The progressives are the up-to-date, well-informed, and correctly oriented scholars whose new views are correct. The middle-of-the-roaders are those who for one reason or another do not support the conservatives but lack the nerve to join themselves overtly with the progressives.

At stake is the issue of the magisterium, the authority of the church, and how far that extends in terms of the subjects covered. While visiting the University of Southern California School of Religion after he was severed from the American Catholic University faculty, Curran wrote an article for the *Los Angeles Times* in which he explored the matter. He recognized the need for authority, for the magisterium, but argued that it is not ultimate. "It is not superior to the word of God, but is its servant."[4] This sounds like Martin Luther. But the Roman church claims to be the infallible interpreter of Scripture and at the head of the process lies the pope. Obviously there will always be differences of opinion on any subject, but who is to decide what the right answer is? Thus it should be clear that when the pope speaks, his views and his office suffer greatly if those views are said to be incorrect. Curran argued in effect that his views are better than those of the head of the church. This leads inevitably to the same sort of situation we have focused on in the Protestant churches: each person is his or her own theologian and all and any views, even when they are opposite, are acceptable. This does not comport easily with the Roman Catholic hierarchical structure of authority.

Curran asserted, "Theological dialogue and discussion are necessary if the word and work of Jesus are to be meaningful in the contemporary circumstances." This leaves unanswered the question of which items are explorable for scholars and which ones are not. Curran is quite right in saying that "official hierarchical teaching has been wrong in the past, even in the area of morality."[5] The ultimate question is whether Curran can overturn the judgments of those who are his hierarchical superiors. Since he has been removed from his teaching post, it appears that the Vatican holds the upper hand and from the perspective of ecclesiastical power he is the loser.

Marjorie Hyer of the *Washington Post* reported the case of Father Dorn: "Father William Dorn, Jr., has been ordered to take an indefinite leave of absence in Crookston, Minn., because his views on homosexuality clash with church teachings, a church official said. Dorn has disclosed that he is a homosexual."[6] The rightness of homosexual intercourse is a crucial issue for which there are Catholics on both sides, but one view or the other must prevail. Curran, who is loose on this same question for he approves of homosexual conduct, is faced with a difficulty. If the church did, in effect, remove Dorn from his post, how can Curran argue that he should be free to teach what the church objects to in the case of Dorn? Why should he continue in good standing when the church by its action has condemned Curran as well as Dorn?

The current struggle in the Roman Catholic church is again made obvious by the recent row involving Archbishop Raymond G. Hunthausen of Seattle, who was also disciplined by the Vatican, by the pope John Paul II. Rome took away from the archbishop responsibility and authority in five sensitive pastoral areas including liturgy and homosexual issues. Anyone could argue that the archbishop had every right to disagree with church teaching in these areas, but this would once again do violence to the governance structures of the church. Hunthausen had the support of many bishops and scholars in the church. But when the showdown came, the bishops clearly acknowledged their subordination to the Bishop of Rome, the pope, and to the Vatican.

All of this shows that the Roman Catholic church is just as

much involved in the stream of the Enlightenment and that the views springing from that movement have infiltrated that church just as much as the Protestant churches. This church is in disarray too and what the future holds for its remains to be seen. This makes it appear that the church of Jesus Christ in history is in distress. But that is not the whole story.

INDEPENDENT CHURCHES

Another factor should not be overlooked in the midst of what may appear to be a bleak picture. There are a number of theologically orthodox smaller denominations that have remained true to the faith. And there are literally thousands of independent Bible churches to be found in the major and minor cities of America. Some of the largest churches in southern California fit this pattern. In Wheaton, Illinois, a town of more than forty thousand people, the two largest churches are independent. The Moody Church in Chicago remains large and faithful. The largest church in New England, the Grace Chapel of Lexington, Massachusetts, is an independent church. And so is the Park Street Church in downtown Boston, which has a flourishing radio ministry to most of New England and one of the largest missionary programs of any church in America. The black Twelfth Baptist Church of Roxbury, led by Michael Haynes, is a shining example of an independent work that has harnessed its forces among the blacks and has been part of a seminary training program for multilingual servants of God in this highly diverse community.

Moreover the missionary outreach of evangelical faith groups of the Interdenominational Foreign Mission Association and the Evangelical Foreign Missions Association of the National Association of Evangelicals support together more than five times as many missionaries overseas as do all of the denominations in the National Council of the Churches of Christ in America.

While the major denominations generally are in a state of decline, God has raised up other groups and churches that are vital, vigorous, and vibrant witnesses to the saving gospel of Jesus Christ. Parachurch organizations should not be overlooked either. The Billy Graham Evangelistic Association, Campus Crusade for Christ, Youth for Christ, and many other similar groups populate the horizon and lead many pagans to a saving knowledge of Jesus Christ. Evangelical radio and TV missions bring the gospel message in ways that put the mainline denominations to shame. Every major city in America also has evangelical rescue missions to the derelicts, the alcoholics, the drug addicts, and the disenfranchised.

Some of America's churches are dead and some are dying; others are somewhere in between, and still others are making an impact on society. God is alive and well and in His divine sovereignty is doing work in the midst of a pagan world that ensures the continuance of God's church now and until Jesus comes. But until the consummation what is the church of Jesus Christ called to do?

THE CHURCH AND EVANGELISM

The church has an inward and an outward calling. In its inward calling it is responsible for shepherding the flock by the work of conservation, maturation, and education. It is a resource center for the equipping of the people of God for its outward reach to the community and to the world. It exists for the worship of God, the celebration of the ordinances or sacraments of baptism and the Eucharist, fellowship, and the care and oversight of its children.

In its outward calling the church has been given the Great Commission from the lips of Jesus. Its people are to bring the good news of salvation and eternal life to all the nations of the world. The Great Commission has certain presuppositions built into it. First, all people everywhere who are not members of the body of Christ are sinners, separated from God, and on their way to eternal perdition. Second, the Christian faith is the only means of salvation. Third, all other religions and ways of life are false. Fourth, the teaching of universalism, found so largely in the World Council of Churches and among those influenced by the theology of Karl Barth, raises the question of whether the preaching of the gospel is really essential since all are already in Christ Jesus whether they know it or not. And at last all will be redeemed. Fifth, God so loved the world that He sent His only Son who offered Himself as an atonement for sin on the cross of Calvary. He thus opened the gates of heaven to all who respond to the divine initiative and receive Christ as their Savior.

The field is the world and the church has been sent into that world to reach all people with the good news. This is the church's primary business. When it fails to do this, it is disobedient to the will of God and can expect God to judge it. Universalism is a key reason why the churches fail to obey the Great Commission. This false teaching always cuts the nerve of missions and turns those churches who hold this viewpoint to the work of social amelioration, that is, the improvement of society in the political, economic, and social realms of life.

Evangelicals who have a one-dimensional view of the mission of the church are criticized roundly by nonevangelicals and by those evangelicals who declare that social action is an integral component of the gospel. This result springs from the failure to distinguish with care the difference between the mission of the church, which is world evangelization, and the work of individual Christians, who have a twofold relationship as members of the Kingdom of God and of Caesar's kingdom. Jesus declared that His kingdom is not of this world and the church, which is in the world and sent to witness to the world, is not of the world.

One of the scandals of the present age is that many in the church have been conformed to the Zeitgeist of the world. They are not countercultural; rather, they follow the lead of the world and either have no vision for world evangelization as the primary work of the church or they have lost the vision they once had. They fail to see that it is not the mission of the church to change the world. This does not mean that God is uninterested in changing the world and conforming it to His revealed will and to the life-style consonant with the principles of Christian ethics. It only means that it is not the business of the church *qua* church to do this.

The great evangelical revival in England in the eighteenth and nineteenth centuries did change the English landscape for a while, but the social and humanitarian gains did not derive from the Church of England per se but from individuals who were members of that or other churches and who stood in the forefront battling for social legislation at the level of the House of Commons. How do we then understand what happened and what should be done in this generation?

The church is one-dimensional as to its outward mission to the world. Its people are two-dimensional. They are not only members of the kingdom of God; they are also members of the kingdom of Caesar, that is, of whatever nation they reside in. As citizens of those nations Christians have a twofold responsibility. They are called upon to evangelize through the gospel and they are called to be world-changers by bringing their biblical insights into the political and other spheres and so conform society to the commandments of God, which will bring healing and health to a people.

There is no Marxist nation in the world where the churches are permitted to influence and affect the political sphere. At best all they can do is to witness through the medium of the gospel for the salvation of their own people. Although the churches cannot participate in matters political, individual Christians as individuals have made an impact in some of the Marxist nations. In the Soviet Union many Christians have been sent to the gulags for their faith. They have refused to conform to laws the doing of which would compromise their Christian convictions. They clearly affirm by their actions that when Caesar's laws conflict with God's laws, they must obey God rather than humans. This is as it should be.

Christians always have as their guide the examples of the apostles, who when they stood before human tribunals said: "Whether it be right in the sight of God to hearken unto you more than unto God, judge ye. For we cannot but speak the things we have seen and heard" (Acts 4:19, 20). Let the Christian citizens of Caesar's kingdoms stand before the heads of states, the legislators of the lands, the judges in the courts, and the agents of law enforcement proclaiming the necessity for them to obey God rather than humans and to uphold biblical principles rather than to yield to the paganism of a lost, dying, and persecuting age. In the doing of this they are pronouncing judgment on any nation that defies the law of God by countenancing any way of life that is forbidden by the Holy Scriptures.

Martin Luther faced a similar situation when he was called upon to recant of those things he believed were taught in Scripture. He boldly said, "I can do no other. So help me God." Indeed Christians, not the church per se, are called upon to be world-changers. But they need to set their sights from the Word of God, to which they are to cling fixedly and unashamedly whatever the cost. By this sort of Christian action will paganism yield to the claims of God. And unjust structures will be eroded and justice and righteousness shall have their day.

THE CHURCH AND EDUCATION

If the church is thought of as a staging compound out of which will come those who will preach the gospel and influence pagan society, it must also be a bulwark for its people and their children. In this sense it becomes a closed community, a self-contained unit separated from the world and fitting its people to live and to retain their convictions against all of the many options that contradict the Word of God.

Paganism and Christianity are irreconcilable enemies. When believers are taught and nurtured by pagans, no matter how nice and amiable, there is a seductive influence that functions by osmosis. It penetrates the minds of Christians, who may then be rendered inoperative or even removed from the faith by a rising tide of unbelief. Pagans do not regard the Bible as a sure Word from the living God and are not bound by its precepts. Thus it is dangerous for the children of Christians to be exposed in depth or over time to influences antagonistic to the faith of their forebears.

Paganism always parades from a platform that looks askance at indoctrination. From one perspective indoctrination is essential even for paganism. Mathematics, chemistry, and physics must be taught from an indoctrination viewpoint. Students must learn that two and two are four. They must be so indoctrinated that they will not jump off the top of a ten-story building as though they would not fall and die when they hit the pavement. Every chemistry laboratory workbook indoctrinates students as to what they can do and what they cannot do. Explosions do occur when certain chemicals come together and students must know what will happen if they do certain things and be warned not to do them. This is indoctrination.

When it comes to religion, indoctrination is the bane of the academic community. Here relativism prevails and the notion of absolute truth is regarded with skepticism at best and denial at worst. The idea that there are moral and ethical principles that must be taught as transcendent and forever true is threatening to the pagan mind. But the opposition to Christian ethics and morality is in itself a form of indoctrination against Christianity. Indoctrination *against* something is just as much indoctrination as indoctrination *for* something.

It is dangerous indeed for the children of Christians whose minds are not yet firmly fixed in the truths of Scripture to be educated in an environment that is neutral and tentative or one that is determined to direct the minds of the young away from the faith of their forebears. Even if the home situation is ideal, this is no guarantee that young minds will be able to evaluate hidden pagan presuppositions and be strengthened in their faith rather than having it corrupted. Since the public educational processes at all levels function in full accord with the pagan Weltanschauung and Zeitgeist, it becomes essential for the church and for Christians to provide educational facilities that are dynamically Christian, educationally sound, and biblically challenging.

Here we must interpose one sad observation. There are many Christian institutions beyond the grade and high-school levels that profess to be Christian but are no longer trustworthy citadels of biblical orthodoxy. Generally the Christian primary and secondary schools established by conservative churches remain faithful. It is at the higher collegiate and seminary levels where the major problems exist. In these institutions the same eighteenth and nineteenth century rationalistic criticism of the Bible has penetrated the faculties, so that they have become mediating, concessive, and face in two directions at the same time. In virtually all of these instances the point of departure has to do with bibliology, that is, whether the Bible is trustworthy or has errors in it at least minimally in matters of science, history, and the cosmos. At worst these institutions have fallen prey to a hermeneutic that interprets the Bible in ways quite contrary to orthodoxy. Source, form, and redaction criticism of a virulent type can be found in schools that label themselves as evangelical. In this sense the paganism from without promoted by those hostile to the Christian faith is assisted by changing approaches within orthodoxy similar to those that led to the defeat of the Christian church after the Enlightenment. This marks such institutions as halfway stations between orthodoxy and Christian paganism.

In the present world in America and around the globe it should be plain that the future of the church depends in a substantial manner on how the education of the church's children is conducted. Sunday church schools and worship services cannot meet the challenge presented by secular and quasi-Christian schools. When we add to this extraneous factors such as we have already mentioned—TV, radio, magazines, secular music, and leisure activities—the pervasive non-Christian elements exert a strong formative and conditioning power that affects and influences the people of God, young and old, away from the Christian way of life and thought.

There is no reason to think that the churches in any land and their people will in the near future live in a society governed by the Judeo-Christian viewpoint. The influence originating from Pentecost took more than three centuries to produce Western civilization based on the Judeo-Christian faith. It may be in the providence of God that a Christian civilization based on Christian principles may never rise again. If, on the other hand, such a change were to take place, it is not currently in the offing. Therefore Christians and Christian churches must learn how to function in a pagan world so as to enjoy the Christian heritage, preserve it through their offspring, and pass it on to generations as yet unborn. If historic orthodoxy is to continue it will not come by accident. It will take insight, planning, determination, and access to the power of the Holy Spirit to bring it to fruition.

Moreover, the conservation of the faith will require as never before an apologetic that will first of all maintain the integrity of the Bible and make it a wellspring from which all of the principles and acts of life come. This can only be done if, second, the people of God raise up and support scholars equipped and qualified to defend all aspects of the Christian faith against old and new heresies. In a rapidly changing world where advances in all fields of learning come at an ever increasing rate, a new kind of scholarly endeavor is called for. Beyond those who are steeped in the biblical fields such as Hebrew, Greek, Old and New Testament studies, church history and Christian education, there is a need for a different kind of scholarship rarely found in the evangelical world today.

We need scholars in all the disciplines of the day—physics, chemistry, biology, sociology, economics, history, anthropology, archeology, and the like. We have many Christians who are well versed in these fields, but few of them are more than Sunday Christians. They are not competent in theological matters, so they are incapable of relating the heretical and non-Christian presuppositions in these fields to the theology of the Bible. Plainly we need Christians who are not only leading thinkers in economics but also leading thinkers in the Christian thought world to relate revelation to these secular fields of learning, so that the average Christian can be helped and his or her faith strengthened. The scholars of which I speak must be men and women for all seasons.

Even more than this, there is a pressing need for cooperative scholarly endeavors in which people from diverse fields of learning can together forge an apologetic not simply to respond to non-Christian viewpoints. They must also reinforce, clarify, and improve the thought lives of serious Christians who labor in high places and in the highways and byways of life. The need of the hour is for an endowed institute that will bring scholars together for a joint and unified endeavor on a long-term basis. It is not enough to bring collegiate teachers and scholars together for a short span of time. We need those who will spend their lives together in a community where their financial and family needs are cared for, so that they can invest their lives on the frontiers of the faith and of secular learning, to forge a continuing Christian apologetic generation after generation. Perhaps the term "think tank" is a good indicator of what is needed.

This sort of endeavor would and should serve two purposes. It should exist for the sake of the church's own people, who need what this think tank can produce to conserve the church today and in the future. But it also should be ready and able to challenge the views of any and all opponents of the Christian faith to show their inadequacies in the light of divine revelation. It makes no difference whether pagans agree with these findings, but it will at least make clear to all what the defects of their non-Christian views consist in and leave them with no ground to stand on. Logic is something that can be used by friend and foe alike. When the laws of logic are applied, those who entertain Christian convictions have nothing to fear. A valid case can be made for the Christian faith and the non-Christian options can be shown to be false. All of this is a work of great magnitude and is something that is urgently needed at this time in the history of the Christian church.

THE CHURCH AND THE SOVEREIGNTY OF GOD

The Scriptures teach that God is sovereign and that He is in control of the church of Jesus Christ. This has been true in the past and it will be true in the future. The Old Testament bears witness to the activity of God at times when Israel seemed on the edge of the abyss. God raised up great leaders who were divinely used to change situations and to continue the work of God.

The New Testament eloquently witnesses to the divine work of God after the resurrection. Peter, Paul, and the other apostles carried on the work of evangelization with mighty power with the help of the Holy Spirit. The apostolic period was followed by one in which there emerged eminently qualified people who left their mark on the history of the church: Augustine, Aquinas, Wycliffe, Huss, Calvin, Luther, Melanchthon, Zwingli, Latimer, Ridley, Wesley, Spurgeon, Edwards, Moody, Fuller, and Graham to mention just a few.

At this junction point in the history of the church, when the evangelical leadership of the last generation is moving off the stage, there is need for new and dynamic leadership that is evangelical and faithful to the Word of God. The God who has raised up new leaders in times of peril in the past neither sleeps nor is unconcerned. He can and will do it again. The world still waits to see what God to can do through men and women who are wholly yielded to Him. More often than not, this comes when the people of God fall on their knees and beseech God for help. And it usually comes when there are Spirit-filled believers who are ready to follow God wherever He wants them to go and are prepared to pay any price necessary to fulfill the divine will for their lives. Such leadership can effect change: the historic Judeo-Christian tradition will once more supplant and replace the New Paganism by which every nation in the world is surrounded. If this does not take place, we can anticipate that the judgment of God will fall upon humankind in a manner as yet unknown in the history of the church. But we can pray that the God who changed things before will change things again. But the change will not come to pass until the people of God see what the problem is and then give themselves to the resolution of it. What needs to be done can be done and it will be done, if the people of God set themselves to do it.

"Two cities," said St. Augustine, "have been created by two loves: the earthly city by love of self even to contempt of God, the heavenly city by love of God even to contempt of self. The one city glories in itself; the other city glories in the Lord. The one city glories in its own strength; the other city says to its God, 'I will love Thee, O Lord my strength.' " Perhaps there has never been a time in Christian history when that contrast has been more sharply felt than it is now—the contrast between that view of man's situation and meaning, in which the emphasis falls on humanity, its vast desires and wonderful achievements, even to contempt of God; and the view in which the emphasis falls on God's transcendent action and over-ruling will, even to contempt of self. St. Augustine saw, and still would see, mankind ever at work building those two cities; and every human soul as a potential citizen of one or the other. And from this point of view, that which we call the "interior life" is just the home life of those who inhabit the invisible City of God: realistically taking up their municipal privileges and duties, and pursuing them "even to contempt of self." It is the obligation and the art of keeping the premises entrusted to us in good order; having ever in view the welfare of the city as a whole.[7]

Appendix I

JOHN DEWEY

Never before in history has mankind been so much of two minds, so divided into two camps, as it is today. Religions have traditionally been allied with ideas of the supernatural, and often have been based upon explicit beliefs about it. . . . They agree in one point: the necessity for a Supernatural Being and for an immortality that is beyond the power of nature.

The opposed group consists of those who think the advance of culture and science has completely discredited the supernatural and with it all religions that were allied in belief in it. . . .

I shall develop another conception of the nature of experience, one that separates it from the supernatural and the things that have grown up about it. I shall try to show that these derivations are encumbrances and that what is genuinely religious will undergo an emancipation when it is relieved from them; that then, for the first time, the religious aspect of experience will be free to develop freely on its own account. . . .

Geological discoveries have displaced creation myths which once bulked large. Biology has revolutionized conceptions of soul and mind which once occupied a central place in religious beliefs and ideas, and this science has made a profound impression upon ideas of sin, redemption and immortality. Anthropology, history and literary criticism have furnished a radically different version of the historic events and personages upon which Christian religions have built. Psychology is already opening to us natural explanations of phenomena so extraordinary that once their supernatural origin was so to say, the natural explanation.

The significant bearing for my purpose of all this is that new methods of inquiry and reflection have become for the educated man today the final arbiter of all questions of fact, existence, and intellectual assent. . . .

There is but one sure road of access to truth—the road of patient, cooperative inquiry operating by means of observation, experiment, record and controlled reflection. . . . Equally significant is the growing gulf between fundamentalists and liberals in the churches. What is not realized—although perhaps it is more definitely seen by fundamentalists than by liberals—is that the issue does not concern this and that piecemeal *item* of belief, but centers in the question of the method by which any and every item of intellectual belief is to be arrived at and justified.

Dewey arrives at a not so surprising conclusion when he writes:
All purpose is selective, and all intelligent action includes deliberate choice. In the degree in which we cease to depend upon belief in the supernatural, selection is enlightened and choice can be made in behalf of ideals whose inherent relations to conditions and consequences are understood. Were the naturalistic foundations and bearings of religion grasped, the religious element in life would emerge from the throes of crisis in religion. Religion would then be found to have its natural place in every aspect of human experience that is concerned with estimate of possibilities, with emotional stir by possibilities as yet unrealized, and with all action in behalf of their realization. All that is significant in human experience falls within this frame.[2]

HERMANN J. MULLER AND ANTON J. CARLSON

I am in full agreement with the statement that "the scientist cannot dogmatically dismiss the miraculous or the new." But however true this may be of us who profess the Christian faith, it is not true of the world of science on the whole. Just ten years ago Hermann J. Muller, Nobel Prize winning geneticist from Indiana University, wrote an introduction to the lecture pamphlet of Professor Anton J. Carlson, onetime physiology professor at the University of Chicago and president of the American Association for the Advancement of Science. Carlson lectured to student audiences everywhere on the subject "Science and the Supernatural." He was opposed to it. He was not neutral as science is supposed to be. "Here," he said, "is the confession of a physiologist (note, he is not saying a man; he is identifying himself as a scientist and speaks as one in this connection) of lack of faith in the supernatural and his reasons." In his conclusion he states "The supernatural has no support in science, it is incompatible with science, it is frequently an active foe of science." Professor Muller says of this lecture: Carlson "gives you in a straightforward way the line of argument about science versus theology and supernaturalism that in fact most scientists would concur in. However, most scientists don't care to risk public disapproval and perhaps the loss of status and their jobs that might follow if they revealed their inner thoughts so openly. . . . After all these views (of Carlson) are shared not only by scientists, but also by many other enlightened [sic] people." It was Professor Anton Carlson who was one of the signers of the original Humanist Manifesto which opted for atheism and denied the supernatural.[3]

GORDON HADDON CLARK

T. H. Huxley asserted that the foundation of morality is to renounce lying and give up pretending to believe unintelligible propositions for which there is no evidence and which go beyond the possibilities of knowledge. In a similar vein W. K. Clifford said, "It is wrong always, everywhere, and for anyone to believe anything on insufficient evidence." The import and context of these statements is a general repudiation of theism in favor of a scientific method that obtains indisputable truth. Or, reference might have been made to more detailed scientific works, such as *The Mechanistic Conception of Life* by Jacques Loeb, the volumes on behaviorism by J. B. Watson, and more fundamentally the physics of LaPlace, Haeckel, or even Ernst Mach, all of whom in one way or another construct a scientific worldview that makes theism impossible. . . .

A. J. Carlson is a distinguished scientist. . . . One must note what he says on the nature of science as well as what he says on its relation to religion. He writes, "Probably the most common meaning of science is a body of established, verifiable, and organized data secured by controlled observation, experience, or experiment. . . . The element in science of even greater importance . . . is this—the rejection *in toto* of all nonobservational and nonexperimental authority in the field of experience. . . . When no evidence is produced (in favor of a pronouncement) other than personal dicta, past or present 'revelations' in dreams, or the 'voice of God,' the scientist can pay no attention whatsoever, except to ask: How do they get that way . . . Many intelligent people . . . retain a distillate of the supernatural in form of beliefs in a 'moral purpose' in the universe. And having injected human ethics into an obviously amoral universe, they endow man with personal immortality. . . . Even this form of the supernatural has no sanction in science or analyzed human needs, as I understand them."[4]

THE VELIKOVSKY CASE

Immanuel Velikovsky wrote his *Worlds in Collision* years ago. At the time of its publication, there was a great upheaval among his colleagues in the scientific fraternity. Horace Kallen of the New School for Social Research stated that Velikovsky's work was "deserving of the careful attention of scholars. . . . If his theory should prove valid, not only astronomy but history and a good many of the anthropological and social sciences would need to be reconsidered for their content and explanation." Kallen made this statement to the famed Harlow Shapley of Harvard, then director of the Harvard Observatory. Shapley said in turn that "If Dr. Velikovsky is right, the rest of us are crazy." He had not read the manuscript yet but called Velikovsky's celestial mechanics "complete nonsense." He pressed Macmillan not to publish it and threatened them with professional blackmail—scientists would not buy their textbooks for classroom use. Dean McLaughlin, astronomy professor at Michigan, wrote to G. P. Breet at Macmillan: "Can we afford to have 'freedom of the press' when it permits such obvious rubbish to be widely advertised as of real importance? . . . Can we afford 'freedom of the press' when it can vitiate [debase, my addition] education, as this book can? . . . No, I have not read the book . . . and I do not intend to waste my time reading it." All of this encourages the notion that often the scientific fraternity is not scientific and freedom of speech does not extend to those who disagree with the prevailing Weltanschauung of the moment.

But most of the theories advanced by Velikovsky and objected to by the leading scientists have now been shown to be correct. Only a few years ago *Harper's* magazine ran a substantial article indicating how Velikovsky's views have been validated by time and further inquiry.

It is this Velikovsky who devotes space in his book *Worlds in Collision* to corroborate the biblical account that there was such a long day in Joshua's time, that the earth actually did stand still [see chapter 1]. One of the important steps he took to verify the notion of a long day was to check out a long night on the other side of the planet. He found adequate extant evidence to show that people on that day on the other side of the globe recorded a night as long as the long day on Joshua's side.

By no means should anyone avoid asking the question whether Joshua believed that the sun revolved around the earth. He spoke of the sun rising as though the sun itself moved. The answer to that question is not too difficult. Joshua was using phenomenological language. He used the same kind language we use today in various situations. The renowned Anton J. Carlson of the University of Chicago, whom I quoted earlier has a curious statement in his famed lecture against the supernatural. He says: "He is like the rooster who crows every morning before daybreak, notices that a little later the sun rises, and then concludes that it is his crowing which brings the sun above the horizon." Clearly Professor Carlson knows that the sun does not rise. But are we to conclude that he believes it does because he used language similar to that of Joshua who preceded him by more than three millennia?[5]

PAUL TOURNIER

The modern world has honestly decided to exclude everything emotional, moral, and religious. On November 10, 1619, in the course of a real mystical crisis, Descartes caught a glimpse of a new civilization in which men, in order to be able to tolerate themselves, would establish a science founded upon reason and common sense, a dependable science free from those moral value judgments which in his conviction had been the cause of all their previous controversies. . . .

Thus modern man appears to be disgusted with the religion for which he nevertheless feels a homesickness. He has repressed it, banished it from his life, proclaimed the exclusion of everything beyond the reach of his senses. He has consummated a great rift between the spiritual and the temporal world. And ever since, he has lived in a tragic duality.[6]

Dr. Tournier notes a "fundamental demarcation between science and religion." They exist as separate domains and the boundary line between them should never be erased. Says Dr. Tournier: Today this scientific dogma is almost unanimously accepted. A man can believe what he wishes; this is only his affair. But as a scientific scholar, a builder of civilization, he dare not give any consideration to his faith. He must confine himself exclusively to the ground of objectivity. Faith is the domain of hypothesis which one can go on discussing forever. Only objectivity leads to sure and effective knowledge.[7]

ALEKSANDR SOLZHENITSYN

I heard a number of older people (in Russia) offer this explanation for the great disasters that have befallen Russia: "Men have forgotten God; that's why all this has happened." . . . I could not put it more accurately than to repeat: "Men have forgotten God."

What is more, if I were called upon to identify the principal trait of the *entire* 20th century, I would be unable to find anything more precise than to reflect once again on how we have lost touch with our Creator. . . .

Dostoyevsky warned that great events could come upon us and catch us intellectually unprepared. That is precisely what has happened. The 20th century has been sucked into the vortex of atheism and self-destruction. . . . It was Dostoyevsky, once again, who said of the French Revolution and its seething hatred of the church that "revolution must necessarily begin with atheism." But the world had never before known a godlessness as organized, militarized and tenaciously malevolent as that practiced by Marxism. . . .

But the West, too, is experiencing a drying up of religious consciousness. Since the late Middle Ages, the tide of secularism has progressively inundated the West. This gradual sapping of strength from within is a threat to faith that is perhaps even more dangerous than any attempt to assault religion violently from without.

The meaning of life in the West has ceased to be seen as anything more lofty than the "pursuit of happiness," a goal that has even been solemnly guaranteed by constitutions. The concepts of good and evil have long been banished from common use. It has become embarrassing to appeal to eternal concepts, embarrassing to state that evil makes its home in the individual human heart before it enters a political system. . . .

All attempts to find a way out of the plight of today's world are fruitless unless we redirect our consciousness, in repentance, to the Creator of all. . . .

The laws of physics and physiology will never reveal the indisputable manner in which the Creator constantly participates in the life of each of us. And in the life of the entire planet the Divine Spirit surely moves with no less force.

To the ill-considered hopes of the last two centuries, we can propose only a determined quest for the warm hand of God, which we have so rashly and self-confidently spurned. Only in this way can our eyes be opened to the errors of this unfortunate 20th century and our hands be directed to setting them right.[8]

DALE MOODY

Conflict between science and religion is far from over. State laws against the teaching of evolution still exist, and some religious leaders would like to pass others. On the one hand, children are learning about man 1.75 million years ago, or even 2.5 million years, while they read religious literature and hear sermons about the first man being made about six thousand years ago. This condition is not able to continue. Biblical interpretation must reckon with science or prove it wrong, and the latter is not likely. . . .

Adjustment of biblical faith to modern science is not as catastrophic as many imagine. The most catastrophic thing for fundamentalism, still very much alive, is to adjust to the historical study of Scripture. The story of Cain in Genesis, an ancient Kenite account preserved by the Yahwist writer of Israel's first history, has statements impossible to harmonize with the assumption [sic] that only three human beings were left after the death of Abel. The origin of Cain's wife is an old debate, but the mark of Cain assumes the presence of other tribes that would attack Cain as he went as a vagabond through the earth. It is little help to hear the fundamentalists explain how this would be done by his brothers and sisters born later or his nieces and nephews. The famous four (Adam and Eve, Cain and Abel) are only representative human beings at the dawn of civilization, not the only human beings. There is plenty of room here for L. B. S Leackey's [sic] discoveries in *Adam's Ancestors*. . . .

A symbolic interpretation of Adam and Eve yields profound insight. Adam is made from the earth, but this does not rule out the long process described by scientific anthropology. The Hebrews believed God created every man, not just the first man, and they knew very well that this did not rule out the biological process in a mother's womb (cf. Job 10:9–11). Why should conservative Christianity attempt to rule out the long biological process described with no little evidence from scientific anthropology?[9]

M. D. AESCHLIMAN

Any rational mind must boggle at this assertion [that man is a part of nature, in the same sense that a stone is, or a cactus, or a camel is]. After all, do cactuses or camels or stones dress up and troop down to the Museum of Natural History to hear eminent scientists lecture? Do they buy and read books by the same? . . . It doesn't take an Aristotle to recognize that the proponents of scientific naturalism are always busily sawing off the branch of rationality on which they are sitting and from which they confidently pontificate. But then, as Whitehead said, "scientists animated by the purpose of proving that they are purposeless constitute an interesting subject for study.[10]

Aeschliman goes on from there to say:

The willful, ostentatious contempt for elementary standards of rational consistency on the part of Darwinian fundamentalists justifies the suspicions that were voiced 25 years ago in the introduction to a centennial edition of *The Origin of the Species* by the eminent biologist W. R. Thompson. Thompson wrote that "the success of Darwinism was accomplished by a decline in scientific integrity."

In his own time this lack of rational consistency and integrity in Darwin's work was demonstrated by Sedgwick and Martineau, and it has been documented in our time by what Jaki calls a "respectable minority of life scientists," including Pierre Grasse, eminent zoologist and former president of the French Academy of Sciences. It has also been documented by two outstanding scholars who can hardly be accused of being in the Biblicist camp: Jacques Barzun's *Darwin, Marx, and Wagner* and Gertrude Himmelfarb's *Darwin and the Darwinian Revolution* are devastating critiques and exposés of the internal inconsistencies and willful obfuscations that have characterized Darwinism from the beginning. Upon first publication both of these books earned the highest praise. The London *Times Literary Supplement,* for instance, said of Himmelfarb's "thorough and masterly book" that "no one should presume henceforth to speak on Darwin and Darwinism" who had not read and studied "this authoritative volume." Yet Philip Appleman's Norton Critical Edition of *Darwin,* which reprints numerous modern essays and selections from books on Darwin (including two of Appleman's own), contains no selection from either Barzun or Himmelfarb, and it does not even *mention* Himmelfarb's book in the extensive bibliography. Is it any wonder, then, that plenty of people other than Biblicists are suspicious of the integrity of Darwinism and of its proponents? . . .

Nevertheless, there are some outstanding present-day essays (especially those of Gilkey, Gingerich, and Pope John Paul II), as well as one reprinted from the nineteenth century in which the great botanist Asa Gray points out that "the momentous question of theism or nontheism" ultimately turns upon "issues of philosophy rather than of science." As for the truth of the hallowed philosophical "argument from design," which is at the root of most of the current controversy, return to our own time and listen to the great physicist and mathematician Sir Fred Hoyle: "A commonsense interpretation of the facts suggests that a superintellect has monkeyed with physics, as well as with chemistry and biology, and that there are no blind forces worth speaking about in nature. The numbers one calculates from the facts seem to me so overwhelming as to put this conclusion almost beyond question."[11]

HENRI J. M. NOUWEN

When Paul Dudley, fellow of Harvard College and Chief Justice of Massachusetts Bay Colony died in 1751, he left to Harvard 133 pounds, 6 shillings, and 8 pence for the establishment of an anniversary sermon or lecture. Now considering the fact that Paul Dudley expected the lecturer to repudiate Catholicism, to expose the idolatry of the Roman Church, and to defend the non-Episcopal ordained ministers, he might be quite surprised to discover that 233 years later one Roman Catholic priest is introducing another in his name! But although there are many turnings in the grave going on these days, it is a real joy for the living that the many who have spoken as Dudleian lecturers reflect a deep spiritual journeying and yearning for community and unity among those who search for some light in the darkness. And your presence among us, Gustavo, as one of the Dudleian lecturers, is truly life-giving. Your work as pastor and theologian, your personal preferential option for the poor, your intense participation in the struggle for the liberation of your people, your very strong support for the many ministers who work with you in your own country, Peru, your very strong love for Jesus Christ, and especially your deep faithfulness to the Church in a time when you became aware that being in the Church without being of it is as hard as being in the world without being of it: all of that is a real gift to us.

I must say, personally, that the most important thing you and your colleagues in the Instituto Bartolome de las Casas in Peru showed me was your willingness to live through many conflicts, divisions, accusations, and misunderstandings within the Church while holding on to the conviction that without that same Church liberation theology and liberation spirituality will not be able to bear fruit. And I know the pain and the agonies it has cost you and others, but I also know that that pain and agony is what makes your presence here so hopeful. You have given us a lot already and we are sure you will give us a lot more. But we also want to give something to you: We want to give you our affection, our support, our friendship, our help, in any way we can, so that you will be free to continue on that road of liberation on which you have embarked. We want to travel with you. In your latest book, *We Drank from Our Own Wells,* you describe the spiritual life as a life in which we become increasingly free to love; and we hope and we pray we offer you the experience in which you can give us some of that freedom but in which you also can receive from us some of that freedom in return. Welcome.[12]

CAN CHRISTIAN MARXISTS REMAIN CHRISTIAN?

In the September 1, 1980, issue of *Forbes* magazine editors carried on a dialogue with Paulo Evaristo Cardinal Arns, archbishop of São Paulo. The archbishop, in response to their questions, spoke of "savage capitalism." "The Church," he said, "criticizes the consequences of economic systems when they damage large segments of society." He called for improved social welfare and indirectly criticized Pope John Paul II when he said, "It's true that the workers, some of them, felt that the Pope stood aside from their cause when he preached against class struggle." The editors, in their introduction, acknowledged that in the church in Brazil some "have been backing the incorporation of Marxist thought into the 'liberation theology' that has been spreading rapidly among Catholics over the past decade." The editors ended the article by observing that "Church radicals heap invective on a capitalist system on whose further development the welfare of their flock and the freedom of the Church depend."

In the October 1, 1976 issue of the *National Catholic Reporter* an article appeared titled "Vatican: Can Christian Marxists Remain Christian?" In the same issue another article titled "U.S. Marxists for Christ" appeared. In the August 10, 1976, issue of *The Washington Post* an article was devoted to Catholic socialists and their use of the theology of liberation as the starting point for their views.

Wherever one goes and whatever one reads about Roman Catholics, it appears that socialism of the Marxist variety is a live option and a favorite topic for discussion, books, articles, and propaganda. Apart from Catholic Poland, all of Western Europe has been deeply infiltrated by socialism among Catholics, and Latin America most of all. The United States has its hard-liners for socialism or soft-liners who are closet socialists.[13]

JOSÉ MIGUEZ-BONINO

José Miguez-Bonino from the Argentine is a Methodist and one of the presidents of the World Council of Churches. He is a Protestant advocate of the theology of liberation.

In his book *Christians and Marxists, the Mutual Challenge to Revolution,* he says: "This book is written from the point of view of a person who confesses Jesus Christ as his Lord and Saviour." Then he speaks of his second presupposition:

"A second presupposition belongs to the level of history: as a Latin American Christian I am convinced—with many other Latin Americans who have tried to understand the situation of our people and to place it in world perspective—that revolutionary action aimed at changing the basic economic, political, social and cultural structures and conditions of life is imperative today in the world. Ours is not a time for mere development but for basic and revolutionary change (which ought not to be equated necessarily with violence). The possibility for human life to remain human on our planet hangs on our ability to effect this change."

Here is his third presupposition:

"Still in another level lies the presupposition—which I shall try to argue throughout the book—that the socioanalytical tools, the historical horizon of interpretation, the insight into the dynamics of the social process and the revolutionary ethos and programme which Marxism has either received and appropriated for itself are, however corrected or reinterpreted, indispensable for revolutionary change."

Bonino heartily endorsed a statement made by Juan Rosales:

"He is an Argentine Marxist author who has given careful attention—and much incisive criticism—to the role of religion in our society. [Rosales] makes this rather startling assertion: 'The bringing about of a true revolutionary transformation in our country . . . is for us [communists] *inconceivable* without the resolute participation of a renewed and engaged Christianity which is equipped to make its specific contribution to the revolutionary baggage.'

"Latin Americans and foreign observers are equally arrested by this new phenomenon: not a Christian-Marxist dialogue but a growing and overt common participation in a revolutionary project, the basic lines of which are undoubtedly based on a Marxist analysis.

"Two characteristics of this relation should be immediately underlined. The first is that the relationship is quite lucid and conscious—at least among the leading participants. The Puerto Rican professor of theology Luis N. Rivera quotes with approval the remark of the Italian Waldensian Mario Miegge. 'I *confess* that I am a Christian, but I *declare* myself a Marxist.' This position, adds Rivera, represents that of many Latin American Christians 'who find in Marxism a language of liberation adequate to articulate their revolutionary intention. . . . It should be inconceivable for progressive Christians to envisage a revolution without the orientating contribution of Marxism-Leninism or without the protagonistic activity of the working class.' "

Bonino goes on from there to endorse socialism (of the Marxist brand) and to damn capitalism. He dares to assert:

"When we look at the history of socialist movements in this light some facts acquire a theological significance. While Asia continues to be visited by the apocalyptic horseman called hunger, communist China has practically eliminated malnutrition, illiteracy, and premature mortality for 800 million people in less than thirty years. While the Caribbean countries, constantly 'helped' by the USA, continue to stumble from economic crisis to economic crisis, frequently in the grip of terror, instability and inflation, the island of Cuba, subjected to economic blockade, has been able to develop in less than twenty years the basis of prosperous agriculture and cattle raising, has established universal education and is beginning to develop new forms of political participation of the people in public life."

This blatantly false statement is not the end of the matter. Bonino's unadulterated endorsement of Marxism from the Christian perspective permeates the entire book. His heroes are communists such as Ernesto (Che) Guevara. He quotes from the writings of Ernst Bloch about the "Red hero":

"He confesses up to his death the cause for which he has lived and clearly, coldly, consciously, he advances toward the Nothingness in which he has learned to believe as a free spirit. His sacrifice is different from that of the ancient martyrs: these died almost without an exception with a prayer on their lips, confident that they had thus merited Heaven. . . . But the Communist hero, whether under the Tsars, under Hitler, or under any other power, sacrifices himself without hope of resurrection. His Good Friday is not sweetened—much less absorbed—by any Easter Sunday in which he will personally return to life. The Heaven to which the martyrs raised their arms amidst flames and smoke, does not exist for the Red materialist. And nevertheless he dies confessing a cause, and his superiority can only be compared with that of the very early Christians or of John the Baptist."

Then Bonino draws this conclusion of his own:

"Nobody who is acquainted with the tortures, the suffering, the death of thousands of communist revolutionaries—as we are today in Latin America—will want to retract or revitalize a single word of this moving homage. 'Greater love has no man than this, that a man lay down his life for his friends' " (John 15:13).[14]

DEAN RUPP

Preparing people to go out and preach the gospel and save souls would be much more compelling to many religious constituencies. But that conception would not be attractive to many of our students, faculty, alumni/ae, and friends. . . .

It certainly is the case that there is a resurgence of traditional religious piety. It has a quite different *ethos* than does this school, although at its best moments the School is open to all, including that kind of religious commitment, in the total mix here. But given the fact that there is a mix here, there is also a level of skepticism toward all unqualified claims about religious or absolute truth. That skepticism contrasts with the assurance evident in the movements you just described.

I am confident that this School is closer to the long-term development of religious life and thought than is that resurgent fundamentalist or authoritarian commitment. . . . This School is thoroughly comparative and critical in the way in which it approaches religion, and in the long run—I mean now the very long run, maybe 500, 700 years in the future—the set of attitudes and approaches toward religion that this School embodies will be more consonant with the development of religion than the nostalgia represented in resurgent fundamentalist movements. . . .

It seems to me that for an understanding of the future of religion, the outcome of that struggle is absolutely fundamental. Even though it's a numerically much smaller and less powerful force within contemporary religious life than, for example, the resurgence of the religious right, it has in germ the future of religious commitment within it, because if that struggle cannot have a positive outcome, then religious communities are not viable. Unless people can maintain the kind of comparative, critical approach to religion and still remain vigorously committed people of faith, then religion will be just a cultural lag, a phenomenon in which there will outbursts of frenzied reassertion of authoritarian religion but to which fewer and fewer people will be susceptible.[15]

DONALD G. BLOESCH

Because [Gustafson] approaches ethics from a contextual or historicist perspective, it follows that there are no absolute, timeless truths but only historically and culturally conditioned insights that need to be tested scientifically. . . .

At the same time Gustafson is also admittedly naturalistic. He sees God not as a transcendent personal being who intervenes in nature and history but instead as an impersonal power (or powers) that works through the processes and patterns of nature and history. His court of appeal, moreover, is not divine revelation but human experience that is tested by the scientific method. . . .

In this scenario, biblical theology fades into insignificance. The Bible is a source of support for Gustafson only as a record of the religious experiences of a particular people in history. We can learn from this record how people in another day responded to the awesome powers that shape the cosmos, but we cannot be bound to their myths, which are the product of a particular historical matrix and are now shown to be outdated, though not irrelevant. Gustafson almost completely ignores the Old Testament. . . . At the same time, he rejects the Jesus Christ of orthodoxy—the preexistent Son of God made flesh—as well as the resurrection of Jesus from the grave. He also denies any kind of life after death and is content to face the future with the courage to live and endure in a world of uncertainty. . . .

What Gustafson has given us is a refurbished natural theology that makes a place for law, even for rules, but not for the gospel. . . . At the price of being relevant to the world of science and philosophy, Gustafson depersonalizes the God of Scripture and ends with a philosophical construct that may well arouse the curiosity of the world but certainly cannot command its allegiance.[16]

Appendix II

WHAT IS ENLIGHTENMENT?

No one figure embodies the Enlightenment, but if one could be singled out, it would be Immanuel Kant. Born at Königsberg, East Prussia, in 1724, he was educated there, taught there, and died there—he traveled, widely and deeply, but only in the mind. As a young philosopher, he followed the dogmatic rationalism of the German metaphysicians, notably Christian von Wolff. But his reading of Newton, Hume, and Rousseau caused him to revise his views and look at philosophical questions in new, more radical ways. Newton set him his life's task: to work out the philosophical implications of the Newtonian system of the world. Hume gave that task its spice and shape: Hume's moderate but fundamental skepticism about human certainty compelled Kant to justify the very possibility of scientific knowledge. And Rousseau showed him the relevance of the common man for the political philosopher.

After publishing some impressive work on cosmology in the 1760s, Kant was appointed to the chair of logic and metaphysics in 1770, and began to work out his Critical system. In a celebrated trilogy, the Critique of Pure Reason *(published in 1781), the* Critique of Practical Reason *(1788), and the* Critique of Judgment *(1790), he gave a comprehensive account of human knowledge and the foundations of ethics and aesthetics. These books were critiques in the largest possible meaning of the word; Kant saw it as his task to establish the foundations on which men could build dependable knowledge, to make it, in the best sense of that term, "scientific." It was a towering achievement, but Kant in addition wrote shorter elucidations of his ideas, including some popular articles. The best known of these, often quoted—and justifiably so—is the essay reprinted in large part below. Here Kant seeks to penetrate to the very heart of enlightenment, and finds it in human autonomy. No one was to state the case better than this.*

The last years of Kant's career were a pathetic anticlimax to his glorious middle years. In 1793–94 he published his Religion Within the Bounds of Reason Alone *and was silenced by the Prussian government for his daring. He kept silence, at least on religious questions, from then on. In any event, his mind was declining, and even before his death in 1804 he was reduced to a shadow of his former self. But he lived, vigorously, long enough to experience and applaud the French Revolution.*

Enlightenment is man's emergence from his self-imposed nonage. Nonage is the inability to use one's own understanding without another's guidance. This nonage is self-imposed if its cause lies not in lack of understanding but in indecision a.id lack of courage to use one's own mind without another's guidance. *Dare to know! (Sapere aude.)* "Have the courage to use your own understanding," is therefore the motto of the Enlightenment.

Laziness and cowardice are the reasons why such a large part of mankind gladly remain minors all their lives, long after nature has freed them from external guidance. They are the reasons why it is so easy for others to set themselves up as guardians. It is so comfortable to be a minor. If I have a book that thinks for me, a pastor who acts as my conscience, a physician who prescribes my diet, and so on—then I have no need to exert myself. I have no need to think, if only I can pay; others will take care of that disagreeable business for me. Those guardians who have kindly taken supervision upon themselves see to it that the overwhelming majority of mankind—among them the entire fair sex—should consider the step to maturity not only as hard, but as extremely dangerous. First, these guardians make their domestic cattle stupid and carefully prevent the docile creatures from taking a single step without the leading-strings to which they have fastened them. Then they show them the danger that would threaten them if they should try to walk by themselves. Now, this danger is really not very great; after stumbling a few times they would, at last, learn to walk. However, examples of such failures intimidate and generally discourage all further attempts.

Thus it is very difficult for the individual to work himself out of the nonage which has become almost second nature to him. He has even grown to like it and is at first really incapable of using his own understanding, because he has never been permitted to try it. Dogmas and formulas, these mechanical tools designed for reasonable use—or rather abuse—of his natural gifts, are the fetters of an everlasting nonage. The man who casts them off would make an uncertain leap over the narrowest ditch, because he is not used to such free movement. That is why there are only a few men who walk firmly, and who have emerged from nonage by cultivating their own minds.

It is more nearly possible, however, for the public to enlighten itself; indeed, if it is only given freedom, enlightenment is almost inevitable. There will always be a few independent thinkers, even among the self-appointed guardians of the multitude. Once such men have thrown off the yoke of nonage, they will spread about them the spirit of a reasonable appreciation of man's value and of his duty to think for himself. It is especially to be noted that the public which was earlier brought under the yoke by these men afterward forces these very guardians to remain in submission, if it is so incited by some of its guardians who are themselves incapable of any enlightenment. That shows how pernicious it is to implant prejudices: they will eventually revenge themselves upon their authors or their authors' descendants. Therefore, a public can achieve enlightenment only slowly. A revolution may bring about the end of a personal despotism or of avaricious and tyrannical oppression, but never a true reform of modes of thought. New prejudices will serve, in place of the old, as guidelines for the unthinking multitude.

This enlightenment requires nothing but *freedom*—and the most innocent of all that may be called "freedom": freedom to make public use of one's reason in all matters. Now I hear the cry from all sides: "Do not argue!" The officer says: "Do not argue—drill!" The tax collector: "Do not argue—pay!" The pastor: "Do not argue—believe!" Only one ruler in the world says: "Argue as much as you please, and about what you please, but obey!" We find restrictions on freedom everywhere. But which restriction is harmful to enlightenment? Which restriction is innocent, and which advances enlightenment? I reply: the public use of one's reason must be free at all times, and this alone can bring enlightenment to mankind.

On the other hand, the private use of reason may frequently be narrowly restricted without especially hindering the progress of enlightenment. By "public use of one's reason" I mean that use which a man, as *scholar,* makes of it before the reading public. I call "private use" that use which a man makes of his reason in a civic post that has been entrusted to him. In some affairs affecting the interest of the community a certain [governmental] mechanism is necessary in which some members of the community remain passive. This creates an artificial unanimity which will serve the fulfillment of public objectives, or at least keep these objectives from being destroyed. Here arguing is not permitted: one must obey. Insofar as a part of this machine considers himself at the same time a member of a universal community—a world society of citizens—(let us say that he thinks of himself as a scholar rationally addressing his public through his writings) he may indeed argue, and the affairs with which he is associated in part as a passive member will not suffer. Thus, it would be very unfortunate if an officer on duty and under orders from his superiors should want to criticize the appropriateness or utility of his orders. He must obey. But as a scholar he could not rightfully be prevented from taking notice of the mistakes in the military service and from submitting his views to his public for its judgment. The citizen cannot refuse to pay the taxes levied upon him; indeed, impertinent censure of such taxes could be punished as a scandal that might cause general disobedience. Nevertheless, this man does not violate the duties of a citizen if, as a scholar, he publicly expresses his objections to the impropriety or possible injustice of such levies. A pastor too is bound to preach to his congregation in accord with the doctrines of the church which he serves, for he was ordained on that condition. But as a scholar he has full freedom, indeed the obligation, to communicate to his public all his carefully examined and constructive thoughts concerning errors in that doctrine and his proposals concerning improvement of religious dogma and church institutions. This is nothing that could burden his conscience. For what he teaches in pursuance of his office as representative of the church, he represents as something which he is not free to teach as he sees it. He speaks as one who is employed to speak in the name and under the orders of another. He will say: "Our church teaches this or that; these are the proofs which it employs." Thus he will benefit his congregation as much as possible by presenting doctrines to which he may not subscribe with full conviction.

He can commit himself to teach them because it is not completely impossible that they may contain hidden truth. In any event, he has found nothing in the doctrines that contradicts the heart of religion. For if he believed that such contradictions existed he would not be able to administer his office with a clear conscience. He would have to resign it. Therefore the use which a scholar makes of his reason before the congregation that employs him is only a private use, for, no matter how sizable, this is only a domestic audience. In view of this he, as preacher, is not free and ought not to be free, since he is carrying out the orders of others. On the other hand, as the scholar who speaks to his own public (the world) through his writings, the minister in the public use of his reason enjoys unlimited freedom to use his own reason and to speak for himself. That the spiritual guardians of the people should themselves be treated as minors is an absurdity which would result in perpetuating absurdities.

But should a society of ministers, say a Church Council, . . . have the right to commit itself by oath to a certain unalterable doctrine, in order to secure perpetual guardianship over all its members and through them over the people? I say that this is quite impossible. Such a contract, concluded to keep all further enlightenment from humanity, is simply null and void even if it should be confirmed by the sovereign power, by parliaments, and by the most solemn treaties. An epoch cannot conclude a pact that will commit succeeding ages, prevent them from increasing their significant insights, purging themselves of errors, and generally progressing in enlightenment. That would be a crime against human nature, whose proper destiny lies precisely in such progress. Therefore, succeeding ages are fully entitled to repudiate such decisions as unauthorized and outrageous. The touchstone of all those decisions that may be made into law for a people lies in this question: Could a people impose such a law upon itself? Now, it might be possible to introduce a certain order for a definite short period of time in expectation of a better order. But while this provisional order continues, each citizen (above all, each pastor acting as a scholar) should be left free to publish his criticisms of the faults of existing institutions. This should continue until public understanding of these matters has gone so far that, by uniting the voices of many (although not necessarily all) scholars, reform proposals could be brought before the sovereign to protect those congregations which had decided according to their best lights upon an altered religious order, without, however, hindering those who want to remain true to the old institutions. But to agree to a perpetual religious constitution which is not to be publicly questioned by anyone would be, as it were, to annihilate a period of time in the progress of man's improvement. This must be absolutely forbidden.

A man may postpone his own enlightenment, but only for a limited period of time. And to give up enlightenment altogether, either for oneself or one's descendants, is to violate and to trample upon the sacred rights of man. What a people may not decide for itself may even less be decided for it by a monarch, for his reputation as a ruler consists precisely in the way in which he unites the will of the whole people within his own. If he only sees to it that all true or supposed [religious] improvement remains in step with the civic order, he can for the rest leave his subjects alone to do what they find necessary for the salvation of their souls. Salvation is none of his business; it *is* his business to prevent one man from forcibly keeping another from determining and promoting his salvation to the best of his ability. Indeed, it would be prejudicial to his majesty if he meddled in these matters and supervised the writings in which his subjects seek to bring their [religious] views into the open, even when he does this from his own highest insight, because then he exposes himself to the reproach: *Caesar non est supra grammaticos* [Caesar is not above grammarians]. It is worse when he debases his sovereign power so far as to support the spiritual despotism of a few tyrants in his state over the rest of his subjects.

When we ask, Are we now living in an enlightened age? the answer is, No, but we live in an age of enlightenment. As matters now stand it is still far from true that men are already capable of using their own reason in religious matters confidently and correctly without external guidance. Still, we have some obvious indications that the field of working toward the goal [of religious truth] is now being opened. What is more, the hindrances against general enlightenment or the emergence from self-imposed nonage are gradually diminishing. In this respect this is the age of the enlightenment and the century of Frederick [the Great].

A prince ought not to deem it beneath his dignity to state that he considers it his duty not to dictate anything to his subjects in religious matters, but to leave them complete freedom. If he repudiates the arrogant word *tolerant,* he is himself enlightened; he deserves to be praised by a grateful world and posterity as that man who was the first to liberate mankind from dependence, at least on the government, and let everybody use his own reason in matters of conscience. Under his reign, honorable pastors, acting as scholars and regardless of the duties of their office, can freely and openly publish their ideas to the world for inspection, although they deviate here and there from accepted doctrine. This is even more true of every other person not restrained by any oath of office. This spirit of freedom is spreading beyond the boundaries [of Prussia], even where it has to struggle against the external hindrances established by a government that fails to grasp its true interest. [Frederick's Prussia] is a shining example that freedom need not cause the least worry concerning public order or the unity of the community. When one does not deliberately attempt to keep men in barbarism, they will gradually work out of that condition by themselves.

I have emphasized the main point of the enlightenment— man's emergence from his self-imposed nonage—primarily in religious matters, because our rulers have no interest in playing the guardian to their subjects in the arts and sciences. Above all, nonage in religion is not only the most harmful but the most dishonorable. But the disposition of a sovereign ruler who favors freedom in the arts and sciences goes even further: he knows that there is no danger in permitting his subjects to make public use of their reason and to publish their ideas concerning a better constitution, as well as candid criticism of existing basic laws. We already have a striking example [of such freedom], and no monarch can match the one whom we venerate.

But only the man who is himself enlightened, who is not afraid of shadows, and who commands at the same time a well-disciplined and numerous army as guarantor of public peace—

only he can say what [the sovereign of] a free state cannot dare to say: "Argue as much as you like, and about what you like, but obey!" Thus we observe here as elsewhere in human affairs, in which almost everything is paradoxical, a surprising and unexpected course of events: a large degree of civic freedom appears to be of advantage to the intellectual freedom of the people, yet at the same time it establishes insurmountable barriers. A lesser degree of civic freedom, however, creates room to let that free spirit expand to the limits of its capacity. Nature, then, has carefully cultivated the seed within the hard core— namely, the urge for and the vocation of free thought. And this free thought gradually reacts back on the modes of thought of the people, and men become more and more capable of acting in freedom. At last free thought acts even on the fundamentals of government, and the state finds it agreeable to treat man, who is now more than a machine, in accord with his dignity.

Notes

CHAPTER 1

1. Donald Grey Barnhouse, *The Invisible War* (Grand Rapids, MI: Zondervan, 1965), 15, 16, 18.

CHAPTER 2

1. Albert Henry Newman, *A Manual of Church History* (Philadelphia, PA: American Baptist Publication Society, 1899, 1933), 1:20, 21.
2. Ibid., 24.
3. Ibid.

CHAPTER 3

1. John Calvin, *Institutes of the Christian Religion*, 7th American ed., trans. John Allen (Philadelphia, PA: Presbyterian Board of Christian Education, 1841, 1936), 1:22.
2. Ibid., 1:26.
3. Ibid., 1:33.
4. Ibid., 4:303.
5. Ibid., 4:314–15.
6. Newman, *Church History,* 2:410.

CHAPTER 4

1. Peter Gay, *The Rise of Modern Paganism*, vol. 1 of *The Enlightenment: An Interpretation* (New York: W. W. Norton, 1977), 3, 8.
2. Ibid., 154.
3. Ibid., 162, 163.
4. Lucretius, *Georgics* 2.490–92.
5. Gay, *The Rise of Modern Paganism*, 46.
6. Ibid., 156–57.
7. Ibid., 157.
8. Norman Sykes, *From Sheldon to Secker* (Cambridge: Cambridge University Press, 1959), 187.
9. Francis Bacon, *The Novum organum Scientiarium* (London: M. Jones, 1913), part 1, section 1, aphorism 1.
10. Gay, *The Rise of Modern Paganism*, 314.
11. *Encyclopaedia Britannica*, "John Locke," 14th ed., 14:188.

12. Gay, *The Rise of Modern Paganism*, 321.
13. Ibid., 391–92.
14. Ibid., 188.
15. Ibid., 337.
16. Ibid., 340.
17. Ibid., 341.
18. Ibid., 212.
19. Williston Walker, *A History of the Christian Church*, 4th rev. ed. by Richard A. Norris, David W. Lotz, and Robert T. Handy (New York: Scribner, 1985).
20. Newman, *Church History*.
21. Ronald Nash, *The Word of God and the Mind of Man* (Grand Rapids, MI: Zondervan, 1982), 21–22.
22. *Encyclopaedia Britannica*, "Edward Gibbon," 15th ed., 8:154.
23. Peter Gay, *The Science of Freedom*, vol. 2 of *The Enlightenment: An Interpretation* (New York: Knopf, 1977), 523.
24. Ibid., 172.
25. Ibid., 174.
26. *Encyclopaedia Britannica*, "Herman Samuel Reimarus," 15th ed., 8:487.
27. See Peter Gay, *The Enlightenment: A Comprehensive Anthology* (New York: Simon and Schuster, 1973), 223–28.
28. Albert Schweitzer, *The Quest of the Historical Jesus* (New York: Macmillan, 1948).
29. Jonathan Edwards, *The Works of President Edwards*, vol. 1 of *A History of the Work of Redemption* (New York: American Tract Society, 1850), 467.
30. Fawn M. Brodie, *Thomas Jefferson: An Intimate Biography* (New York: W. W. Norton, 1974), 98.
31. Ibid., 131.
32. Ibid., 361.
33. Ibid., 382.
34. Ibid., 453.
35. Ibid., 447.
36. Page Smith, *John Adams* (Garden City, NY: Doubleday, 1962), 2:667.
37. Ibid., 2:668.
38. Brodie, *Thomas Jefferson*, 98.
39. Smith, *John Adams*, 2:1078.
40. Ibid.
41. Thomas Paine, *Age of Reason*, (part i 1794; part ii 1796).
42. *Encyclopedia Britannica*, "Thomas Paine," 14th ed., 17. 37.
43. Carl Van Doren, ed., *Benjamin Franklin's Autobiographical Writings* (New York: Viking, 1945), 785.
44. Ibid., 257.
45. Ibid., 784–85.
46. Gay, *Enlightenment*, 383.
47. Ibid., 384–89.

CHAPTER 5

1. Newman, *Church History*, 2:443.
2. Francis Brown, Samuel Rolles Driver, and Charles Augustus Briggs, *A Hebrew and English Lexicon of the Old Testament* (Oxford: Clarendon Press, 1952).

3. James Hastings, ed., *Dictionary of the Bible* (New York: Scribner, 1963).
4. Gerhard Maier, *The End of the Historical–Critical Method* (St. Louis, MO: Concordia, 1977), 8.
5. Ibid., 15.
6. *Good News* (May–June 1986): 21.
7. J. I. Packer, *God Speaks to Man: Revelation and the Bible* (Philadelphia: Westminster Press, 1965), 12.
8. C. S. Lewis, *Christian Reflections* (Grand Rapids, MI: Eerdmans, 1967), 153.
9. Ibid., 153, 154, 157.
10. Ibid., 162.
11. Ibid., 158.
12. Ibid., 159, 160.
13. *The Yearbook of American and Canadian Churches* (Nashville, TN: Abingdon, 1985), 244–45.
14. Harold Lindsell, "The Major Denominations Are Jumping Ship," *Christianity Today*, September 18, 1981, 1189–90.
15. Benton Johnson, "Liberal Protestantism: End of the Road?" *Annals of the American Academy of Political and Social Science* (July 1985): 39–52.
16. Phillip E. Hammond, "The Curious Path of Conservative Protestantism," *Annals of the American Academy of Political and Social Science* (July 1985): 53–62.

CHAPTER 6

1. Charles Hartshorne, *The Divine Relativity* (New Haven, CT: Yale University Press, 1982), 150.
2. Carl F. H. Henry, *God, Revelation and Authority*, 6 vols. (Waco, TX: Word, 1983), 6:53.
3. Ibid., 6:66.
4. Quotations on the back jacket of Hartshorne, *Divine Relativity*.
5. John Dewey, *Democracy in Education* (New York: Macmillan, 1916), 270.
6. *Los Angeles Times*, August 19, 1986, Part I, 1.
7. Gleason L. Archer, *Encyclopedia of Bible Difficulties* (Grand Rapids, MI: Zondervan, 1982).
8. *Good News* (March-April 1985): 42.
9. Karl K. Turekian, from "Spirit of Iniquity," *Wheaton Alumni Magazine* (June–July 1986): 7.
10. Stanley L. Jaki, *Angels, Apes, and Man* (LaSalle, IL: Sugden, Sherwood, 1983).
11. Roland M. Frye, ed., *Is God a Creationist: The Religious Case Against Creation Science* (New York: Scribner, 1983).
12. Jacob Bronowski, *The Identity of Man* (Garden City, NY: Natural History Press, 1965).
13. Robert Royal, review of *Lost in the Cosmos: The Last Self-Help Book* by Walker Percy, *National Review*, September 16, 1983, 1149.
14. Peter Medawar, *The Limits of Science* (New York: Harper & Row, 1984).
15. Daniel Lazich, "How Science Discovered Creation," *Ministry* (November 1985): 29. See also *Ministry* (January 1986): 27f.
16. William LaSor, David Hubbard, and Frederic Bush, *Old Testament Survey* (Grand Rapids, MI: Eerdmans, 1982), 72.

17. Randy Maddox, "Biblical Authority and Interpretation," *Theological Students Fellowship Bulletin*, (September–October 1984): 6.
18. Allan C. Brownfeld," Monitoring Marx on Campus," *America's Future* 28, no. 2 (February 1986): 2.
19. Ibid.
20. Florence Skelly, "To the Beat of a Different Drum," *Harvard Magazine* (March–April 1986): 21.
21. *Los Angeles Times*, March 29, 1986, Part I-A, 1.
22. James M. Gustafson, *Ethics from a Theocentric Perspective* (Chicago: University of Chicago Press, 1984).
23. *Time*, January 20, 1986, 71.
24. Paul Tillich, *Systematic Theology*, 3 vols. (New York: Harper & Row, 1967), 2:158, 164.
25. Allen Spraggett, interview with William Hamilton, *Toronto Daily Star*, April 2, 1966, 15.
26. Carolyn See, review of *The Passion of Ayn Rand* by Barbara Branden, *Los Angeles Times Book Review* (September 7, 1986): 1.
27. Ibid.

CHAPTER 7

1. *Los Angeles Times*, July 19, 1986, Part I, 10.
2. *The World Almanac 1985*, 779.
3. William F. Buckley Jr, "The Porn Report: How to Evaluate It," *National Review*, August 15, 1986, 55.
4. *International Herald Tribune*, July 4, 1986.
5. Ludwig Edelstein, *The Hippocratic Oath: Text, Translation and Interpretation*. Baltimore: The Johns Hopkins Press, 1943).
6. *Encyclopedia Britannica*, Hippocrates, "History of Medicine and Surgery," 14th ed., 15:95.
7. "Humanist Manifestos I & II," *The Humanist*, (September–October 1973).
8. Karl Barth, *Church Dogmatics: A Selection* (New York: Harper & Row, 1962), 213–215.
9. Joseph Sobran, "The Politics of AIDS," *National Review*, May 23, 1986, 24.
10. *International Herald Tribune*, July 2, 1986, 1–2.
11. *International Herald Tribune*, July 4–5, 1986, 4.
12. Richard John Neuhaus, "God Save This Vulnerable Court," *National Review*, August 15, 1986, 40.
13. Edward John Carnell, *Television: Servant or Master?* (Grand Rapids, MI: Eerdmans, 1950).
14. Alan Soble, "Pornography: Marxism, Feminism, and the Future of Sexuality," *Yale Books in Philosophy* (1986): 4.
15. *Interntional Herald Tribune*, July 9, 1986, 3.
16. Kerby Anderson, "The Text Book Bias Against Religion," *Lampasas Dispatch Record*, February 13, 1986, 4.

CHAPTER 8

1. Bernard Ramm, *After Fundamentalism: The Future of Evangelical Theology* (San Francisco: Harper & Row, 1983), 27.

2. Ibid.
3. Ibid., 3.
4. Ibid., 31.
5. Charles Hartshorne, *Insights and Oversights of Great Thinkers* (Albany, NY: State University of New York Press, 1983), 2, 375.
6. Ramm, *After Fundamentalism*, 32.
7. Ibid., 47.
8. Ibid., 121.
9. Ibid., 103.
10. Karl Barth, *Church Dogmatics*, ed. and trans. T. F. Torrance and G. W. Bromiley (United Kingdom: T & T Clark 1956–1969) I, 2:528, 529.
11. *The New Catholic Encyclopedia* (New York: McGraw-Hill, 1967), 2:384.
12. Ramm, *After Fundamentalism*, 77.
13. Carl F. H. Henry, "My Encounter with Karl Barth," *Theological Students Fellowship Bulletin* (May–June 1986): 10.
14. Ramm, *After Fundamentalism*, 167.
15. Ibid.
16. Ibid., 169.
17. Ibid., 171.
18. Ibid.
19. Kenneth Kantzer, "Thank God for Karl Barth but . . . We Need to Read Him with Our Eyes Open," *Christianity Today*, October 3, 1986, 15.
20. Ramm, *After Fundamentalism*, 127.
21. Gordon H. Clark, review of *After Fundamentalism* by Bernard Ramm, *Fundamentalist Journal* (June 1983): 52.
22. Kantzer, "Thank God for Karl Barth," 15.
23. Ramm, *After Fundamentalism*, 26.
24. Ibid., 74.
25. Ibid., 82–83.
26. Ibid., 84.
27. Clark, review, 53.
28. George Hunsinger, "Response to William Werpehowski," *Theology Today* 43, no. 3 (October 1986): 356.
29. Carl F. H. Henry, *God, Revelation and Authority*, 6 vols. (Waco, TX: Word, 1976), 1:191.
30. David Hume, *Essays Moral, Political and Literary* (New York: Oxford, 1963), 520.
31. Ibid., 542.
32. Ibid.
33. Vladimir Ilyich Lenin, "Letter from Lenin to A. M. Gorky," *Selected Works* (London: Lawrence & Wishart, 1939), 11:675–76.
34. *Encyclopaedia Britannica*, "Humanism," 15th ed., 8:199.
35. Henry, *God, Revelation and Authority*, 5:33.
36. Gordon H. Clark, *The Philosophy of Science and Belief in God* (Nutley, NJ: Craig Press, 1964).
37. John W. Robbins, "The Scientist as Evangelist," *Trinity Review* (The Trinity Foundation, P.O. Box 169, Jefferson, MD 21755), (January–February 1986): 2, 3.
38. Robbins, "The Scientist as Evangelist," 2. For Russell, see his essays "Limitations of the Scientific Method," "Science and Education," "The New Physics and Relativity," "Science and Values," and "Non-Demonstrative Inference"

in Robert E. Egner and Lester E. Denonn, eds., *The Basic Writing of Bertrand Russell* (New York: Simon & Schuster, 1961). The quotation used by Robbins can be found on p. 622.

39. Ronald W. Clark, "Einstein the Man Behind the Genius," *Reader's Digest* (August 1972): 28. See also A. P. French., Ed., *Einstein: A Centenary Volume* (Cambridge, MA: Harvard University Press, 1979), in which Einstein is quoted as saying: "There is not a single concept of which I am convinced that it will stand firm, and I feel uncertain whether I am in general on the right track" (p. 158).

40. Karl Popper, *Conjectures and Refutations: The Growth of Scientific Knowledge* (New York: Harper & Row, 1968), vii.

41. Ibid., 138, 151.

42. Robbins, "The Scientist as Evangelist."

43. David A. Forte, "Natural Law and Natural Laws," *The University Bookman*, vol. xxvi, no. 4 (Summer 1986): 77.

44. Everett F. Harrison, ed., *Baker's Dictionary of Theology* (Grand Rapids, MI: Baker, 1960), 150.

45. *Los Angeles Times*, November 25, 1978, II, 13.

46. Robert Gundry, *Matthew: A Commentary on His Literary and Theological Art* (Grand Rapids, MI: Eerdmans, 1982), 26–27.

47. Ibid., 623.

48. William LaSor, David Hubbard, Frederic Bush, *Old Testament Survey* (Grand Rapids, MI: Eerdmans, 1982), 71–74.

49. Quoted in Gordon Clark, *A Christian View of Men and Things* (Grand Rapids, MI: Baker, 1981), 199–200.

50. Ibid., 201.

CHAPTER 9

1. John Hick, ed., *The Myth of God Incarnate* (London: SCM Press, 1977).

2. *Los Angeles Times*, February 28, 1987, Part II, 16.

3. *Los Angeles Times*, July 26, 1986, Part II, 22–23.

4. *Los Angeles Times*, October 16, 1986, Part II, 13.

5. Ibid.

6. *Los Angeles Times*, November 8, 1986, Part I, 29.

7. Evelyn Underhill, *The House of the Soul* (Minneapolis, MN: Seabury Press, 1929), 10.

APPENDIX I

1. John Dewey, *A Common Faith* (New Haven, CT: Yale University Press, 1934), 1–2, 31–32.

2. Ibid., 57.

3. Harold Lindsell, "The Biblical Faith and Modern Science," *Review and Expositor* 71, no. 2 (Spring 1974): 243–48.

4. Gordon H. Clark, *A Christian View of Men and Things* (Grand Rapids, MI: Baker, 1952), 198–99.

5. Lindsell, "Biblical Faith and Modern Science," 247, 248.

6. Paul Tournier, *The Whole Person in a Broken World* (New York: Harper & Row, 1977), 10, 78.

7. Ibid., 80.
8. Aleksandr Solzhenitsyn, "Men Have Forgotten God," *Reader's Digest* (September 1986): 21–25. Originally printed in the July 22, 1983 issue of *National Review.*
9. Dale Moody, "Tabletalk on Theology Tomorrow," *Review and Expositor* (Summer 1967): 71, 72.
10. M. D. Aeschliman, review of *Angels, Apes, and Man* by Stanley L. Jaki and *Is God a Creationist: The Religious Case Against Creation Science,* ed. Roland M. Frye, *National Review,* September 21, 1985, 47–48.
11. Ibid., 49–50.
12. Henri J. M. Nouwen, "Introduction," *Harvard Divinity School Bulletin* 14, no. 5 (June–August 1984): 4.
13. Harold Lindsell, *Free Enterprise: A Judeo–Christian Defense* (Wheaton, IL: Tyndale, 1982), 36–37.
14. José Miguez-Bonino, *Christians and Marxists, the Mutual Challenge to Revolution* (Grand Rapids, MI: Eerdmans, 1976), 2, 7, 8, 15, 16, 88, 135, 136.
15. George Rupp, "Community and Commitment," *Harvard Divinity School Bulletin* 15, no. 4 (April–June 1985): 12.
16. Donald G. Bloesch, review of *Ethics from a Theocentric Perspective* by James M. Gustafson, *Theological Students Fellowship Bulletin* (November–December 1986): 34.

APPENDIX II

1. Immanuel Kant, "What Is Enlightenment?," trans. Peter Gay in *Introduction to Contemporary Civilization in the West,* 2 vols., 2nd ed. (New York: Columbia University Press, 1960–61) 1:1071–76.

Bibliography

Archer, Gleason L. *Encyclopedia of Bible Difficulties*. Grand Rapids, MI: Zondervan, 1982.

Barnhouse, Donald Grey. *The Invisible War*. Grand Rapids, MI: Zondervan, 1965.

Barth, Karl. *Church Dogmatics*. Edited by T. F. Torrence and G. W. Bromiley, translated from the German. United Kingdom: T & T Clark, Fortress, 1956–1969.

————. *Church Dogmatics: A Selection*. New York: Harper & Row, 1962.

Becker, Carl L. *The Heavenly City of the Eighteenth-Century Philosophers*. New Haven, CT: Yale, 1932.

Brodie, Fawn N. *Thomas Jefferson: An Intimate Biography*. New York: Norton, 1974.

Bronowski, Jacob. *The Identity of Man*. Garden City, NY: Natural History Press, 1965.

Brown, Francis with cooperation of Samuel Rolles Driver and Charles Augustus Briggs. *A Hebrew and English Lexicon of the Old Testament*. Oxford: Clarendon Press, 1952.

Cairns, Earle E. *Christianity Through the Centuries*. Grand Rapids, MI: Zondervan, 1981.

Calvin, John. *Institutes of the Christian Religion*. Translated by John Allen, American Edition. Philadelphia, PA: Presbyterian Board of Christian Education, 1841, 1936.

Carnell, Edward John. *Television: Servant or Master?* Grand Rapids, MI: Eerdmans, 1950.

Clark, Gordon Haddon. *A Christian View of Men and Things*. Grand Rapids, MI: Baker, 1952.

————. *The Philosophy of Science and Belief in God*. Nutley, NJ: Craig Press, 1964.

Dewey, John. *A Common Faith*. New Haven, CT: Yale, 1948.

Edwards, Jonathan. *A History of the Work of Redemption*. New York: American Tract Society, 1850.

————. *The Works of President Edwards*. 2 vols. Andover, MA: Morrill and Wardwell, 1842.

Frye, Roland M., ed. *Is God a Creationist: The Religious Case against Creation Science*. New York: Scribner, 1983.

Gay, Peter. *The Enlightenment: An Interpretation: The Rise of Modern Paganism*, Vol. 1. New York: Norton, 1977.

———. *The Enlightenment: An Interpretation: The Science of Freedom*, Vol. 2. New York: Norton, 1977.

Gay, Peter. ed. *The Enlightenment: A Comprehensive Anthology.* New York: Simon and Schuster, 1973.

Gundry, Robert. *Matthew, A Commentary on His Literary and Theological Art.* Grand Rapids, MI: Eerdmans, 1982.

Gustafson, James H. *Ethics from a Theocentric Perspective.* Chicago: University of Chicago Press, 1984.

Gutierrez, Gustavo. *The Theology of Liberation.* Maryknoll, NY: Orbis Books, 1973.

Harrison, Everett F., ed. *Baker's Dictionary of Theology.* Grand Rapids, MI: Baker, 1960.

Hartshorne, Charles. *Insights and Oversights of Great Thinkers.* Albany, NY: State University of New York Press, 1983.

———. *The Divine Relativity.* New Haven, CT: Yale, 1948.

Hastings, James, ed. *Dictionary of the Bible.* New York: Scribner, 1963.

Henry, Carl F. H., *God, Revelation and Authority.* 6 vols. Waco, TX: Word, 1976–1983.

Hick, John, ed. *The Myth of God Incarnate.* London: SCM Press, 1977.

Hume, David. *Essays Moral, Political and Literary.* London: Oxford, 1963.

Kilpatrick, William Kirk. *Psychological Seduction.* Nashville: TN: Nelson, 1983.

———. *The Emperor's New Clothes.* Westchester, IL: Crossway Books.

LaSor, William Sanford, David Allen Hubbard, and Frederic William Bush, *Old Testament Survey.* Grand Rapids, MI: Eerdmans, 1982.

Lenin, Vladimir Ilyich. *Selected Works.* London: Lawrence and Wishart, 1939.

Lewis, C. S. *Christian Reflections.* Grand Rapids, MI: Eerdmans, 1967.

Lindsell, Harold. *The Battle for the Bible.* Grand Rapids, MI: Zondervan, 1976.

———. *The Bible in the Balance.* Grand Rapids, MI: Zondervan, 1978.

Jaki, Stanley L. *Angels, Apes, and Man.* La Salle, IL: Suglen, Sherwood & Co., 1983.

Maier, Gerhard. *The End of the Historical-Critical Method.* St. Louis, MO.: Concordia, 1977.

Medawar, Peter. *The Limits of Science.* New York: Harper & Row, 1984.

Miguez-Bonino, José. *Christians and Marxists, the Mutual Challenge to Revolution.* Grand Rapids, MI: Eerdmans, 1976.

Minnery, Tom, ed. *Pornography a Human Tragedy.* Wheaton, IL: Tyndale House, 1986.

Montgomery, John Warwick. *The Shaping of America.* Minneapolis, MN: Bethany House, 1981.

Nash, Ronald. *The Word of God and the Mind of Man.* Grand Rapids, MI: Zondervan, 1982.

Newman, Albert Henry. *A Manual of Church History.* Philadelphia, PA: The American Baptist Publication Society, 1899, 1933.

Packer, J. I. *God Speaks to Man: Revelation and the Bible.* Philadelphia: Westminster Press, 1965.

Percy, Walker. *Lost in the Cosmos: The Last Self-Help Book.* New York: Farrar, Straus & Giroux, 1983.

Popper, Karl. *Conjectures and Refutations: The Growth of Scientific Knowledge.* New York: Harper & Row, 1968.

Ramm, Bernard. *After Fundamentalism: The Future of Evangelical Theology.* San Francisco: Harper & Row, 1983.

Russell, Bertrand. *The Basic Writings of Bertrand Russell.* New York: Simon & Schuster, 1961.

Schweitzer, Albert. *The Quest of the Historical Jesus.* New York: Macmillan, 1948.

Smith, Page. *John Adams.* Garden City, NY: Doubleday, 1962.

Soble, Alan. *Pornography: Marxism, Feminism, and the Future of Sexuality.* New Haven, CT: Yale, 1986.

Sykes, Norman. *From Sheldon to Secker.* Cambridge, MA: Cambridge University Press, 1959.

Tillich, Paul. *Systematic Theology.* New York: Harper & Row, 1967.

Tournier, Paul. *The Whole Person in a Broken World.* New York: Harper & Row, 1977.

Underhill, Evelyn. *The House of the Soul.* Minneapolis, MN: Seabury Press, 1929.

Van Doren, Carl, ed. *Benjamin Franklin's Autobiographical Writings.* New York: Viking, 1945.

Walker, Williston, Richard A. Norris, David W. Lotz, and Robert T. Handy, *A History of the Christian Church.* New York: Scribner, 1918, 1959, 1970, 1985.

Index